# LIVING IN THE CONSTELLATION OF THE CANON:

## The Lived Experience of African American Students Reading Great Book Literature

By

Dr. Anika T. Prather

*with a forward by Eva Brann*

LIVING WATER PRESS

First published 2017
by Dr. Anika T. Prather



Library of Congress
TXu002041515 / 2017-03-05

ISBN: 9798833185513

Printed in the United States of America

# TABLE OF CONTENTS

# Dedication

This work is dedicated to:

GOD

Jesus looked at them and said, "With man this is impossible, but not with God; all things are possible with God." Mark 10:27

## ACKNOWLEDGEMENTS

To my soul mate, best friend and my intellectual muse Damon Prather, I am so thankful to you for keeping me inspired, babysitting, cooking, running the house, etc.,all so I could write. Thank you for taking a personal interest in this research so we could dialogue and you could keep me challenged to be sure I'm clear in sharing my passion. I love you more than words can say.

To my parents, Lorenzo and DeLoris McKinney, my thankfulness to you goes beyond words. Thank you for urging me to go as far as education can take me so that I could be in the position to offer my children the world. Thank you for introducing me to reading the Great Books as an African American and showing me how this literature is relevant to all of us. Thank you for introducing me to W.E.B. DuBois' *The Souls of Black Folk* which is where the first epiphany began.

To Dr. Sais Kamalidiin, for showing me as a Masters student years ago that I was smart enough to do this. Thank you for talking me out of quitting on too many occasions. Wherever you are, please know that you will forever be in my heart as the one who pushed me to start the journey. To Lawanda Kamalidiin-Saddler, for taking up the mantle. Your prayers and constant support breathed life into me constantly.

To Dr. Francine Hultgren, I cannot believe how you were so faithful to stand by me during this long journey. Thank you for never giving up on me. Thank you for giving me the space to find my way, but ALWAYS being there to push me forward. Thank you for believing in this topic enough to guide my way, even as I felt so alone in this passion. You have seen me get married, birth 3 kids and through it all you held out your hand to me, guiding me to the light of my phenomenon. I will forever be grateful for your strong presence in this journey.

To Dr. Donna Wisman, thank you for lifting me from a low place in the early part of this journey and validating where my heart was leading me. Your warmth and support of me during my entire PhD journey has been a constant shining light of hope.

To my committee, Dr. Sharon Fries-Britt, Dr. Wayne Slater and Dr. Jennifer Turner, thank you for your excitement and support. In so many ways, each of you have been my cheerleaders along the way and have provided the fuel to keep going.

To St. John's College for welcoming me into the community and celebrating the relevance of these books to the African American people with me. To Marilyn Higuera for that one day in front of McDowell Hall where we recited W.E.B. DuBois together and found that common ground.

To Dr. Jean Snell, the first person to challenge me to pursue my research interest at any cost.

To Dr. Charles McKinney for always reminding me to "Focus and Finish."

To Dr. Duane and Traci McKinney, for giving me the fun space to cry about the journey. The smiles you guys brought to me as you struggled with me, energized me to push forward.

To Natalie Burton, who in this last leg of the journey put my arms around her shoulder and carried me to the finish line, by helping with the school on days I needed to escape and write.

To the McKinney Family for the legacy of valuing education so much that it is forever imprinted on my brain. Your stories of your persistence in your educational journey, your cards, prayers, emails, etc. encouraged me in the darkest times.

To Zorah, Arthur Scott, Sophia, Ray Charles and Zeke, thank you for opening your hearts and minds to me that I may understand the lived experience.

To my students of WCCS and The Living Water School, my time with you is the reason I took this journey in the first place. Teaching you has inspired me in ways that are too deep to describe. Thank you for letting me take the journey of wonder and learning with you.

## Forward

Writings on educational rectitude are, in my experience, sometimes weighed down by respectable earnestness. Anika Prather's *Living in the Constellation of the Canon* is about the best study matter and the right way to teach it, but it is neither heavy-handedly banal nor academically correct but exuberantly fresh and unabashedly individual. For example, her term "Constellation" replaces, suggestively, the tired term "context." Again the work is dedicated to none of its heroes, Frederick Douglass, W.E.B. Du Bois—and Martin Heidegger (it is very much about having heroes), but, directly and simply, to God, with whom "all things are possible." So also the central chapter, on Phenomenology and Heidegger, is headed by all five stanzas (I didn't know it had five) of "Twinkle, Twinkle little star / How I wonder what you are / Up above the world so high / Like a diamond in the sky." The relation to Heidegger is then disclosed in a quotation. He says: "To think is to confine yourself to a simple thought that one day stands still like a single star in the world's sky." Here's a witty melding of the sublime and the simple in that easy association which is a precondition, if the largely unprepared young are to make friends with high and sophisticated matter.

The single fixed focus of the book is announced in its subtitle: *The Living Experience of African American Students Reading Great Books Literature*. "Living Experience" is the animating breath of the work. Dr. Prather has discovered from her own experience as a graduate student at a Great Books college and as the principal teacher of a Great Books school she herself founded that this designation does indeed form a class, one whose members make demands on its readers and render life-enhancing, even life-changing returns. From teachers they demand gentle but firm direction.

Perhaps the phrase itself sounds a bit like a marketing mantra, yet it is full of meaning not subject to dictionary definition. I went to Brooklyn College, a public school, where I had a professor who once told us, apropos Homer: "You'll recognize a great book when the back of your neck begins to prickle." I've never been told a better criterion.

Let me stop a moment describing *Living in the Constellation* to say who, I hope, will read this book: All the world of teachers and learners, but especially members of African American communities: parents, ministers, teachers, principals, and perhaps even some professors of Schools of Education—in short all who care for the souls, and particularly the intellects, of the young.

The work has that scope and yet that focus because it brings together two desires: "a desire to discover / our common humaneness and inner selves" (from Dr. Prather's own poem), and a desire to testify to a presently not particularly popular truth: our common humanity is the most secure basis on which our tribal identity flourishes and flourishes soundly.—Thus being cosmopolitan in studies and parochial in allegiance—cosmic citizen and African American—are mutually enhancing conditions.

It follows, and Dr. Prather's book is full of examples, that school learning should be alive with variety (a more peaceful and substantial term than diversity). Without losing illuminating distinctions, the categories ought to be permeable: a prose exposition should be hospitable to poetry, a logical treatise to analogy; the off-beat might mingle with the canonical, the expert consort with the amateur.

Some books, when taken seriously, make the world worse. Some so taken keep it steady on course, and some, if they gained influence, would do real local good. Dr. Prather's book seems to me to be of the last sort.

Eva Brann
Senior Faculty and Dean Emerita
St. John's College, Annapolis

**Finding *Anam Caras***

From different worlds we came together

Around a table

Around the books

Of yesteryears and present day

From different generations we came together

Around a desire to learn

Around a desire to discover

Our common humanness and inner selves

From different backgrounds we came together

Around a space of dialogue

Around a curiosity to understand

How our souls are joined

How our minds, hearts and very essences are joined

How we are *Anam Caras*

With those of yesterday, today, tomorrow…

and each other

(Prather, 2017)

# CHAPTER 1:
# THE JOURNEY TO MY STAR

The Road Not Taken
Two roads diverged in a yellow wood,
And sorry I could not travel both
And be one traveler, long I stood
And looked down one as far as I could
To where it bent in the undergrowth;

Then took the other, as just as fair,
And having perhaps the better claim
Because it was grassy and wanted wear,
Though as for that the passing there
Had worn them really about the same,

And both that morning equally lay
In leaves no step had trodden black.
Oh, I kept the first for another day!
Yet knowing how way leads on to way
I doubted if I should ever come back.

I shall be telling this with a sigh
Somewhere ages and ages hence:
Two roads diverged in a wood, and I,
I took the one less traveled by,
And that has made all the difference.
(Frost, 1921, p. 9)

The journey I am on now was not the path I intended to be on when it all began, and yet the detour I took has brought me into my destiny, a destiny I had no idea would be mine. I often am baffled about my passion for teaching African American high school students the Great Books of Western Civilization. How did I, an African American woman, find myself so passionate about teaching these books to my students? The spark first took flame when I started teaching a high school Great Books class 7 years ago. One incident comes to mind as the first opportunity to see the power of these books and how that power is revealed through discussion and engagement with the books.

My students and I had just finished reading "The Bacchae." I'd set the class up so that it fostered open discussion and engagement, even if the students disagreed with my thoughts or opinions. There was a line towards the end of "The Bacchae" that said, "…his name was not honored in Thebes…" I thought that it was talking about the character Pentheus, but my students (all African American males) thought it was talking about Dionysius. We went back and forth about it, until Raymond (the student who often seemed the most disengaged and uninterested) said out loud, "I think it was talking about Dionysius." I asked him "Why?" and he pointed to a line when Dionysius says, "My name has not been honored in Thebes…" This was a break through. I did not have to coax him into speaking out, but he did and was able to point to evidence in the text. This moment, this moment when that one student who always seemed so angry, so disengaged, so un-phased by the class, shone the light that pulled me into the phenomenon of African American students engaging in the Great Books of Western Civilization. The light glared and would not let me go. And so here I am 7 years later trying to put that moment, and the many other moments like it, under a microscope, in order to come to understand **the lived experiences of African American students reading Great Books literature.**

## Raymond, the Star That STARted It All

I have chosen to name the above student Raymond after one of the characters from the

Disney movie, "The Princess and the Frog." In the movie, Raymond is a firefly. He's an old, battered and torn firefly. In fact he has to shake his little rump from time to time in order to keep his light glowing. He is small with a big heart and a love for Evangeline. Evangeline is the Evening Star, but he thinks it is another firefly. All throughout the movie he looks at the Evening Star and talks of his love for her. He dreams that one day they will be together. At the end of the movie, Tiana and Prince Naveen are about to be killed by the Shadow Man, but Raymond flies quickly to the Shadow Man and takes the source of his power from around his neck (it's a necklace that he wears). Eventually, the Shadow Man swats Raymond to the ground and steps on him with his foot. At the end of the movie, when the Shadow Man is vanquished (thanks to Raymond), the characters of the movie all gather around Raymond as he's breathing his last breath. He dies and they all have a funeral for him. After the funeral, they notice another smaller star shining brightly next to the Evening Star (Evangeline) and everyone is happy. They see that the new star is Raymond who will now shine for eternity, next to his true love.

I looked up the name Raymond in a name meaning website and it means "advice" (Baby Names World, 2011). I then looked up the word "advice" in the etymological dictionary and it comes from the Latin word *visum*, which means "to see."[1] Throughout the movie, Raymond served as a guide to find the woman who could reverse the Shadow Man's spells. He was also the one to

---

[1] From this point on all etymological references will come from www.etymonline.com.

discover the source of the Shadow Man's power. Once he revealed that to everyone, the Shadow Man was easily destroyed. Raymond helped the characters of the movie to see the solution to their problems. So I have named my student Raymond, because his story has been a light of inspiration for my long journey, and his "star" light still reminds me of being called to my phenomenon.

**Inviting "Others" to the Conversation**

I have been on this path for a long time, trying to understand the experiences of African-American students engaging in the Great Books of Western Civilization. I feel that the year I chose to focus on one student was a breakthrough for me. During the year that I chose to just focus on Raymond, I decided to mix in some African-American literature that I felt would compliment the Great Books reading list. These books complimented the Great Books list, because the authors all cited from the Great Books in their writings. I must say that more than any of the previous years, I noticed a heightened interest and engagement in the literature from the students in general. I did not realize that it would have this effect on the students, especially Raymond. Maybe it was because the students could see how past African Americans were able to connect these books to their lives, and as a result, were able to create their own literature. Now, the literature seemed more relevant, because they could see that other African Americans from all walks of life saw the relevancy of these books. Some of the authors had even been former slaves (e.g., Phyllis Wheatley), and others came from a more affluent background (e.g., W.E.B. DuBois). Raymond confirmed my thinking when he said:

> I think the English class impacted me the most this past year. I think it's because you

> had us read African-American literature along with the Great Books. I was able to see the whole story of African-Americans. When I read about our struggles through slavery and our mistreatment in this supposedly Christian nation, it made me think differently.

**Raymond Lights the Way**

Raymond is a lot like the firefly in "The Princess and the Frog." He, too, seemed insignificant, and many times he struggled to let his "little light shine." There was a time when Raymond would barely speak or participate in class. He would not complete homework. His overall performance in school was poor. I wonder if the root of my struggles with him had something to do with his self-esteem. When I asked him why his motivation in school had been low in the past, he said, "I think I had a low confidence or something." I wonder if my Great Books class somehow provided a way for him to work through this struggle. Could engaging in the literature have provided a way for him to see that he could learn, that he was capable of succeeding at something? When I asked him how the books made him feel, he said:

> Reading these books made me see that unlike the slaves, I don't have to be ignorant. I can change what I know. I have access to books and the Internet and things like that. The English class caused me to not just read, but to comprehend and apply what I'm reading. Reading about Frederick Douglass really inspired me. It made me

> appreciate how I have access to different books and the slaves were not allowed to read. Now in my time, I can just pick up a book and read it… anywhere.

What I notice about this is his repeated use of "I can…" Before, I think that he must have felt like something was holding him back. Could reading about the slaves have caused him to see that if they could overcome the chains of slavery, he could overcome whatever was holding him back? He just had to believe in himself.

> I didn't really have a desire to learn anything. It wasn't that I wasn't smart, but I didn't want to use what I knew to my advantage. My mom was trying to get me to do better. She kept talking to me, but it didn't matter. I had to want it for myself. I finally got it in my head that I want to do good and then I started to try. The more I began to try, the more I wanted to learn. The more I wanted out of life. (Raymond)

There came a point when Raymond formulated a belief in himself and that belief pushed him to want to make something out of his life. As stated earlier, he found some of his motivation in the literature he read (i.e., when reading about Frederick Douglass). Seeing these changes in him confirmed what I hoped would happen through my literature class. When I first started teaching Raymond, he was not headed towards a bright future, but I hoped that engaging in the literature would help him to change his direction. Through reading the books, Raymond's thirst for knowledge began to grow.

> You had us read the Constitution and now I know my rights and the different laws…different things like that. Now I can understand the history of things. African-American and US history is very important. It's important, because if you don't know your history then you can't know how to change certain things. You can't know how to react to things. Reading the African-American literature and the Great Books showed me how the different subjects relate to each other. They all come together. (Raymond)

Knowledge became useful for him in different ways. He saw knowledge as a way to understand the world better, and he also began to see knowledge as a way to accomplish something.

> The knowledge I gain through reading, learning…going to college can inspire me to create something, like a dance, a play…It's always more than what appears. You have to go deep. It's more than just reading…it's comprehending and application and you can't do the application without reading and gaining the knowledge. (Raymond)

I feel that this thirst for knowledge was an outward showing of what was happening to Raymond on the inside. I remember watching him reading a book after school as he waited for his mom to pick him up. I recall how he would come to class and tell me something interesting he had read the night before. This thirst for knowledge showed that Raymond had definitely been reborn. He was becoming my bright star, shining his light on the path I should take, just as Raymond in "The Princess and the Frog" shined his light on the path that led them to freedom from the Shadow Man's spell. Observing and chronicling Raymond's process and his transformation in my class gave me a foundation for researching **the lived experiences of African American students reading Great Books literature.**

## Discovering a New Way of Teaching and Learning

Surprisingly, I found myself drawn to the philosophy of classical education well before my passion for the Great Books took root. It all happened by accident, myself being slowly pulled into this particular understanding of teaching and learning. In fact, as I was pulled deeper and deeper into learning more about classical education, I found myself pulled away from a total focus on what had always been my first love—arts in education. Even still at the end, I found that I was not pulled completely away from arts in education, but I gained a more encompassing understanding of education that involves not just literacy, but the various forms of expressing that literacy (i.e. writing, speaking and even the arts).

I had been teaching for Montgomery County Public Schools for about 6 years when I was accepted into the music education program at Howard University. At this time, I realized that I wanted to take a break from teaching full time in order to continue studying the arts in education. As this was happening in my life, my parents were starting a journey of their own, for they were in the process of starting a private school. Our journeys intersected when they began looking for a part time music and drama teacher. They agreed to hire me if I agreed to learn about the educational philosophy upon which they decided to base the school.

My study of classical education involved reading *The Lost Tools for Learning* by Dorothy Sayers (1948) and *A Well Trained Mind* by Susan Wise and Jesse Wise-Bauer (1999). Reading these books allowed me to see the different cognitive phases that students move through during their years of education. According to the philosophy of classical education, a child's intellectual development involves a three part process of training the mind (Wise &Wise-Bauer, 1999, p. 43). Classical education believes that the primary role of the teacher is to show the student how to think by guiding them through these phases. When a child is educated in a classical school, they go through each of these stages (grammar, logic and rhetoric) with the end product being children who can think and articulate that knowledge for themselves and others.

Classical education provides a rigid structure for how children should progress through school. The Grammar phase has students focusing on memorization of facts that are foundational to most common knowledge (i.e., parts of speech, parts of the body, naming the states, naming the countries, mulitiplication facts, etc.). Teachers of this phase are teaching grades K through 6, and during this time they are primarily focusing on encouraging memorization of these facts. The Logic phase has students taking those facts that were memorized during the Grammar phase and then coming to understand the "why's" behind those facts. They also learn how to articulate their comprehension of those facts in their own words. The introduction of argument/debate takes place in this phase as well. Teachers of this phase are working with students in grades 7 to 9. The Rhetoric phase has students take the facts and the comprehension of those facts and then use them to formulate their own theories, philosophies, and world view. Students learn to present theses in which they argue their own personal beliefs and theories.

I studied and practiced this philosophy for over 10 years, but as I became more focused on teaching the Great Books class, I came to a place where I did not feel bound by keeping students within the confines of those phases. I do find these phases helpful to me in understanding and naming how students are learning, thinking, growing and being, but I also realize that students should be allowed to progress through these phases at their own pace. For example, my 5 year old son is already in the rhetoric phase. I can read a Great Book text with him and he is able to discuss it with me as if I am talking to one of my high school students. His learning of addition is actually progressing through comprehension of what addition means, as opposed to just memorizing his addition facts. This is how he learns. He is my "why" baby. A child's educational journey is a very personal one and should be allowed to take place as the child is learning to learn. I also believe that a child's progression in education is all about exposure. As I used to feed my students texts like *A Mid Summer Night's Dream*, even though it seemed so far away from who they were, I feed my son the stories of slavery, even though he is only 6. My students connected to Shakespeare, just as my son has recently become interested in African culture and stories of slavery. Exposing African American students to the Great Books expands them beyond their culture, beyond their life, beyond their personal belief systems, etc. Including African American authors in this type of learning keeps them connected to their heritage, invites their ancestors into the Great Conversation, along with themselves.

**The Connections Made**

It did not matter to my students that most of the authors were of European descent. They were able to connect to the literature for many reasons, one reason being that these books address topics that are relevant to every human being. For example, I cannot forget the response of my students after they read Plato's *Symposium*. The students became engrossed in discussing the tactics that Socrates used to get people to think and discuss their understandings of various concepts. In fact, they started to find Socrates very provocative in how he was always asking questions and getting people all turned around. They also got involved in a deep discussion based upon a question that was posed in *The Sypmposium*: "What would it be like if there were no sexes…if everyone was the same?" The students discussed the differences between men and women, why each one is necessary, and what the world would be like with each one. They got so involved with this discussion that I could not move forward with my planned lesson. By including the Great Books into my lessons, my students were able to take part in the thought processes of human kind over the centuries.

The majority of African American students I worked with seemed to find a stronger sense of self-worth as a result of being "allowed" to take part in this centuries long and worldwide "think tank." I'll never forget what one of my students said in relation to what I've just shared. A teacher made a comment that caused this student to feel that she was putting him down for being a poor reader. The student replied to her, "If we can't read, then how come we readin' college level books?!" Even though he was being disrespectful, I could not help but smile. It was at this moment that I began to see that not only would engaging in the literature help them with their reading and comprehension, I was also able to see that engagement in the Great Books could increase self-esteem. This incident gave me a glimpse into something that was taking place within the students. I wonder what it means to these students to "be" in this place of literacy?

I know that giving credence to these texts and even saying "The Great Books of Western Civilization" can conjure up some critical questions, questions of race and superior attitudes, questions of isolation and degradation, questions of pluralism and multiculturalism. Even still, I sought to understand why the school where I was teaching, that was primarily populated by African American students, made them an integral part of their program. To grasp this, I felt I needed to look deeper into why they were considered "great." I really had to look past my own thoughts on race and cultural relations in this country and face some realities that are evident throughout history. Although our founding fathers were slave holders, they are the authors of the Constitution. Can we still learn from them? What can be learned from other writers and thinkers of the past, regardless of their racial background? How can I use these texts to pose questions about the historical conflicts to question racism more directly, and how can I draw in literature from African American authors to help address those questions? By having this type of inclusive dialogue with the Great Books authors, African American authors and others, would I be able to help my students still appreciate these texts as truly "great," especially now that I am inserting them and their heritage into the Conversation? Could we even begin to identify those texts not included on the Great Books list that should be included?

## The Greatness of the Great Books

The Great Books are rhetoric in action (Wise & Wise-Bauer, 1999). Students get to read the works of great minds from ancient times to present day. By studying the arguments of these ancient to contemporary thinkers, high school students are able to analyze how they are able to articulate and defend their belief systems (Wise & Wise-Bauer). Classical education is more than a pattern of learning, but it is language focused. Students learn through the written and spoken word. Reading the texts of those who lived before them, writing their thoughts on the subject, and finally speaking with conviction on those topics they have read and studied is the ultimate goal of classical education. It is through facilitating the immersion in the literature of the thinkers, authors and philosophers of the past and present, that classical education helps to develop a well-trained mind.

Even though most of the books are from Western culture, they are still relevant to the African American student. Classical education believes that each student should develop a greater understanding of their own civilization, country and place in time (Wise & Wise-Bauer, 1999). This can only be done by understanding that which has come before us. David Hicks (1981) says, "The old books lay a foundation for all later learning and life" (p. 138).

I have mentioned the "Great Conversation" previously. When Mortimer Adler and his colleagues compiled the list of Great Books, they had an understanding that a Great Conversation was going on between all of the great thinkers of the past and present. In order to reveal this dialogue through the centuries, Adler and his colleagues catalogued the topics of the books (Gwinn, 1993). Reading through the pieces of literature one can see that the authors seem to be responding to the writings of those authors who came before them. This is why I believe that the Great Books are "rhetoric in action" (Wise & Wise-Bauer, 1999, p. 453). When students begin to read them, understand them, and even form their own opinions about them, the students become a part of that dialogue, that Great Conversation. This dialogue is the dialogue of every person, and specifically it is a discussion that is relevant to every American. My students are given an opportunity to join the human conversation, instead of being isolated from it, as has been done in the past.

## My Way to the Great Books

Coming to understand classical education and why the Great Books are an integral part of this educational philosophy has been a long and arduous pilgrimage, and I needed a guide to help me tease out an understanding of my journey. I found that guide in Martin Heidegger. In his short autobiographical essay, "My Way to Phenomenology" (1962), I was provided a framework whereby I can write about my experience with teaching the Great Books. Heidegger begins his essay at the very beginning of his academic career, and he carefully charts the steps, detours, twists and turns that led him to phenomenology and the study of Being. In the end, he found himself in a place he had not planned to be, but he had stepped into his educational and career destiny. Throughout this chapter, I refer to excerpts from this essay in order to provide a mirror of what took place for me in my journey. In this way, I hope to reveal my trying to understand **the lived experience of African American students reading Great Books literature.**

### The Spell

We never come to thoughts. They come to us. (Heidegger, 1962/1993, p. 368)

> My academic studies began in the winter of 1909-10 in theology at the University of Freiburg. But the chief work for the study in

> theology still left enough time for the philosophy which belonged to the curriculum anyhow. Thus both volumes of Husserl's Logical Investigations lay on my desk in the theological seminary ever since my first semester there. These volumes belonged to the university library. The date due could be easily renewed again and again. The work was obviously of little interest to the students. But how did it get into this environment so foreign to it? (Heidegger, p. 251)

When I first read the above lines, my mind took a trip back in time to the day I first met the Great Books and the philosophy underpinning their compilation. Martin Heidegger planned to study theology, and yet a piece of literary work grabbed his attention so strong that his educational and career path changed completely. Before I had my first experience with seeing the response of my students to Great Books literature, something had to call me away from my previous path of arts education. Something had to draw my attention to it. What draws our attention to something is that thing that is such a mystery that it almost seems to "withdraw" from us. The understanding of that thing is so veiled that it eludes us. In essence, we become drawn into what withdraws from us (Heidegger, 1968). The mystery of it, the unknown of it, is what draws us in. It feels or seems like a spell, an all-consuming power that overwhelms your thinking. It would have to be a spell for me, because I was completely focused on music and theatre in education, but on one fateful day, I stumbled upon something that changed my course forever.

It was about my fifth year teaching music and drama when I happened to be walking down the hall and I stumbled upon the school's high school English class. The class was made up of four African-American male students (the school was quite small), and they were disengaged. Actually, they were not really reading or writing at all. They would just lean back in their chairs and pass the time. I had to do something about it. I went to the principal and shared with him what I had observed. I was told that the literature program was too difficult for the students and that the school maybe should look into other literature for them to read. The principal's words haunted me in the days to follow, and I became consumed with trying to figure out how to get these students to become interested in the texts. It was not long before I had to relinquish myself to the spell that was slowly taking control of my heart, soul and mind. I asked if I could have a try at teaching the Great Books class and the rest is history.

Heidegger describes his interest in Husserl's work as a "spell":

> Still I remained so fascinated by Husserl's work that I read in it again and again in the years to follow without gaining sufficient insight into what fascinated me. The spell emanating from the work extended to the outer appearance of the sentence structure and the title page. (Heidegger, 1962, p. 251)

On the surface, it seemed that the spell that took control of me found its power in my pondering how I could engage disinterested students. No, that was just the "call" to the phenomenon. The spell actually emanated from the books themselves. These ancient texts passed on from generation to generation over thousands of years, that discussed those issues relevant to all humankind, are what put me under a spell. To discover their relevancy to my students, I had to study the books for myself, and in reading them, I became fascinated with them as Heidegger found himself fascinated with Husserl's work.

I am reminded of Abram's writing on the word *spell*:

> Perhaps the most succinct evidence for the potent magic of written letters is to be found in the ambiguous meaning of our common English word "spell." As the Roman alphabet spread through oral Europe, the Old English word "spell," which had meant simply to recite a story or tale, took on the new double meaning: on the one hand, it now meant to arrange, in the proper order, the written letters that constitute the name of a thing or a person; on the other it signified a magic formula or charm. Yet these two meanings were not nearly as distinct as they have come to seem to us today. For to assemble the letters that make up the name of a thing, in the correct order, was precisely to effect a magic, to establish a new kind of influence over that entity, to summon it forth! To spell, to correctly arrange the letters to form a name or a phrase, seemed thus at the same time to cast a spell, to exert a new and lasting power over the things spelled. (Abram, 1996, p. 133)

*Spell*. Most of us when we see that word, we imagine witches standing over a large open book, chanting words in a set order that magically cause something they desire to happen. Those specific words bring about an effect, and so it is with the words found in these books. In these books lies the secret to opening my African American students' eyes to a broader, more inclusive literacy. They are the Bible, Shakespeare's plays, Aristotle's philosophy, Socrates' logic, the Constitution, Abraham Lincoln's speeches. They are the words of the gods and of humankind who have survived the ages, because someone simply wrote them down. Knowing these words, the specific words found in these books, helps us to understand who we are and where we live.

For African-Americans who for centuries have struggled with solidifying their identity in this country, it is imperative for them to know the specific words (their order, their construct, their meaning) in the context of THIS country. These books hold these specific words, the words that are the life and breath of every American. Knowing these words helps to break the spell of anonymity that has plagued the African American since being forced to live here hundreds of years ago. By simply reading the words, reciting the words, talking about the words, meditating on the words, found in these books, a new spell takes over. Like lightening striking the darkness and my students, my people can see who they are, here, in America and that is simply—human. To see themselves as human, equally human in America seems simple, but the roots of their beginnings here did not define them as such. So, for my students to read these books, and to have their heritage included in the Conversation of these books, helps them to articulate their own and others' humanness. Realizing this, created in me the desire to teach the class. It became a personal mission. The power of the spell was upon me.

## The Light of Freedom through Liberal Education

The books consumed my every thought. The recurring thought that began to manifest itself was that these very books played an important role in the educational journey of many notable African Americans, for example like Anna Julia Cooper, James Baldwin, Marva Collins, Frederick Douglass, W.E.B. Du Bois and many others. I began thinking of these books and those people who were affected by them. As I reflected on this, a poem came to me:

> A-B-C-D…the Great Books are for you and me
> **A**nna my friend thought so
> **B**aldwin did too
> **C**ollins used them in her classroom
> **D**u Bois danced with the authors
> A-B-C-D…the Great Books could be the key to our literacy
> **A**nna my friend used them as a tool to teach
> **B**aldwin used them as a map to new identity
> **C**ollins used them to exercise young minds
> **D**u Bois had a love affair with their words and thoughts
> A-B-C-D…the Great Books were read by these four and now me
> Because there was a time where we couldn't
> Weren't allowed to
> And were kept from understanding who we are now…in America
> Not Africa.
> (Prather, 2007)

When I think of these men and women who also found themselves touched by the books, I realize that their attraction to this literature was that the books somehow helped them to become literate, not just with regards to the written or spoken word, but they also became literate in American culture.

I have found that the term "classical education" is interchanged with the term "liberal education." I thought it essential briefly to share why these terms are synonymous, because as I have been reading about African American education history, the terms are often used interchangeably. Liberal education is the art of apprehending, understanding and knowing (Nelson, 2001). This is what our ancestors understood, and in the past, to train students to think for themselves was the goal of every teacher. The human mind thinks through symbols, those symbols mainly being words and numbers (Nelson). Together, words and numbers help humankind develop the mentality, the culture, and the traditions that stand the test of time. These traditions are what tell the human story, what bind us together in America, Africa, Europe or elsewhere. In education it is imperative that students continue to understand the traditions of humankind and how they are relevant to the present day. Reading the classics is one way for a student to capture this understanding.

This is the kind of education that has been taking place over the centuries. This is the education that came to America with the settlers, the education that George Washington, Thomas Jefferson, Benjamin Franklin and others had. This is the education that was hidden from the slave, and even today, is out of reach for many African American students. In *Democracy and Education* John Dewey provides another understanding of liberal education. He believed that ALL children within this free country must be given an equal educational opportunity (Adler, 1982). They must all receive the same quality of education. Yet, this country continues to have different strains of education, depending on location, depending on socioeconomic status, or depending on race. To this dilemma, Mortimer Adler responds:

> We should have a one-track system of schooling, not a system with two or more tracks, only one of which goes straight ahead while the others shunt the young off onto sidetracks not headed toward the goals our society opens to all. (2001, p. 5)

I have been asked the question, "Why would you want to encourage your students to read mainly the books written by dead white males?" The truth of the matter is that America was founded and established by a group of "dead white males." They established this country's religions, scientific and artistic traditions (Postman, 1995). Whether or not this all took place in an ethical way, does not erase the fact that there is a literacy that should be embraced by African American students in order for them to thrive in this country.

Frederick Douglass understood the importance of inserting himself into the dialogue with the Great Books and he felt that by doing this he could help to articulate the unethical ways that African Americans were being treated. Those African Americans who have been able to stand before all races in order to push for equality have used these texts to help them formulate the argument. For example, Martin Luther King's "Letter from a Birmingham Jail" includes the words and thought of St. Thomas Aquinas (my students and I did a comparative reading and study of it along with St. Thomas Aquinas' *Summa Theologica*). Even Huey P. Newton (co-founder of the Black Panther) was inspired by this collection of books in some way. Although he did not learn to read until he graduated from high school, he taught himself to read by studying Plato's *Republic* (http://www.penguin.com/author/huey-p-newton/234951). Understanding the importance of reading, comprehending and joining in the conversation of the Great books has been instrumental in the racial uplift of the African American people. Having knowledge and understanding of the Great Books does not cause us to forget our culture and our past, but it empowers us to rise above the dark spaces of our past, so we, too, can become a part of the Great and HUMAN Conversation.

## The Lights on My Journey

Our founding fathers were proficient in the Great Books, and you can even find excerpts from these texts in many American documents. Reading the Great books provides a gateway to becoming literate in American society and culture. As an educator who primarily focuses on educating African American students, I find this quite intriguing. Over my 12 years of working in classical education and having students come across my path, I have never failed to have high school students who struggled with cultural and academic literacy. Realizing this and then watching the transformation that happened once I began to take students on a journey through the Great Books, I could not help but find myself drawn deeper and deeper into analyzing the importance of immersing African-American students into this compilation of literature.

In my delving deeper into this study, I discovered that there are several who have lit the way for me, inspiring me to keep pressing on with exploring this phenomenon. Either through their life and/or their life's work, the relevancy and power of the Great Books were revealed to me. Whether they were alive or historic, their lives shed light on my path.

### Back to Raymond

Clarence Major's (1997) "On Watching a Caterpillar Become a Butterfly" is a poem that struck me as I reflected on Raymond's metamorphosis, who I discussed previously.

> It's a slow, slow process
> Sitting here on the porch

Just watching a clumsy male
Milkweed caterpillar

Slowly turning itself
Into a graceful butterfly

Hanging from the underside
Of a withered leaf dark with
life
(Gates & McKay, 1997, p. 2246)

At the end of Raymond's senior year and the end of my time being his Great Books teacher, he told me, "I feel like I'm starting my life…like I'm just being born." Watching him evolve from the disengaged, angry, and uninterested student to becoming the student hungry for knowledge and anything on the written page, was a long, difficult and amazing experience. As his intellect, understanding and literacy were cultivated in my class, he began to develop into his own individual "butterfly."

Changing itself
as it hangs from the bottom

Of this green leaf
Wedged tightly

As though bolted
With metal springs

Throwing off that light
A light of silver-purple

Outlined in gold-
Golden trimmings
(Gates & McKay, 1997, p. 2247)

It has been several years since I chronicled Raymond's progress through my Great Books literature class. A few months ago, I was browsing his mom's Facebook page and her status that particular day was the following:

> It's a wonderful feeling to hear my second born, Raymond, talk about what he learned at the Washington Classical Christian School (7th thru 12th grades). How they taught him how to research. And literally how to teach his self. How he uses logic and rhetoric. How the massive reading assignments are paying off. The conversations he reflects on from the teachers that have made him wiser. I told him that the day would come when he would realize why I wanted him to attend there. THANK YOU WCCS TEACHERS!!!! I had an extreme passion and belief in their vision for my son.

Just a few days later, I was browsing Raymond's Facebook page and I read the following post from him:

> On the surface I'm a youngsta with dreads, tattoos and sometimes some flashy clothes. They don't see the deep thoughts, knowledge obtained over the years, or the search for wisdom and guidance. I represent the struggle but I know there is always a chance to increase. There is always room for growth spiritually, professionally and personally. I want to tell you, whoever you are, you can do whatever you want and be who you want

> to be. The person you are today is the person
> you choose to be.

Tears welled up in my eyes after reading these two postings. They caught me by surprise. Here it is years later and he has grown so much. He is a completely different person. I asked him about his Facebook status yesterday and this now 22-year-old young man said to me that he is able to use everything he learned in his life today. I believe he is able to connect the positive place he is in today, with reading and discussing the literature to which I exposed him. Raymond is truly my star, my RAY of light guiding me, inspiring me, as I seek to capture the lived experience of others who have gone through my Great Books literature class.

**My Predecessors in Great Books Education**

The interest in looking closer into this phenomenon also drew me to past African Americans who shared a similar journey. I needed these sojourners of education to come alive for me, guiding me to a place of understanding why this was so important.

**W.E.B. DuBois.** It was early in my tenure teaching the Great Books literature class when one evening, while relaxing in the basement of my parents' home, I looked over on the shelf and discovered W.E.B. DuBois' *Souls of Black Folk.* I had no idea what my eyes discovered, until the pages literally fell open to the essay, "On the Education of Black Men." Here is the one passage in this essay that has become my anthem on this journey:

> I sit with Shakespeare and he winces not.
> Across the color line I move arm in arm
> with Balzac and Dumas, where smiling men
> and welcoming women glide in gilded
> halls….I summon Aristotle and Aurelius and

> what soul I will, and they come all graciously with no scorn nor condescension. So, wed with Truth, I dwell above the Veil. Is this the life you grudge us, O knightly America? Is this the life you long to change into the dull red hideousness of Georgia? Are you so afraid lest peering from this high Pisgah, between Philistine and Amalekite, we sight the Promised Land? (Du Bois, 1903/2005, p. 108)

When I read this, I felt as if this was Du Bois' opus to the Great Books. Here he expresses why these books can be seen as relevant to the African-American. Since being brought to America as slaves, African Americans have wrestled with inclusion and equality. DuBois found in these books a world where he was considered equal. He also discovered knowledge and understanding of the culture he was living in, because the language was no longer hidden from him. This passage drove me to want to unpack its relevance to my current study. It became my personal Polaris in my research, guiding me to a full understanding of why the Great Books are relevant to the African American people. It did not take me long to begin to delve into whatever Dubois had written on education and literacy for the African American, and as I read more from DuBois, I discovered a woman, his contemporary, that they call "The Female DuBois," Anna Julia Cooper.

**Anna Julia Cooper**. Anna Julia Cooper was born into slavery in Raleigh, North Carolina in 1858. Her mother was a slave and her father is said to have been her mother's master. Anna, along with her mother, remained a slave until emancipation in 1863. In 1868, at just 10 years of age, Anna enrolled in the newly established St. Augustine's Normal School and Collegiate Institute.

It was here that Anna began her academic training in liberal or classical education. St. Augustine's was founded by the Freedman's Bureau and the Episcopal Church.

Anna's mother earned meager wages as a domestic worker, but she sacrificed greatly in order to send Anna to school. In order to help her mother in providing an education for herself, Anna began to work as a peer teacher at St. Augustine's at just 10 years of age. A gifted student, she was one of the first female students employed by the school. Anna was so hungry to learn that she wanted to also take more nontraditional courses like Greek and Latin, but there was opposition to her doing so, because the administration thought that only men seeking to be ministers could take these classes. She fought this mandate, however, and was eventually granted permission to take these courses. She graduated with her diploma in 1877, and she continued to study and teach at St. Augustine's until 1881.

Even though Anna Julia Cooper often had to fight for her right to further her education at St. Augustine's, she credits her time there to her overall development and maturity:

> That school was my world during the formative period, the most critical in any girl's life. Its nurture and admonition gave shelter and protection from the many pitfalls that beset the unwary. (in May, 2012, p. 16)

Not long after graduation, Anna married George A. C. Cooper (whom she met at St. Augustine's) who died very soon after they were married. She would never marry again, but she would continue to further her studies. She hungered for a college degree and to continue her studies in classical education, so she enrolled in Oberlin's Gentleman's course which provided her with a classical education that was the same as the male students of Oberlin. She was part of the first cohort of African American women to graduate from Oberlin, and from this cohort came other notable educators, such as Mary Jane Patterson who became the first African American female principal of the M Street School. Anna Julia Cooper would eventually serve as principal there (May, 2012, p. 12).

Anna's story is the telling of the life and educational journey of a former slave girl. From slavery, she was placed in a classical school and continued on this educational path for the rest of her life. The woman on this journey is the same woman who when you would walk the halls of the M Street School you could hear her enthusiastically read in Latin, the "Aeneid." Her teaching of the works of Cicero to African American high school students was life-changing for those very students. She went on to become a professor, a principal, a lecturer, philosopher, feminist, activist and essayist. When you read her essays and speeches, they are littered with the words of the Great Books authors, for she uses these authors to help her make sense of her place in America. She was the fourth African American woman to earn a PhD in the United States. Her immersion in classical studies which included the reading of the Great Books, helped to shape her into the educator that she became. In fact, she passed this type of learning on to her students at the M Street School in DC, giving them the best education she could offer them. She says:

> There is no social activity that more vitally concerns the life of a people than the problem of education. The Colored people

> of the United States…want for themselves and their descendants…all the advantages and opportunities of education as the term is interpreted and understood in the most favored groups in our American civilization. (in Johnson, 2000, p. 65)

I wonder if Anna's background, coming from slavery to being a leader in education, helped to infuse her with the passion for educating African American students in the way that she did? The journey she went on for herself, reminds me of my journey at St. John's. Her journey into educating other African American students also reminds me of my time with my Great Books class. I wonder why she placed such an emphasis on teaching this literature to her students? Did we share the same experiences as we watched "something" happen to our students when they engaged? It is said that she spent so much time teaching, that she had too little time to really write about her educational philosophy. I can only speculate to a point, but the tidbits I glean make me question and wonder.

## Dwelling in the Constellation of the Canon

We Wear the Mask
We wear the mask that grins and lies
It hides our cheeks and shades our eyes,---
This debt we pay to human guile;
With torn and bleeding hearts we smile
And mouth with myriad subtleties

Why should the world be overwise,
In counting all our tears and sighs?

Nay, let them only see us, while
We wear the mask.

We smile, but, O great Christ, our cries
To thee from tortured souls arise.
We sing, but oh the clay is vile
Beneath our feet, and long the mile;
But let the world dream otherwise,
We wear the mask!
(Dunbar, 1895, p. 896)

Reading the works of Anna Julia Cooper causes me to understand the process of my students seeking to connect to these texts. The oppression African Americans have suffered over the past hundreds of years is one of "deep-down-in- the-soul" pain. As a coping mechanism many turned to the literature of the oppressor, putting it on as one would a coat or a shell or a mask in order to find some way to dwell within these unfortunate circumstances. Anna and others did not read these texts in order to forget their history. Neither did they read these texts in order to become someone else, but they read them to place their situation in some type of context, in order to survive, to protect their mentality and even to cover up the hurt. They read the literature to make some sort of sense of it all and to be able to communicate that comprehension amongst themselves and any other who would listen and could understand the English language. Discussing their situation in conjunction with the texts that all of America shared provided a context whereby all persons, no matter their race, could maybe understand. It gave them a language to dialogue about their lowly state that was common to all.

To reveal more of what I am trying to convey, I have selected an excerpt from one of her essays entitled "Has America a Race Problem; If So, How Can It Best Be Solved?" in order to show an example of how she was able to have a written dialogue about race that included excerpts from the Great Books. The following excerpt gives her views on the organic nature of race conflict. She contrasts it to the utopian world created in *Looking Backward* by Edward Bellamy in order to unveil how the racial conflict of America is a part of the natural order of things:

> Progressive peace in a nation is the result of conflict; and conflict, such as is healthy, stimulating, and progressive, is produced through the co-existence of radically opposing or racially different elements. Bellamy's ox-like men pictured in *Looking Backward*, taking their daily modicum of provender from the grandmotherly government, with nothing to struggle for, no wrong to put down, no reform to push through, no rights to vindicate and uphold, are nice folks to read about; but they are not natural; they are not progressive. God's world is not governed that way. The child can never gain strength save by resistance, and there can be no resistance if all movement is in one direction and all opposition made forever an impossibility. (Cooper, 1988, p. 151)

She took another step to get at the root of racial conflict by going back in history to the rise of the dominant Western culture. The next excerpt reveals how she was able to see that the rise and fall of dominant cultures was part of the natural flow of humanity, but as she quickly reminds us, "…equilibrium, not repression among conflicting forces is the condition of natural harmony, of permanent progress and of universal freedom" (Cooper, 1988, p. 151). She shares in her essay that the Europeans were descended from the early barbarians (Goths, Huns, Vandals, Danes, Angles, Saxons, Jutes, etc.) and that no one could forsee these untamed people ruling and reigning. She goes on to remind the reader that ALL of the American people came from somewhere else, even the dominant culture.

> Who are Americans?" comes rolling back from ten million throats. Who are to do the packing and delivering of the goods? Who are the homefolks and who are the strangers? Who are the absolute and original tenants in fee-simple? The red men used to be owners of the soil---but they are about to be pushed over into the Pacific Ocean. They, perhaps, have the best right to call themselves "Americans." (Cooper, 1988, p. 163)

In Cooper's process of dialoguing with herself and writers past and present about the race problem, she argues with De Tocqueville when she says:

> De Tocqueville, years ago, predicted that republicanism must fail in America. But if republicanism fails, America fails, and somehow I cannot think this colossal stage was erected for a tragedy. I must confess to being an optimist on the subject of my country. (Cooper, 1988, p. 165)

In her quoting the texts of those from Western thought, Cooper still wove in the thoughts of African American thinkers, inviting them to join in the dialogue.

> I believe with our own Dr. Crummell that "the Almighty does not preserve, rescue, and build up a lowly people merely for ignoble ends." (Cooper, 1988, pp. 173-174)

As I read through Cooper's struggle about America's race problem, I thought of Paul Lawrence Dunbar's poem "We Wear the Mask." This conversation with herself and writers of the past was a common occurrence within the African American community. The reading of the texts that help to place the oppression of the African American people in a context void of just anger and bitterness, was necessary. It was a mask of sorts. It hid the pain that is constantly grappled with by African Americans. Talking about it helped to cover the wounds, the sadness, the anger. We could be the sad clown with the face painted to look happy, but the sadness can be seen somehow. Yet, we live on. We thrive. We manage. The literature helped us to manage and to somehow make sense of it all. Maybe inserting ourselves in the conversation with the great thinkers somehow lifted our heads?

This essay was one in many examples of Anna dwelling in the constellation of the canon. It was from her and W.E.B. DuBois that I came to understand how that can take place. Their writings helped me to design my literature class. It was no longer a matter of students' minds being jammed with the literature so we could say they read it. After being introduced to these two, I came to understand that the literature could be used as a tool for my students to work through their own struggles and life-confusion. Whether it is about race, love, hate, family, nature, talking through this literature that is written by humans just like us, somehow provides a dwelling place for the thoughts that flood our minds to rest and work themselves out.

**Dwelling**

The word "dwell" has its roots in the Old English *dwellan* which means to "mislead or deceive." In light of my discussing "We Wear the Mask," I am intrigued by this etymology. These books cover us. They cover our original roots and our feelings about our history. They in no way reflect what is inside of our souls. However, like a mask, we wear them (the Great Books), we dwell in them, as a hermit crab dwells in its shell. The African American people are like "the hermit crab that goes to live in abandoned shells" (Bachelard, 1958, p. 126). We were taken from one home and then somehow found a way to make ourselves at home in another space. Reading these books does not cause us to forget, but they help us to dwell here. Bachelard (1958) explains what this means:

> Everything about a creature that comes out of a shell is dialectical. And since it does not come out entirely, the part that comes out contradicts the part that remains inside. (p. 108)

Yet, the African American must dwell here (in America) under this "double consciousness" and under the weight of this foreign shell upon our backs. One way that we have been able to do that is through our engagement with the Canon. Dwelling in the constellation of the Canon, through drawing our lives as African Americans into the centuries-long dialogue, has helped us to dwell here. W.E.B. DuBois (2005) discusses the dilemma in his essay "Of Our Spiritual Strivings":

> After the Egyptian and Indian, the Greek and Roman, the Teuton and Mongolian, the

> Negro is a sort of seventh son, born with a veil, and gifted with second-sight in this American world—a world which yields him no true self-consciousness, but only lets him see himself through the revelation of the other world. It is a peculiar sensation, the double-consciousness, this sense of always looking at one's self through the eyes of others, of measuring one's soul by the tape of a world that looks on in amused contempt and pity. One ever feels his twoness—an American, a Negro; two souls, two thoughts, two unreconciled strivings; two warring ideals in one dark body, whose dogged strength alone keeps it from being torn asunder. (p. 7)

Is the shell the hermit crab? Yet the hermit crab cannot live without it. When I think of Anna Julia Cooper, W.E.B. DuBois and others that are discussed later in this chapter, I see an example of African Americans who found a way to survive the pain of living this duplicitous life. They crawled into the shell of this new world, chose to dwell in the literature that revealed the mentality of the new world and found a way to make a home for themselves. They made a mask for themselves. They made a shelter for themselves that protects them from a person or an inner feeling telling them they do not belong. These books help us to feel that we, too, are a part of the conversation and thus a part of America. My engaging students in the Great Books was my way of seeking to help them go through that same process, not only working through their African and American identities, but also so they could engage in dialogue about other issues relevant to human nature. I chose this path instead of having them only read culturally relevant literature because I wanted students to insert themselves and their cultural background into the Great Conversation. If St. Augustine is from Africa and many of the authors from the Bible, for example, are from the Middle East, are these really about Western thought? If the topics discussed in this particular literature are really about human nature, isn't there room for my students' cultural background in the conversation?

There was another African American like Anna Julia Cooper and W.E.B. DuBois who had an appreciation for the Great Books. Although he was a slave, he developed a love for the works of Cicero, Shakspeare and others. However, unlike the others he was not able to garner any formal educational training. His engagement in the Great Books was a completely self-propelled journey and it changed Frederick Douglass' life as well as America's.

**Discovering Douglass**

I am amazed at how this journey has come together for me. By reading about W.E.B. DuBois and Anna Julia Cooper, my mind became aflutter with excitement. I felt that I had stumbled upon some unrealized treasure, with regards to the educational history of the African American people. DuBois led me to Cooper, and for a while, these were the only two that fueled my passion for reading the Great Books and teaching my students to engage in these books. Then, yet again, Providence would have me stumble upon another African American who saw the value of reading and engaging in these books.

It was around my third year teaching the Great Books and I decided to take a break from our assigned list. I decided that we should read the *Narrative of the Life of Frederick Douglass.* I had no idea about his passion for reading classic literature. In order to support our reading of the book, I took the students to the Frederick Douglass House in DC. In his foyer sat a bust of Cicero. Then I slowly walked into his library and I saw floor to ceiling books. There was Shakespeare and a host of other Great Books authors. Then we walked into his parlor and there was a painting of a scene from "Othello." By the time I stood in front of the painting of "Othello" I could barely contain myself. I kept thinking, "You too Frederick??" I could not understand how or why he came to love and appreciate these books, because he was a former slave and had not had any formal education. At that moment I set in my heart and mind to understand why. Why was he connected to these books? What role did they play in his life? How and/or why would a slave want to read the literature of the master? How was he able to read this literature and not lose sight of his own heritage? Might looking deeper into this somehow reveal something that my students needed? Could these revelations unveil something to me about how I was teaching?

Like most slaves, Douglass was severed from all roots (when he was sold away from his mother), and "the means of knowing" were withheld from him. Douglass was left as a blank slate of sorts. When he was still a young boy, he was sent to be a slave for the Auld family in Baltimore. Going to Baltimore gave Douglass the chance to recreate his heritage, and this process began when his new master's wife started to teach him to read. She had never owned a slave before and initially was a very kind mistress. Without any hesitation on her part, she set out to teach him his ABC's, how to spell small words, etc., and just as he really began to progress, the master found out and put a stop to it:

> If you give a nigger an inch, he will take an ell. A nigger should know nothing but to obey his master---to do as he is told to do. Learning would spoil the best nigger in the world. If you teach that nigger (referring to Douglass) how to read, there would be no keeping him. It would forever unfit him to be a slave. He would at once become unmanageable, and of no value to his master…it would make him discontented and unhappy. (Douglass, 1845/1995, p. 20)

Mr. Auld made the above statement as a young Douglass (around 6 years old) was sitting there. Little did the master know that in saying this, he taught Douglass a lesson that would change his life forever. This statement provided the fire Douglass needed to continue his studies of literacy at any cost:

> These words sank deep into my heart, stirred up sentiments within that lay slumbering, and called into existence an entirely new train of thought. It was a new and special revelation, explaining dark and mysterious things, with which my youthful understanding had struggled, but struggled in vain. I now understood what had been to me a most perplexing difficulty…From that moment, I understood the pathway from slavery to freedom…Though conscious of the difficulty of learning without a teacher, I set out with high hope and a fixed purpose, at whatever cost of trouble, to learn how to read. (Douglass, 1845/1995, p. 20)

The above quote from Douglass is quite popular, and many of us have read it and found inspiration in the act of a young slave boy teaching himself to read; however, this time when I read this statement and also reflected on the various items I discovered in his house, I could not help but ask myself, “So once he learned to decode, WHAT did he read? What books shaped his thinking?” Douglass did more than just “learn HOW to read,” he also learned WHAT he should read. His house reflected what literature to which he was drawn.

I do not feel that Douglass was alone. The more I read, the more I discover that this was common amongst slaves and former slaves. Being taken from their homeland, ripped from a mother or a father, not knowing their birthday, not knowing their roots, slaves had to somehow reconstruct their heritage. Earlier I talked about the process of the African American learning to “dwell” here, and I also discussed how the word “dwell” is connected to some type of mask or covering that hides their “lostness.” James Baldwin’s text below describes this mask so well to me:

…I brought to Shakespeare, Bach, Rembrandt, to the stones of Paris, to the cathedral at Chartres, and to the Empire State Building, a special attitude. These were not really my creations, they did not contain my history; I might search in them in vain forever for any reflection of myself. I was an interloper; this was not my heritage. At the same time I had no other heritage which I could possibly hope to use--I had certainly been unfitted for the jungle or the tribe. I would have to appropriate these white centuries, I would have to make them mine--I would have to
accept my special attitude, my special place in this scheme--otherwise I would have no place in any scheme. (Baldwin, 1998, p. 7)

In order to reconstruct their heritage, slaves had to make America their dwelling, their heritage, their culture and as I look through the educational history of the African American people, I find a common thread—the Great Books of Western Civilization.

Reading about DuBois, Cooper, and Douglass ignited a fire within me that caused me to realize a sense of urgency with regards to teaching my students. Before coming to my parents' school, these students had not even read an entire book before, and the little bit they had read was literature that was directly opposed to understanding the role and place of EVERY person who resides in America. Some would call it culturally relevant literature, but it was only relevant to the African American culture, not the overall American culture. Everything I was reading about African Americans and classic literature, took place hundreds of years before I was born. I needed something more contemporary to solidify the belief that was developing within me. Soon after my discovery at the Frederick Douglass Home, I got a call from my mom, telling me to turn on the T.V. to watch a story about a woman named Marva Collins.

**Embracing My Phenomenon through Marva**

> Why won't people accept that just good old fashioned teaching works, no matter if the children are rich, poor, white, or black.
> (From "The Marva Collins Story*,"* 1981)

The above quote from "The Marva Collins Story" was made after a news reporter came to visit her school and asked her, "What's the secret?" He had just observed her teaching the students about Socrates, Hera, Marcus Aurelius and others from classic literature. He walked in while the class was engaged in a lively discussion about them. This is "good old fashioned teaching."

Discovering Marva, was the final transition in my "turning." Van Manen describes the turning: "Every project of phenomenological inquiry is driven by a commitment of turning to an abiding concern" (van Manen, 1997, p. 31). Up until this point, I was doing a great deal of wondering about this phenomenon of engaging African American high school students in the Great Books. It was a thought that was ever present in the deep recesses of my mind. However, when I saw Marva Collins portrayed by Cicely Tyson in a movie, the wondering turned into one solid thought that literally glared in my mind and consumed it. The definition of "glare" is "(of the sun or an electric light) shining with a strong or dazzling light" (Google). This thought was now at the forefront, its light blinding my mind from pondering anything else.

I think of a short poem written by Heidigger, that is foundational to my project: "To think is to confine yourself to a single thought that one day stands still like a star in the world's sky" (Heidegger, 1971, p. 4). When I started this journey, I was interested in the Great Books AND how the arts could be implemented in my Great Books class, but as the journey progressed, even the arts fell by the way side, and I just became fascinated with the overall story of the experience my students had reading the literature. I believe looking at that will draw out the arts, but writing, speaking, living, and being as well. I realized that I actually was not focusing on the arts in my class as much as just getting the students to be immersed in the literature, and my interest is what that experience looks like for the students. I found that the arts still came back to the light, but so much more than the creation of art happened when the students engaged in this literature, and I wanted to capture that. In fact, watching Marva was like a mirror reflecting what also happened in my class. I could not articulate it, and maybe I couldn't even understand it, but watching this movie revealed that SOMETHING does happen. It was such an amazing process to spend time sorting through what that "something" was.

My mom first introduced me to Marva Collins and this was a true gift from heaven for me. It synthesized and gave validity to all of the ponderings and wonderings that had been taking place surrounding this phenomenon. I'll never forget the moment I picked up the phone when she called me: "Nika! Nika! You have got to turn on your T.V. right now! There's a movie about a lady who believes in teaching black kids about the Great Books!" I ran to the television, and there was Cicely Tyson, playing Marva Collins. The moment I turned on the T.V. was a powerful one. There I saw an African American little boy standing up next to his desk reading an essay he'd written. He could not have been more than 8 years old. His essay was on Socrates' speech before his death. The student focused on one major quote: "I'm a citizen, not of Athens or of Greece, but of the world." After reading the quote, he was able to connect it to his life and he says, "I am a universal student of the world, and my duty is to pass on my knowledge to the world." Here you have a student who grew up in one of the worst neighborhoods in Chicago, being able to connect his life to the life of Socrates. I remember thinking as I watched him, "That's what my kids do too!" They were able to see that this literature solidified their place in this world, and most importantly, in this country.

The entire way she structured her class was so similar to min

e (i.e. having the students read the literature and then write essays and give speeches on the literature). My class was modeled after the classes at St. John's College, but being able to see an African American teacher work with students from the inner city of Chicago using a similar model, I felt confirmed in the importance of what I was trying to do. This was the contemporary example I was looking for. What does this history of African Americans reading the Great Books reveal about its relevance to my students' lives? Did the effect of the Great Books on past African Americans look the same with my students? Were my students even impacted at all, as Marva Collin's students or Frederick Douglass or Anna Julia Cooper were by these texts? I wonder about these questions as I am called to this phenomenon, and I look forward to exploring these questions through sharing **the lived experiences of African American students reading Great Books literature.**

### A Detour on the Journey

> After four semesters I gave up my theological studies and dedicated myself entirely to philosophy. I still attended theological lectures in the years following 1911...My interest in speculative theology led me to do this...the tension between ontology and speculative theology as the structure of metaphysics entered the field of my research. (Heidegger, 1962/2003, p. 71)

I mentioned earlier that my Great Books class was modeled after the classes at St. John's College. Teaching the Great Books class that first year also caused me to change my course of study for my doctoral work. After that first year, I discovered a program at St. John's College that would allow me to spend four consecutive summers studying the Great Books, and at the end of the fourth summer, I would earn an MA in liberal arts. In no way did I ever intend to earn yet another master's degree, but I thought this would be helpful to me because each summer I could spend time studying the Great Books and, thus, be more prepared for developing the literature class I was now teaching. However, so much more of an evolution happened to me as a result of becoming a student at St. John's.

**At St. John's: A Rest Stop and New Direction**

Although St. John's is located in Annapolis, which is just under 30 minutes from where I was living, I decided to stay on campus for the summer. I remember my first day on the campus. It was like a monastery. I could hear the local church bell ring, the water of College Creek trickle and people silently walking with books in hand. The air was fresh and I took in a deep breath. I, like Heidegger, continued to be influenced by the power of the spell:

> …I was still captivated by the never ceasing spell of *Logical Investigations*…Husserl came to Freiburg in 1916…Husserl's teaching took place in the form of step-by-step training in phenomenological "seeing" which at the same time demanded that one relinquish the untested use of philosophical knowledge. As I myself practiced phenomenological seeing, teaching and

> learning in Husserl's proximity…my interest leaned anew toward the *Logical Investigations*…(Heidegger, 1962/2003, p. 73)

The spell had brought me here, and by staying on campus, I could yield myself to its magic without any distractions. It was here that I would learn more about these books and why they were considered great.

When you visit the website for St. John's College, the first thing you will see is this statement: "The Following Teachers Will Return to St. John's This Year-Aristotle, Euclid, Plato, Hume…" (http://www.sjc.edu/). Naturally, one would think that statement is referring to us learning from those concepts presented in their writings. However, as I reflect on this statement, I cannot help but think that there is something else we can learn from these great minds of the past. I believe that we as teachers can guide students into realizing that they, too, can join in the dialogue with the Great Books authors.

As stated earlier in the chapter, Mortimer Adler and Robert Hutchins were the ones to head up the committee of scholars in canonizing the collection of literary works that we call the Great Books (Adler, 1993). Canonizing these works and then cataloging them into the Syntopicon, revealed that there was a Great Conversation taking place, a dialogue between authors thousands of years apart (Adler). The authors of each of the writings appear to be responding to the writings of those authors who came before them, and their responses cover common themes, ideas, topics, etc. that are relevant to any and every human being (Adler). Two of Adler and Hutchins' colleagues took the Great Books and designed an entire college program that utilized the texts as the primary curriculum. Their names were Stringfellow Barr and Scott Buchanan. This program was implemented at St. John's College, and it is designed so that students take part in this Great Conversation, along with the authors.

The class sessions at St. John's seek to emulate the Socratic dialogues of ancient times. Plato, once a student of Socrates transcribed the conversations that Socrates had throughout his lifetime. While I was at St. John's, I took a class called "Socratic Dialogues." By participating in this class, I learned a great deal about Socrates and about how the class sessions of St. John's were designed.

Socrates did not deem himself a formal educator or a man of great wisdom. Actually, he was a stonecutter by trade, but he allowed himself to puzzle the great mysteries of life and he invited all who were willing to join him (Adler, 1993). One of the dialogues that Socrates engages in is one in which he and a group of men are searching for the true definition of courage. The dialogue is entitled "Laches." In it he says, "So if you wish, let us too remain persistent and be steadfast in the search, in order that courage herself not ridicule us" (Plato, 1987, pp. 240-268). This is one in the many invitations Socrates gives for individuals to search along with him for the truth. Unfortunately, this puzzling led to his eventual execution. His puzzling eventually led him to question the validity of the Greek gods, and because of this, he was put to death (Barr, 1968).

There is something to be learned from the conversations that Socrates had with the young, the old, the religious, the poor, the rich and whoever else was game for the adventure. Many of those who engaged in the dialogue with Socrates had already heard of Socrates' ability to question so deeply, so intensely that most who engaged in conversation with him, rapidly found themselves befuddled and in doubt of the principles they had always held dear. Meno, one of those who engaged in a dialogue with Socrates said, "Socrates, before I even met you I used to hear that you are always in a state of perplexity and that you bring others to the same state, and now I think you are bewitching and beguiling me, simply putting me under a spell, so that I am quite perplexed" (Plato, 1976/1981, p.12). Socrates did not intend to bring about this perplexity; neither was he motivated by a desire to "win" a debate. His one motivation was to effectuate a hunger for knowledge in the individual. Is this not what we as teachers should desire for our students? As my students and I worked through the literature, I found that a hunger for knowledge grew within them. I first had to become a student at St. John's to learn more about how best to teach my students. Based upon my experience as a student at St. John's, I was able to learn how to lead my class in Socratic dialogue around the literature. My time at St. John's showed me how to teach my students how to delve deep into the literature and also how to connect the thoughts of the literature into their own lives. I learned how to make the literature relevant (allow me to correct that): I learned that the literature WAS relevant to every human. I was just given the tools to be able to reveal that to my students.

While being a student of Husserl, Heidegger had to let go of his original process of philosophical "seeing," in order to embrace phenomenological "seeing." While a student at St. John's, I had to let go of my traditional preparation as a teacher in order to embrace the fact that my students have something to contribute to the teaching and learning process. At St. John's the teachers call themselves tutors, because they consider themselves equal with students in the quest for knowledge. They want to be viewed as merely a guide to understanding, and that is what I desired to take place in my classroom. The Great Books are great, because they facilitate the opportunity to go on the quest for knowledge. They invite us to go on the journey with the author and take part in sharing our experiences and revelations while on the journey.

**Aristotle, My Compass**

> However, the clearer it became to me that the increasing familiarity with phenomenological seeing was fruitful for the interpretation of Aristotle's writing, the less I could separate myself from Aristotle and the other Greek thinkers. Of course I could not immediately see what decisive consequences my renewed occupation with Aristotle was to have. (Heidegger, 1962/2003, p. 73)

It was while under the teachings of Husserl, that Heidegger began to gain an understanding of Aristotle. Heidegger (1962) says, "As I myself practiced phenomenological seeing, teaching and learning in Husserl's proximity after 1919 at the same time *I* tried out a transformed understanding of Aristotle in seminar…" (pp. 253-254). It was while studying at St. John's that I was introduced to Aristotle and learned to work through his writings. My experience learning to comprehend Aristotle is what caused me to experience the process that takes place when my students are invited to engage with this literature. I remember sitting in a seminar and discussing Aristotle's "Parts of Animals" and finding myself drawn into deeply questioning the creation of the different animal species. As much as I love animals (especially dogs), I had never looked so closely into their entire construct. From Aristotle, I learned that everything around us, be it the sun, literature, a song, a bird…anything can evoke questions that draw us deeper and deeper into a thirst for knowledge and understanding. When he wrote "Parts of Animals," he was not just seeking to catalogue the animals and what makes them specific to a particular species. He was seeking for the soul or substantial being of the animal (Lennox, 2001). Also, by looking closely at each animal, he began to wonder about something deeper than himself, or greater (Smith, 1941). In connecting the dots of the parts of animals, he came to realize that every part of an animal is created for a specific cause or purpose.

Upon studying Aristotle's other works, I found that he uses a similar method of questioning. The questioning functions as a shovel, digging deeper and deeper into the subject matter. Aristotle taught me that we never reach a place of mastering all the facts or closing the book on a subject. I really don't think we will ever fully understand anything perfectly, but we continue to fall deeper and deeper into a bottomless pit of wondering, but that wondering is leading us into a place of deeper understanding.

Aristotle has given me license as a teacher to say, "I don't know but let's see if we can find out." And then the students and I go on the journey of discovery together. I can teach my students to enjoy the journey of trying to make that gap between knowledge and lack of knowledge smaller. By wondering, I join Aristotle in wondering first about the strange things near at hand and then going forward little by little, question by question, until we reach an even greater puzzle. Then the cycle begins again, and my students and I can say together, "I don't know, but let's see if we can find out!"

It would appear that Heidegger, too, made this same discovery while studying Aristotle: "Thus I was brought to the path of the question of Being, illumined by the phenomenological attitude…But the path of questioning became longer than I suspected. It demanded many stops, detours and wrong paths" (Heidegger, 1962, p. 254) . I came to St. John's in order to get more prepared to teach my students about the Great Books of Western Civilization. I received more than that. I became a student of these books, and I was inspired by my personal struggle to understand Aristotle to invite my students to join me on the quest to understand these texts. I also came to realize what my greater question was. If reading these Great Books could affect me so powerfully, could my students also be affected through engaging with these books in some way? Through myself, through Raymond, and through the conversations I had with my former students, I was able to gain insight into the possibility.

## Back on the Road: Illuminating the New Path

> Thus I was brought to the path of the question of Being, illumined by the phenomenological attitude… "Professor Heidegger—you have got to publish something now. Do you have a manuscript?"…Now I had to submit my closely protected work to the public. (Heidegger, 1962, pp. 254-255)

Through the years of questioning Aristotle's perception of Being, Heidegger was able to create his seminal work *Being and Time*. Through my years of questioning Aristotle's works and other Great Books, I have found my opportunity to write about my passion for engaging African American students in the Great Books of Western Civilization. "To think is to confine yourself to a single thought that one day stands still like a star in the world's sky" (Heidegger, 1971, p. 4). From the moment Heidegger saw Husserl's *Logical Investigations* on his desk, he found himself drawn to a single thought. That thought continued to mesmerize him until it took over his thoughts and his life's work. In fact, the constant growth of the thought within him caused him to leave the path of studying theology and led him to focus more on the study of philosophy. From the moment I saw those disengaged students 7 years ago evolve into students with a passion for gaining knowledge through the Great Books, I found myself drawn to the single thought of what happens when a group of African American high school students engage in the Great Books of Western Civilization.

**The Headlight: Seeing My Path through Phenomenology**

In the conclusion of Heidegger's "My Way to Phenomenology" he says:

> …phenomenology is not a school (*of philosophy)*. It is the possibility of thinking, at times changing and only thus persisting, of corresponding to the claim of what is to be thought…(Heidegger, 1962, p. 256)

This is what he discovered as he sought to follow his Star (the understanding of Being). He did not find himself trapped by the thoughts of those philosophers who had gone before, but he allowed his interest to guide him, and he only pulled in those philosophers as they spoke to his interest. Van Manen says, "…to orient oneself to a phenomenon always implies a particular interest, station or vantage point in life" (1997, p. 40). I have chosen phenomenology because it has freed me to think for myself and to follow the lead of my star. I am permitted to go on this journey of ups and down, and detours in order to understand: "…our questioning is a kind of light which casts a certain pattern on the phenomenon, while also filling in our expectation in a way that allows us to formulate further questions, and thus to advance our understanding" (Moran, 2000, pp. 236-237). I used van Manen's guidelines to illuminate my way through this journey:

> How can human science research be pursued? Reduced to its elemental methodological structure, hermeneutic phenomenological research may be seen as a dynamic interplay among six research activities: 1). Turning to a phenomenon which seriously interests us and commits us to this world; 2). Investigating experience as we live it rather than as we conceptualize it; 3). Reflecting on the essential themes which characterize the phenomenon; 4). Describing the phenomenon through the art of writing and rewriting; 5). Maintaining a strong and oriented pedagogical relation to the phenomenon; 6). Balancing the research context by considering parts and whole. (van Manen, 1997, pp. 30-31)

In addition, I used the teachings of Martin Heidegger, Hans Gorge Gadamer and others to help me make sense of my students' experiences in my Great Books literature class.

When I first started my PhD, I did not sense this type of freedom to explore my interest. I felt like I had to prove something, like when it was all said and done, I had to have a conclusion. Phenomenology releases me from that and appreciates my desire to wonder, thus inviting others to wonder with me. It appreciates my perceptions, understandings and wonderings. Socrates believed that in wondering we gain knowledge. Phenomenology allows me to explain to others why this particular phenomenon is interesting to me, and maybe in my sharing this lived experience, others will be drawn into the phenomenon as well.

A lot has happened since this journey first began. I have graduated from St. John's and have also completed all of my candidacy requirements. Raymond has graduated from high school and has gone on to complete two successful years of college (although he is currently taking a break since his father passed away suddenly/tragically). The school my parents started has closed down, but still leaves a legacy of students who were impacted by its philosophy and passion for the Great Books. I feel that phenomenology best captures the essence of this story. By this story, I mean the story of **the lived experiences of African American students reading Great Books literature**.

Van Manen (1997) instructs me to "search everywhere in the lifeworld for lived experience material so that upon reflective examination, I might yield something of its fundamental nature" (p. 54). Through phenomenology, I have been able to take a deeper look at the experiences of my former students from my Great Books literature class. By studying my students as a class/group (the students spanning the 6 years I taught this course), I came to a better overall understanding of the lived experiences of African American students reading Great Books literature.

## The Rays of the Star

**What are the lived experiences of African-American students reading Great Books literature?** This is my star. It shines in my mind, and Heidegger's short poem expresses its power in my life:

> To think is to confine yourself to a single thought that one day stands still like a star in the world's sky. (Heidegger, 1971, p. 4)

The star forms the metaphor for my study. What started out as a personal interest in the Great Books, began to evolve into a star with multiple rays. I not only found myself intrigued by the books, but also in the historical influence of these books on the lives of African Americans. Another ray that formed was my interest in seeing if and how my students were affected by the engagement with the books. When I think about this project, I envision a multi-pointed star, each point representing each chapter of the study. To further illuminate the star as a metaphor, each chapter will have some connection to a star (i.e. a story, an astronomical fact, the use of stars in human life or other information related to stars).

In chapter one I have described my journey into studying the lived experience of African American high school students in my Great Books literature class. This turning began with my own experience coming to teach in a classical school, where studying the Great Books was an integral part of the curriculum. In order to prepare for teaching my students better, I enrolled in the graduate program at St. John's College, which allowed me to spend my summers immersed in the Great Books. While there my own literacy began to be challenged and reformed. As a result, I began to wonder if these texts could have some type of effect on my students. From the moment I began to understand philosophers such as Aristotle, I started thinking about my students and what this same experience could do for them.

In chapter two I delve deeper into the historical significance of these books on the lives of the African American people. This is relevant, because after realizing how many notable African Americans relied on these books for their education and freedom, I was able to step outside my personal experience with these books. Unveiling the historical significance of these books also revealed literature from African American authors, that although not included in the list of the Great Books, could show my students how other African Americans have found these books relevant to their lives.

In chapter three, I address the philosophical underpinnings of my study, through the writings of Martin Heidegger, Hans Gorge Gadamer and Max van Manen. It is through these three philosophers that I seek to develop an understanding of my students' lived experiences.

Chapters four and five, provide a rendering of students' experiences in my Great Books literature class. Through conversations with my past students I was draw out themes that were brought together in order to reveal the story of their lived experiences. In addition, the students performed a play that they created which depicts their lived experience in dramatic form. The play also is highlighted in order to provide a visual representation of the students' lived experiences.

Chapter six draws forth the pedagogical insights from the study, addressing such questions as the following: How does this study inspire other teachers to engage African American students in the Great Conversation with Great Books literature? In what ways does this study contribute a better understanding of providing literacy education to

African American students that is rigorous and intellectually stimulating, but also culturally relevant? The historical accounts presented, and the experiences of the students offer some perspective into how these books have been a major source of uplift for the African American people. It is my hope, also, that this study will inspire teachers into discovering ways they can engage their students in the reading of and connection to The Great Books of Western Civilization.

# CHAPTER 2:
# THE GREAT BOOKS AS A POLARIS

From the literature I hoped that a new race
would be born
A new kind of people
A new kind of culture
A new kind of speaking
A new kind of being
A new kind of thinking
From the literature I hoped a new offspring
would be born
That surpassed the stereotypes
That surpassed the destiny of mothers and
fathers
That surpassed the expectations of the
majority
That surpassed even their own limitations
From the literature I hoped that a new nature
would be formed
And a new fate would be determined
(Prather, 2010)

## So What Is Great?

I know from experience that whenever the title "Great Books of Western Civilization" is used, it rubs people the wrong way. In the previous chapter, I gave an historical account as to why these books are great. Exploring the etymology of the word "great" might also expand its meaning further and illuminate the importance of this designation for the classes I taught.

The West Germanic word *grautaz* means coarse, thick, while the root word *ghreu*-means to rub, grind. The Old English verb, *greatian* means to become enlarged and the Middle English word *greaten* means to become larger, increase, grow. It seems odd for some of these words to be connected. When I read this history of the word "great," I was immediately haunted by memories of my own experience of trying to read the Great Books. I was also haunted by memories of my students connecting to the literature. At first our journey was hard. The literature was thick and course. It rubbed at us, frustrated us, made us feel small; it whittled us down to nothing, almost. However, the mind is a magical creation, for unlike the body it has no limit to its growth and development (Adler & Van Doren, 1972). Once we allowed the thickness and coarseness of the books to whittle away our limited comprehension ability and our limited worldviews, our minds began to grow. These books, in whittling away our own prejudices, brought us out of isolation. They gave us the courage to venture out of our African-American background and forced us to make a greater connection with the whole of the human race that dwells in America.

One element that helped to break down the racial barriers that separated us from the books, was Socratic dialogue. I first was introduced to it at St. John's College. Most of the time I was the only African American in the class. The majority of the literature was not written by authors who looked like me. Initially, I felt so isolated. I wondered what I could contribute to the conversation? However, as my tutors use of questioning within dialogue gently drew me into the literature, making a way for me to appreciate the mind of the philosopher and thinkers of the past, the color lines were erased for me. Instead of seeing myself as a black woman in a class of white people, I soon began to see myself as a human being in a room with other human beings. Color lines can sometimes turn into blind folds. Could lines and walls and isolation be a hindrance to us actually hearing, seeing and understanding the thoughts of other human beings? Stepping away from the framework of my own prejudices (of color, cultures, religion, values) was painful for me, but very liberating, and I have not been the same since.

After experiencing the power of this teaching tool through my time as a student in a Great Books class, I brought it back to my own classroom. Mortimer Adler (1982) writes:

> Discussion draws on the student's skills of reading, writing, speaking and listening and uses them to sharpen the ability to think clearly, critically and reflectively. It teaches participants how to analyze their own minds as well as the thought of others, which is to say it engages students in disciplined conversation about ideas and values. (p. 31)

During a Socratic dialogue there is no right or wrong (I think that is what makes it frustrating at first). There is just the license to wonder and conjecture about this or that pertaining to the text. There is the invitation for others to join you in that process of observation, wondering, questioning, understanding, believing, and communicating one's beliefs. Just as I saw my transformation from the books grinding at my comprehension, my belief systems, thoughts and feelings, I began to notice "something" take place with my students. I became somewhat obsessed with engagement in the Great Books. I also became consumed with a desire to use engagement in these texts as a teaching tool.

"Something" begins to happen as we engage in a "conversation" with the authors of the past. For me, I felt my mind *greatian* or enlarge as I pushed through the difficulty of connecting to these books that represent the thoughts of all humankind and even the gods. "Something" did happen with my students as well; I saw "something" happen! But what was "it"? This is what draws me to ask the guiding question of my study: **What are the lived experiences of African American students reading Great Books literature?**

## Rebirth through the Great Books

Paolo Friere (2015) says, "Liberation is thus a childbirth, and a painful one" (http://www.freire.org/paulo-freire/quotes-by-paulo-freire/). As my poem expressed at the beginning of this chapter, I wondered if the same rebirth I experienced during my time at St. John's could also happen with my students? If my journey was not easy, it was not going to be easy for them either. To gain courage to pursue this interest of fostering engagement in the Great Books with my students, I decided to research whether other African Americans had gone through a similar process. I found that many had. Many found that connecting to this literature aided them in their liberation from oppression in America, while the literature also supported their process of coming to really "dwell" in America. How, then, do we live in this contradiction, this place of tension? In the previous chapter I shared a quote from W.E.B. DuBois (1903/2005):

> It is a peculiar sensation, this double-consciousness, this sense of always looking at one's self through the eyes of others, of measuring one's soul by the tape of a world that looks on in amused contempt and pity. One ever feels his twoness—an American, a Negro; two souls, two thoughts, two unreconciled strivings; two warring ideals in one dark body, whose dogged strength alone keeps it from being torn asunder. (p. 7)

By inviting ourselves into the Great Conversation, we are able to work through the entanglement of this "double consciousness." By constantly looking at it in the face, talking through it along with the literature of those who have oppressed, and seeking to comprehend it for ourselves, we bring healing. Comprehending it for ourselves also helps us to clearly articulate who we are and our place in America in a language and understanding that all human beings can ascertain.

I think the challenge is looking at these texts without the stigma of only seeing them written by, about and for Europeans. It is true that the list of authors in this canon is about 90% European (Augustine was not European, and neither were ANY of the authors of the Bible, for example), and those who compiled the selections of books into one canon are of European descent as well. The goal of this chapter is *not* to address the controversy surrounding labeling any set of books as superior to others. This chapter seeks to illuminate the transformative potential this particular set of books had for many notable and influential African-American people. It also explores further the "something" I observed as my students engaged in these very texts.

## The Birth of Light in the Slave's Mind

There are many harrowing tales of how slaves escaped to freedom and of how many helped them to escape. In Jeanette Winter's (1988) *Follow the Drinking Gourd,* we hear of one such tale. Peg Leg Joe was a conductor on the Underground Railroad and he would hire himself out to plantation owners as a handyman. He would then make friends with the slaves and teach them a simple song entitled, "Follow the Drinking Gourd." The song seemed harmless, and slave masters could not decode its deeper meaning. Little did they realize that the song was a guide to freedom. "The Drinking Gourd" symbolizes the Big Dipper, which points to Polaris. Polaris was the star they should follow, along with the trail that Peg Leg Joe had set, in order to get to the North. The word Polaris means "center of all attention" or "a guide" (Schaaf, 2008, p. 48). Slave masters failed to realize that slaves knew observational astronomy, and slaves did an exceptional job of camouflaging their ability to do so (Rall, 1995). It was imperative that slaves understood how to read the night sky, because it could tell the way to freedom. They kept their eyes on Polaris, for it was the "center of all attention" and "a guide" to freedom. The words "Drinking Gourd" had to be used instead of the explicit "Polaris," because the slightest mention of the Big or Little Dipper could reveal the message of the song (Rall, 1995). Polaris is another name for the North Star, and because freedom and Polaris were both located in the north, Polaris became synonymous with freedom for the slave.

In *Anam Cara,* John O'Donohue (1997) gives a poignant rendering of the symbolism of light, and the message of it appears to be relevant to the intellectual freedom of the African American. He writes:

> We are always on a journey from darkness to light. At first we are children of darkness. Your body and your face were formed first in the kind darkness of your mother's womb. Your birth was first a journey from darkness into light. All your life, your mind lives within the darkness of your body. Every thought that you have is a flint moment, a spark of flight from your inner darkness. The miracle of thought is its presence in the night side of your soul; the brilliance of thought is born in darkness...Ultimately, light is the mother of life. Where there is no light, there can be no life...It keeps life awake...Light is a nurturing presence...The soul awakens and lives in light...Once

> human beings began to search for a meaning to life, light became one of the most powerful metaphors to express the eternity and depth of life…thought has often been compared to light. In its luminosity, the intellect was deemed to be the place of the divine within us. (O'Donohue, 1997, pp. 4-5)

This passage reveals the explanation of how light is a metaphor for thought or the intellect. The fact that the slaves knew and understood observational astronomy reveals that in the midst of their dark and oppressive state, they were able to amass knowledge of the most intricate kind, and that knowledge lit the path to freedom. Even still with slaves being forbidden to know how to read, the development of their intellect was limited, and physical freedom was still out of reach.

**A Growing Light Gives Rise to Freedom**

Frederick Douglass broke through that darkness and taught himself to read. The moment he learned to read, the light shined to reveal many truths. Once he learned to read, the books became a guide for him obtaining freedom and following his purpose. Literacy was his Polaris. In reading literature such as the *Columbian Orator*, he yearned for freedom, education and the power to make a difference. The literature he chose to read were the same texts that the master read. By using the literature of the master, he allowed these books to somehow unchain his mind well before he unchained his body from the bonds of slavery.

What was it about the words in this literature that brought about his freedom? How did these words free him? Why did his mind have to be freed before his body?

Are the mind and the body so separate? Levin (2003) says, "What now calls for thought is the bearing of the body, which is...bearing the life of our thinking" (p. 90). I also recall a Bible verse that my mom used to quote to me, when my actions were not what they should be. Before she would quote the verse, she would say, "Nika, what is in your heart?" and then she'd quote Proverbs 23:7: "For as he thinketh in his heart, so is he..." (KJV).

Frederick Douglass first had to come to see himself as a man, not cattle, not three-fifths human, not property, not a slave. He had to first see and think of himself as a free man. His reading of the literature helped to develop that thought within himself. His first book was the *Columbian Orator,* an anthology of various excerpts from the Great Books list. Douglass would say that it was from reading this book that he developed the words needed to speak against slavery, but before he could get there, his thought had to change. His mind had to be freed and it was. Douglass says:

> The more I read, the more I was led to detest my enslavers...As I writhed under it, I would at times feel that learning to read had been a curse rather than a blessing...It had opened my eyes to the horrible pit...I envied my fellow slaves for their stupidity. The silver trump of freedom had roused my soul to eternal wakefulness. (Douglass, 1845/1995, p. 24)

I can identify with this as I reflect on my time at St. John's. I honestly had a very closed view of who I was in America. Even still at 6 years after graduation from St. John's my attitude and relationships with those of other racial and cultural backgrounds is so different, much more open, much more inclusive. I saw some type of transformation happen in Raymond's thinking (who I introduced in chapter one). He went from saying "My dad didn't finish junior high school, so why should I?" to saying:

> I didn't really have a desire to learn anything. It wasn't that I wasn't smart, but I didn't want to use what I knew to my advantage. My mom was trying to get me to do better. She kept talking to me, but it didn't matter. I had to want it for myself. I finally got it in my head that I want to do good and then I started to try. The more I began to try, the more I wanted to learn. The more I wanted out of life.

With Raymond and with my students who participated in this study, I realize that "something" happened to them. Was there a rebirth? A transformation? If so, what exactly does it look like for them individually? What thoughts did they have during the experience? Did that experience bring about some type of action or life change? I will unpack the answers to these questions in the proceeding chapters.

> Levin explains how thought gives birth to action: The etymology of 'bearing' focuses our attention on the manifold nature of the body of thought. 'To bear' means 'to give birth,' 'to gestate.' It indicates, therefore, a gesture or movement which is essentially and intrinsically creative. As we shall see, the one whose bearing understandingly realizes and fulfills his creative gift is one who 'dwells' on the earth in a poetizing way. 'To bear' means 'to give,' 'to bring forth,' 'to make appear.' Thus, the bearing of thought must be understood in relation to

> our skillfulness and our capacity for
> practical activity in general. (2003, p. 91)

There is a pattern of reading, thinking and action that occurs when one encounters these books. I saw with myself. I saw it with Raymond and I saw it with my students who participated in the study. I got a glimpse of my students' thinking through our class discussions years ago, and now I have been given the opportunity to get at the essence of what took place within them as they engaged in the Great Books class. The participants have all graduated from high school now. Most have finished one or 2 years of college already. Engaging in this study allowed me to know (retroactively) the nature of their thinking and experience during that time, and if reading the texts gave birth to an action in their personal lives.

## The Great Books: A Polaris of Freedom and a Call to Action

> If Frederick Douglass can, so can I.
> If Frederick Douglass could learn
> When learning seemed almost impossible
> for a black man, so can I.
> If Frederick Douglass could free our people
> from the bondage of slavery,
> Surely I can free my people from the
> bondage of slavery,
> Surely I can free my people from the
> bondage of ignorance.
> If Frederick Douglass could conquer the
> impossible,
> Surely I can conquer ignorance.
> If Frederick Douglass could deliver
> speeches to thousands of people,
> Surely I can deliver a speech to the few.

> If Frederick Douglass could scale the high wall of success
> Surely I can too. (Marva Collins, student citation in Collins & Tamarkin, 1990, p. 137)

I recounted in the previous chapter, how when you walk into the home of Frederick Douglass in Washington, DC you will immediately see evidence of his emphasis on literacy. Opposite his library is the parlor, and in it hangs the painting of "Othello." Throughout the home are traces of Douglass' love for classic literature (i.e. a bust of Cicero). It was on a tour of his home that I first had my epiphany about the Great Books. Could Douglass' love for classic literature somehow be connected to his call to action in the abolitionist movement? Almost immediately after escaping to freedom, he began to engage in activities that put his new-found thought-life to action: he wrote his own autobiography, traveled across the nation giving speeches, and he established his newspaper, the "North Star." Literacy was an integral part of Douglass' life in the abolitionist movement.

**The Accidental Call to Literacy**

Recounting what has been shared in the previous chapter, Douglass' first encounter with the power of literacy began when he was just a boy of seven or eight (Douglass, 1845/1995). He had just been transferred to a new master, and the wife of his new master began to teach him how to read. The new master found out about it and said:

> If you give a nigger an inch, he will take an ell. A nigger should know nothing but to obey his master…to do as he is told to do. Learning would spoil the best nigger in the

> world…if you teach that nigger how to read, there would be no keeping him. It would forever unfit him to be a slave. He would at once become unmanageable, and of no value to his master. As to himself, it could do him no good, but a great deal of harm. It would make him discontented and unhappy. (Douglass, 1845/1995, p. 20)

Douglass says that from that moment he came to understand why the slaves remained oppressed; it was during that revelation that he became determined to read. This reminds me of what it says in the *Anam Cara* passage: "Every thought that you have is a flint moment, a spark of flight from your inner darkness" (O'Donohue, 1997, pp. 4-5). This encounter with his master provided a "flint moment" where he became aware of something very essential to obtaining his freedom. He says, "From that moment, I understood the pathway from slavery to freedom...I set out with high hope and a fixed purpose, at whatever cost of trouble, to learn how to read" (Douglass, 1845, p. 20).

Douglass' striving for literacy forms a palette for his life story. This is the case, because as long as slaves were illiterate, they could be viewed as inferior to their masters, but Douglass realized that becoming literate was the most powerful way to prove his equality with them (Sisco, 1995). Douglass asserts that his master was right when he said, "Mistress, in teaching me the alphabet had given me the inch, and no precaution could prevent me from taking the ell" (Sisco, 1995, p. 3). That "ell" was more than just obtaining physical freedom, but it involved an unshackling of the slave's mind (MacKethan, 1986). How could literacy accomplish this unshackling? In Douglass' case, literacy must first be understood to be more than his desire to decode words. It was more than his ability to copy the letters of the alphabet. The master's objection revealed that literacy was more than that. His master feared Douglass grasping the authoritative discourse, which is "that language and understanding that is indissolubly fused with authority or political power, an institution or person…it is the word of the fathers" (Sisco, 1995, p. 3). This literacy was not a monolithic thing for Douglass, not simply a skill that he has or doesn't have (Sisco). A better term, perhaps, would be "literateness" (Sisco). There is a continuum between decoding on the one hand and the more complex use of literacy for one's material, intellectual and political advantage on the other (Sisco). Upon reading Douglass' autobiography, one can see him transitioning through that continuum as he used the literature to bring about his liberation and the liberation of others.

## Learning the Dominant Discourse: Tales of Success

In Delpit's "Acquisition of Literate Discourse" (2001), she tells the stories of two successful African-American men. When asked about the secret to their success, they recount that their teachers played a large part in what they achieved. Clarence Cunningham, who is now vice chancellor at the largest historically black institution in the United States, came from a very poor community in rural Illinois (Delpit). As he was showing Delpit a picture of his elementary school class, he pointed out how many of the students from his class grew up to be a successful member of the larger society. She tells a second story about Bill Trent, who is a professor and researcher at a major research

university. He grew up in the inner city of Richmond, VA. Neither of his parents had earned a high school diploma and both were blue-collar workers (a cook and a domestic respectively). With this kind of background, it was difficult for them to see any future for themselves beyond high school. However, many of the students within his 8th grade class grew up to finish college and most were successful, as well as notable (Delpit).
When they were both asked about what contributed to the high percentage of success within their class, they stated that it was because their teachers taught them the "superficial features of middle class discourse," grammar, style, mechanics, etc. (Delpit, 2001, p. 298). But most importantly, these teachers taught the students the fine points of the dominant discourse (the values and beliefs of the dominant culture), which included how to speak and write in correct English, critical thinking, etc. (Delpit). Delpit gave examples of teachers who understood the importance of their role in the literacy classroom:

> They also seek to teach students about those who have taken the language born in Europe and transformed it into an emancipatory vehicle. In the mouths and pens of Bill Trent, Clarence Cunningham, bell hooks, Henry Louis Gates, Paul Lawrence Dunbar and countless others, the "language of the master" has been used for liberatory ends. Students can learn of that rich legacy, and they can also learn that they are its inheritors and rightful heirs. (Delpit, 2001, p. 301)

These teachers saw language and literacy learning as political acts and they realized that literacy was tied to power relations in society (Morrell, 2005). They saw themselves as political agents capable of developing skills, which enable academic transformation and social change. These teachers understood what Frederick Douglass understood as a boy of 7 or 8 years old. In order truly to be free, he had to become literate in the language of the master.

**Literacy as a Political Act**

Viewing literacy education as a political act makes it so much more than the simple task of teaching students to decode or score high on standardized tests or answer a few comprehension questions. Ernest Morrell (2005) speaks of critical English education. Morrell spent years working with urban secondary literacy educators in order to build upon local, situated literacies to facilitate empowered and empowering ways of decoding existing dominant texts and of producing new texts. It is imperative that literacy educators facilitate access to academic literacies, but they must also move towards helping students decode it for themselves and apply it to their own lives. This is what Frederick Douglass had to do. This is what I had to do. This is what my students had to do.

Lisa Sisco (1995) says, "Douglass identifies moments of reclaiming his humanity not in literacy alone, which was dominated by the rules and intentions of the white audience, but with literacy experiences transformed by action and infused with the spirit of an African oral tradition." I recall the thoughts of James Baldwin (1984/1998):

> I would have to appropriate these white centuries, I would have to make them mine--I would have to accept my special attitude, my special place in this scheme--otherwise I would have no place in any scheme. (http://www.nytimes.com/books/first/b/baldwin-essays.html)

Baldwin and Douglass both give clear revelations as to why it is essential for literacy educators to allow for focused study of the Great Books of Western Civilization in the education of African American students. As slaves, African-Americans were forbidden to be educated in any form. Once freed, they had to be taught a new way of life and understanding, and that new life and consciousness were foreign to them. Learning the dominant discourse was like learning a new language. Even though it has been hundreds of years since that time, the need still exists.

In "Toward a Critical Pedagogy of Popular Culture," Ernest Morrell (2002) discusses how he was able to use hip-hop music to help students connect to the texts of the canon. He revealed his reason for using hip-hop as a tool to help students engage:

> Popular culture can help students deconstruct dominant narratives and contend with oppressive practices in hopes of achieving a more egalitarian and inclusive society…Often the failure of urban students to develop "academic" literacy skills stems not from a lack of intelligence, but from the inaccessibility of the school curriculum to students who are not in the dominant or mainstream culture. (Morrell, 2002, p. 1)

Morrell and a colleague developed an English unit where hip-hop music was incorporated in the typical poetry unit of a public high school. Morrell gave lectures about the various time periods of the poetry and the relevant historical facts connected to the poetry. After the series of traditional lectures, students were placed in groups and asked to identify rap songs that connected to various poems. They then had to present those connections to the class. The students were successful in creating quality interpretations, and they also made relevant connections between the canonical poems and the rap songs. In addition, the students wrote their own poems that were personal and reflective of the rap songs and the canonical poems. Morrell was able to lead his students into demonstrating critical literacy. Critical literacy goes beyond reading and writing. It allows for students to gain access to the difficult literature, and it aids them in comprehending the correlation between the power and domination representative of the canonical literature. When students are given the tools to accomplish this, they are empowered. Morrell says, "Critical literacy can lead to an emancipated worldview and even transformational social action" (p. 73).

Could what has been shared above, be what happened when Frederick Douglass began to read *The Columbian Orator*? Douglass says that the text enabled him "to utter my thoughts and to meet the arguments brought forward to sustain slavery" (1845, p. 24). Although Morrell's method of utilizing hip-hop to help students connect to the works of the canon was effective, Frederick Douglass was able to do it as an enslaved, self-taught reader and without the aid of hip-hop. In addition, his focused reading of these texts (it is said that he spent hours in his study just reading these texts) spurred him to action.

## Other Chains Broken by the Great Books

Previously, I shared experiences with Raymond, the student who illuminated the power of the Great Books for me. I was new to the Great Books when he was my student, so we had to grow, learn, read and connect together. Over the subsequent years of teaching the Great Books, after

Raymond graduated from high school, the process for helping my students engage with the texts developed into a more specific pedagogy. I call it "Constellating the Great Books." This is where students read several books from the Great Books list, and in our discussions, the books were connected to each other and to the students' lives.

Constellating the Great Books is not a new concept. When the Great Books of Western Civilization were compiled into a canon, the men who created the compilation realized that the common threads in these books covered similar themes relevant to all of human kind, and each book cited texts that were written previously on the particular theme. These common threads created the context for these men to name this concept the Great Conversation. The citations made it seem as if the authors were engaged in a conversation about a particular theme, and this conversation crossed worlds and time. The authors would often cross-reference each other in their writings. This cross-referencing reveals the Great Conversation. When I invite my students to join in this process, I call it Constellating the Great Books. I call it that, because I am working with predominately African American students who struggle in the area of literacy. This struggle can be very confining for them. To have a forum where they can talk about their thoughts and feelings within the context of a piece of literature, is liberating. Just as the stars and many of the constellations are often used to help people navigate their way to a certain destination, Constellating the Great Books through conversation can help students find their way through the clouds of cultural and literary illiteracy.

**That They Might Soar to the Light**

Oh how the little things
Strengthen my tiny wings
So I can take on the world…

I might even fly
I might even fly
I might even fly
(Sarah Groves, 2005)

**So My Students Can Fly**

The story of when Peter Pan is teaching Wendy and her brothers to fly, causes me to think of the experiences of Frederick Douglass, W.E.B. DuBois, Anna Julia Cooper, Marva Collins, and my time with my students. When Peter Pan told them to fly, they could not. Two things had to happen to them first. First they had to change their thinking. They were told to think wonderful and happy thoughts. They had to think of those things that lifted the spirit. All of us who are mentioned in this rendering of African Americans' experiences reading Great Books literature, had to have something take place from within—in the mind—in the heart—in the soul. But that wasn't enough. It was not enough for them to just think the right way; Peter Pan had to do something as well. He had to sprinkle pixie dust on them. He had to empower them to fly. As the master's wife (even though for just a moment) empowered Frederick Douglass to learn to read or me empowering my students to connect to the literature, someone has to sprinkle the pixie dust.

Ernest Morrell (2002) says, "Often the failure of urban students to develop 'academic' literacy skills stems not from a lack of intelligence but from inaccessibility of the school curriculum to students who are not in the 'dominant' or 'mainstream' culture" (p. 72). These "academic" literacy skills are also considered to be critical literacy. Without Peter Pan providing the pixie dust, Wendy and her siblings would not have been able to fly, no matter how much they thought "wonderful thoughts." It was a joint effort to cause others to fly. My process of engaging my students in the Great Books involved me inspiring my students and revealing why they were important. That was my pixie dust. Something is happening to the dissemination of pixie dust within the classroom and because of that, critical literacy, that literacy that allows students' minds to cause them to fly, is slow to develop.

Ernest Morrell says, "The world needs independent, free thinking, open-minded intellectuals who can come together to collect, process, and produce information that will help to solve the most challenging problems of our time" (Morrell, 2010, p. 149). I am drawn to Morrell's research because of his interest in using the Canon to develop critical literacy in African American students. I am also drawn to him because of his belief in also including culturally relevant texts in this engagement. I believe in the study of the Great Books, but I also feel that it is essential to include culturally relevant literature in the study of these texts. This allows me to insert the African American culture into the Great Conversation. The Great Conversation is about all humankind. This marriage exemplifies that. One reason that I am able to see it in this way, is because I am also African American. I can identify with what a student may need to soar. My story is similar. Unfortunately, the number of ethnic minority teachers is shrinking (Morrell), while the enrollment of ethnic minority students is increasing (Morrell). The challenge is great. There is a shortage of teachers who have the knowledge, background, experience and inspiration to supply the pixie dust to minority students.

In Virginia Hamilton's (1985) black folk tale *The People Could Fly* (a slave narrative), we see this time a slave "sprinkling the pixie dust" on other fellow slaves in order that they may fly to freedom:

> He raised his arms, holding them out to her. "*Kum..yali, kum buba tambe,*" and more magic words, said so quickly, they sounded like whispers and sighs…The young woman lifted one foot on the air. Then the other. She flew clumsily at first, with the child now held tightly in her arms. Then she felt magic, the African mystery. Say she rose just as free as a bird. As light as a feather. (p. 169)

The raising of critical consciousness in people who have been oppressed is a first step in helping them to obtain critical literacy and, ultimately, liberation from oppressive ideologies (Morrell, 2002, p. 89). My bringing my students into engaging with the Great Books, along with drawing in literature that connects to them culturally, is my way of saying *Kum, yali, kum buba tambe*. I cannot truly explain why when I did this, "something" happened. I saw a change and I was amazed, just as the slave master and overseer in *The People Could Fly* stood in awe as they watch slaves leave the fields, flying away to freedom. They were so awed by the phenomenon that they really could not speak of it. They could not speak about what they did not understand. This journey that I am on to understand the phenomenon of **the lived experiences of African American students reading Great Books literature** is my way of putting into words what has happened. Another step towards my gaining insight as to what is taking place, has been through the work of Louise Rosenblatt.

**Why They Might Fly**

The statistics are startling. In "Adolescent Literacy Policy" by Ernest Morrell (2010) he discusses the U.S. Department of Education's (2010) *A Blueprint for Reform: The Reauthorization of the Elementary and Secondary Education Act.* It reveals that although at one time our nation was once one of the most educated nations in the world, now 10 countries have surpassed us. We are beginning to see the results of the deficits in our education, by how our college retention rates are decreasing. The low performance of American schools has pushed our country to implement intense standardized testing, all the while the building of critical literacy in our students is declining. Our nation is desperate for a change, a way to address the problem. I have to agree with Morrell (2010), when he suggests that "Critical Literacy is a matter of life and death" (p. 147). Literacy rates have to be raised. If literacy is proving to be struggling on a grand scale in America, imagine how it is declining within the African American community.

The struggle hits close to home for me. Within the state of Maryland (where I live and work as an educator), recently released data that show widespread gaps in the number of students who are ready for college in each county (Moore, 2015). The report reveals those counties where students score at high academic levels; however, within the county where I live and work (PG County), where most of the population is African American or Latino, 50% of its students score low in academic testing (in the areas of language arts and math). In fact, state wide, 22% of Maryland's African American students score lower than any other race (Moore, 2015).

Here we are in 2015 and the struggle continues. Recently I visited my aunt (she is 97), who was a teacher and is one of the main reasons I went into education. When

I visit her, she and I love to discuss issues in education. On this last visit, she made a poignant statement: "Anika, it's sad to say the struggles we are talking about and the struggles I read about today are the same as they were when I first started teaching." I believe that the historic nature of the struggle is steeped in the African American not experiencing true freedom and equality. Their lives did not matter, their families did not matter, their voice did not matter. When teaching moves forward without freedom, African American students will continue in the habit of not being free, especially in ways where they cannot contribute to the larger society. They will continue to dwell in the realm of isolation. Louise Rosenblatt's work was motivated by a desire to encourage democracy in the classroom. This is what could make students fly. To feel important, heard, appreciated infuses wings with the fuel to fly. Rosenblatt (1960) says:

> *To improve, not simply the quality of books studied, but rather the quality of literary experiences undergone*: this should be the emphasis when we speak of raising standards. To lead the student to have literary experiences of higher and higher quality requires constant concern for what at any point he brings to his reading, what by background, temperament, and training he is ready to participate in. (p. 93)

To invite students to engage in the work, sharing their personal life experiences and also synthesizing the text with other culturally relevant literature, welcomes them into the American culture—into the Great Human Conversation. Also the beauty of Rosenblatt's belief is revealed in how no one is seen as superior to the other. In her teaching of reading, Rosenblatt places emphasis on the dialogue that ensues after students respond fully to the text. The dialogue is not about anyone being more right than the other, but it is about everyone sharing equally, because she realized that every person has a unique perspective and those varying perspectives are what create our society:

> In a turbulent age, our schools and colleges must prepare the student to meet unprecedented and unpredictable problems. He needs to understand himself; he needs to work out harmonious relationships with other people. He must achieve a philosophy, an inner center from which to view in perspective the shifting society about him; he will influence for good or ill its future development. (Rosenblatt, 1995, p. 3)

Rosenblatt saw so much importance in her work. Through equal dialogue around the literature that has shaped American culture, Rosenblatt believed that students were being equipped to become citizens. She felt that if a student could speak well and engage in dialogue effectively, they could stand on their convictions when it comes to making the important decisions in the development of our country. They will be the ones to hold our leaders accountable for leading our country well. Dialoguing about the literature and connecting to their own thoughts and convictions could help them become more than just good citizens of this country but also good persons. Talking about the literature causes students to think about human life and their personal life. They are not driven by just an impulse to please themselves, but they begin to think and care about that which is outside of themselves.

Rosenblatt calls the perspectives created through student dialogue of texts a poem. "Meaning emerges as the reader carries on a give and take with the signs on the page…The two-way, reciprocal relation explains why the meaning is not 'in' the text or 'in' the reader. The poem or the novel or the play exists in the transaction that goes on between reader and text" (Rosenblatt, 1995, p. 27). This explains why my students were often inspired to write a song, a poem, a play, and even a dance that revealed their connection to the text. I even recall a student bringing in music from Lauren Hill to express her connection to a text we were reading in class. This is flying to the light. W.E.B. DuBois speaks of the veil that blocked the African American people from seeing their place in this country, but through engaging in the literature DuBois shares that he was able to ascend the high mountain and see the Promised Land. He was able to touch the sky. I want that for my students. I want them to fly. So like Peter Pan, I sprinkle the pixie dust on them, and as we perch together up high looking forward to our destination of understanding, I can say to them: "There it is, *Students* (Wendy), second star to the right and straight on 'til morning" (Cohn & Fain, 1953).

## Illuminating Our Humanness

Allow me to attempt to paint an image here. Merriam-Webster (2015) defines a constellation as "a group of stars that forms a particular shape in the sky and has been given a name" (http://www.merriam-webster.com/). Another definition that has been given is "a group of people that are similar in some way." If you look through African American history, you will find that the Great Books functioned as stars, shining light on the path to understanding a new culture in which they had been forced to survive. They were able to connect those books in order to develop an image for understanding their new identity on American soil. Constellating the books evoked the name of "human" for themselves, even though they were seen as being less than cattle. As a result, even though the constitution listed them as three-fifths human in America, connecting to the Great Books illuminated the fact that they were, indeed, equal to the master. They were human, equally human. They could view themselves as part of the group of people who were similar in some way, that similarity being humanness.

The Human Family
I note the obvious differences
in the human family.
Some of us are serious,
some thrive on comedy.

Some declare their lives are lived
as true profundity,
and others claim they really live
the real reality.

The variety of our skin tones
can confuse, bemuse, delight,
brown and pink and beige and purple,
tan and blue and white.

I've sailed upon the seven seas
and stopped in every land,
I've seen the wonders of the world
not yet one common man.

I know ten thousand women
called Jane and Mary Jane,

but I've not seen any two
who really were the same.

Mirror twins are different
although their features jibe,
and lovers think quite different thoughts
while lying side by side.

We love and lose in China,
we weep on England's moors,
and laugh and moan in Guinea,
and thrive on Spanish shores.

We seek success in Finland,
are born and die in Maine.
In minor ways we differ,
in major we're the same.

I note the obvious differences
between each sort and type,
but we are more alike, my friends,
than we are unalike.

We are more alike, my friends,
than we are unalike.

We are more alike, my friends,
than we are unalike.
(Angelou, M. http://allpoetry.com/Human-Family)

The Great Books reveal our unified humanness, because they cover the topics relevant to every human being. This is why my students could connect. Being able to understand the literature increased their self-image. As one of my students said, "When I talk to my friends and I tell them the books I have to read for class, I feel so smart because they tell me that they don't have to read such hard books." I recall Frederick Douglass saying something similar. Being able to connect to the literature gave them courage to face their personal struggles because the books reveal the struggles that all humans go through.

When my students had to read *The Count of Monte Cristo*, "Othello," and the story of Joseph (found in the book of Genesis), they came face to face with their struggles of holding a grudge or wanting to take revenge. For the unit, they had to constellate these three books along with their personal interpretations. As a result they picked music, wrote monologues and did a full performance on this topic. What was revealed through our conversations was how a desire for revenge chains us to our thoughts and feelings of anger. When the students chose the following song as the theme for the play they created around this unit, I knew that they realized how letting go of those feelings of anger could liberate them from the darkness of revenge. The song they chose was "Shout" by Kirk Franklin:

Shout. Shout.
Let it all out.
These are the things I can do without
So come on
I'm talking to you
So come on
(Franklin, 2005)

As we planned out the production and began to think of appropriate songs to use for the opening scene, the students picked this song because it addresses the importance of not holding in bitterness, anger, and hurt. The production was called "Revenge Anonymous" which is a play about a support group for those who are holding grudges.

Reflecting on the above unit with my students, I think of O'Donohue (1997) who says, "We are always on a journey from darkness to light…" (p. 4). As my students and I worked through the literature, discussed it and prepared the production, they often shared personal moments of facing a desire for revenge. We discussed how holding in hurt instead of addressing it, creates a desire for revenge. By constellating these texts, they were able to unchain themselves from the grasp of the dark spaces of their lives. I wonder could this same process of self-reflection occur with other human struggles? How would that self-reflection give way to any type of life-change? What other strategies can be used to help students connect to and discuss other literature?

## Literacy Lighting the Path

Douglass began with learning his ABC's through his master's wife. Inspired by his master's objection to him learning to read, he sought any opportunity he could to develop his understanding of the alphabet. One opportunity came through him sneaking into his master's office to copy out of his ledger book. Before long, Douglass had learned to emulate his master's handwriting. From there, he created writing competitions with the local white children he would encounter around the town. He would boast of being a better writer, and the children would write in order to show Douglass how they could write better than he. Douglass set this up in order to continue his mastery of letters and the few words he knew how to write (Douglass, 1845).

Another opportunity came while Douglass was working at the shipyard. When pieces of wood were labeled in order to be assigned to a certain part of the ship (for building the ship), he would use charcoal to copy the labels. In this way, Douglass seized every moment to develop his literacy. There was one major act that demonstrated Douglass' literacy development and his progression on the continuum of literateness. This act gave evidence of his graduation from the rudimentary practice of copying letters of the alphabet or simple words and phrases. In time, on his first attempt to escape slavery, Douglass wrote his own pass, in the same writing style as his master (Douglass, 1845). This was no small accomplishment. Lucinda MacKethan, professor emeritus of English at North Carolina State, says:

> Writing his own pass, for the slave narrator, involved the appropriation of the master's hand, the master's grasp of language, and the master's symbols…a black slave became a man of letters in a country where letters—the ability to make them and make meaning of them—were exclusively a white man's domain. Mastering letters enabled Douglass to write his "pass" and to "pass" into a world where he could no longer be named a slave. (MacKethan, 1986, p. 64)

This evolution in Douglass' life happened well before he actually became physically free. Literacy had liberated his mind (MacKethan, 1986). The pursuit of literacy all began with one moment when his master sought to keep him within the confines of slavery.

This process of Douglass mastering his master's handwriting reveals his comprehension of the master's language. When a person can take a piece of text and make it his/her own, and then develop some sort of creation from that text, it reveals a major step in the building of a person's literacy. Douglass wrote his own pass and it was so well done that it looked exactly as if his master had written it. Another example is when the slaves wrote the Negro Spirituals, they proved to be the first persons of African descent to seek literacy in America. The creation of the Negro Spirituals is surprising because the Spirituals are based on the Bible which is the text slave masters used to justify enslaving another human being. However, when you read the words of the spirituals, you see an embracing of Christianity for themselves.

Douglass creating his own pass and the slaves creating the Negro Spirituals, both remind me of when a student I had wrote a song based on our unit which included Ecclesiastes, *The Iliad,* and *The Peloponnesian War*:

It's all meaningless, meaningless, meaningless
I can climb the highest mountain
I can swim to the deepest sea
But at the end of the day what does it all mean
I can do my very best
Pass every test
Wear victory on my chest
But I still know that it's meaningless
(a student in my Great Books class)

The student wrote the above words, composed the instrumentation, played it and sang it during another one of our class productions. He went over to the keyboard (my class met in the school auditorium) and just started playing and singing this song. This is probably one of my most memorable moments in teaching the Great Books because of the spontaneity of this incident. We read the books and discussed them and he was inspired to write a song about his interpretations of the texts. To demonstrate their comprehension and connection with the literature, my students joined the process of recreating a text as Frederick Douglass did with the master's handwriting and the slaves did with the Bible and the Negro Spirituals. Louise Rosenblatt (1983) says, "Fundamentally, the process of understanding a work implies a re-creation of it" (p. 13).

The process started with us reading the text. We then had a conversation about the texts, sharing ideas, insights and connections about the literature. From this conversation, students were inspired to re-create the texts through a performance. Gadamer (1975/1989) writes:

> Hence reaching an understanding on the subject matter of a conversation necessarily means that a common language must first be worked out in the conversation…To reach an understanding in a dialogue is not merely a matter of putting oneself forward and successfully asserting one's own point of view, but being transformed into a communion in which we do not remain what we were. (p. 371)

This process was the same for the slave, for freed African Americans, for my students. We inserted ourselves, our culture and our backgrounds into the Great Conversation, and as a result, an understanding developed between all of us involved. We did not keep our experiences to ourselves, but we shared them with each other and the authors. The connection was so powerful that something had to be created. As Phillis Wheatley created poetry based on

Greek myths, and as my student created the song "Meaningless," these creations represent the transformation through understanding that took place while sharing the new understandings with others. Could this sharing of their creations be an invitation to join the conversation as well? Is this how the cycle has continued through the ages?

**Home is Where the Heart and Mind Are**

What is it about these books from a different time and culture that continue to inspire us? Phillis Wheatley was born in Africa and brought to America as a young girl to be a slave, and yet she read the Great Books. Most of her poetry is littered with references from the Great Books. This following poem from her is based on the Bible:

> 'Twas mercy brought me from my Pagan land
> Taught my benighted soul to understand
> That there's a God, that there's a Saviour too:
> Once I redemption neither sought nor knew.
> Some view our sable race with scornful eye,
> "Their colour is diabolical die."
> Remember, *Christians, Negros*, black as *Cain*,
> May be refin'd, and join the angelic train.
> (Wheatley, 1773, p. 171)

The African being brought to America was not a matter of choice. We were forced to come here. The struggle to find our place in America has been a constant battle. The slave trade extended from Europe (the Portuguese, Dutch, English, etc.) and went down the West coast of Africa (Stearns, 1956). Anthropologists reveal that the majority of slaves came from the West coast of Africa, especially Senegal, the Guinea coast, Niger delta and the

Congo. Inter-tribal raids in dynastic wars in West Africa fueled the slave trade. The victors of these battles would take their captives and sell them into slavery. The captives were often kings and priests, people who were specialists in their own tribal music and rituals (Stearns). Once here in America, the African tried to adjust to their new home the best way that he could. It was customary for West Africans to adopt the deities and attitudes of whomever conquered them, so creating music that connected to the literature, such as the Bible, (the Negro Spirituals being the first sign of their attempt to connect to the literature) was a revelation of this cultural practice.

America, with one of its major religions being Christian, had many churches, ceremonies and events that gave Africans opportunities to hear the Bible and the ritual music of the church (Stearns, 1956). Upon hearing this, the slave was able to create songs that revealed an embracing of their master's religion. It is interesting that the slave embraced Christianity, because the Christianity that they knew of the Bible contrasted the one that was practiced before them (Johnson & Johnson, 1926). However, the slave connected to Christianity, and it seems that he felt a connection with the story of the Jews in the Bible (Johnson & Johnson). Slaves felt the pain of oppression that the Jews felt, and they also felt that if God saved Daniel in the lion's den, he would save them. As God preserved the Hebrew children in the fiery furnace, he would preserve them. As God delivered Israel out of bondage in Egypt, so he would deliver them (Johnson & Johnson, 1926). These stories within the Bible gave them the strength to endure hundreds of years in bondage on American soil and the spirituals are a testament to this survival.

The Spirituals were essential for the endurance of the slave, for singing these songs helped the slave to toil. African music was always used to accompany work (Stearns, 1956). In Africa, singing took away the drudgery and inspired people to work. Using songs in this way transferred to the African's new life as a slave in America. So the African, illiterate in this country, only had the music of his homeland deep within his soul. Everything else had been stripped from him. The first literature he encountered here was the Bible, presented to him through hymns and recitations of the Bible that the master allowed him to hear.

Creating the Spiritual was the African Americans' first attempt at connecting to the foundational literature of America. In the process, a form of liberation developed within them because it allowed them to be inserted in the conversation through understanding the Bible. It gave them an identity because the one they had, was taken from them. It was one of the few things that the slave could hold on to in order to be pulled out of the darkness. When we read these texts and their light shines in our minds, the liberation we experience is incredible and inspiring. It drives us to create, because in reading them, we find the language necessary to articulate who we are in America. In a previous chapter I shared the thoughts of James Baldwin and it expresses the essence of what I am seeking to illuminate here:

> …These were not really my creations, they did not contain my history; I might search in them in vain forever for any reflection of myself. I was an interloper; this was not my heritage. At the same time I had no other heritage, which I could possibly hope to use--I had certainly been unfitted for the jungle or the tribe. I would have to appropriate these white centuries, I would have to make them mine... (Baldwin, 1998, p. 7)

I am reminded of the song "Home" sung by Diana Ross in the "Wiz" as I write this. The song starts out with her singing nostalgically about a home she used to know. But then the song transitions into her realizing home is within her. Home develops within as she learns to accept and appreciate where she is, even though it is not her original home, even though it is not where she wants to be. The Old English word *ham* means "dwelling place, house, abode, fixed residence." The slaves now had to dwell in America; it was their fixed residence. The creation of the Spirituals reveals to me their early effort to create "home" within themselves first, so that they may actually be able to abide here.

## Remembering Home While Embracing a New Land

When students first enrolled in my class, many had no idea what the Constitution said. Some could tell me that the original documents did not have African-Americans in mind when they were written, and they would get pretty upset about that injustice. BUT what is the case now? As shared earlier, Raymond went through a metamorphosis as he came to accept that the Great Books often do not reflect him, but they do serve a purpose. He said, "Reading the African-American literature and the Great Books showed me how the different subjects relate to each other. They all come together."

As Phillis Wheatley expresse in her poem mentioned previously, she did not forget where she came from. She did not even start to see herself as "less than," but she communicates an acceptance of who and where she is right at that moment, while still remembering where she came from, as expressed in her poem "On Being Brought from Africa to America." When she calls Africa "a pagan land," is she talking as if Africa is bad and America is good? Or is she talking about her embracing of the Christian faith, which in her country was something she did not know? Her new found faith in God is what gave her the light of hope when she was taken from her family as a young girl. Like the lyrics in Diana Ross's song "Home," she was able to learn to appreciate, and accept where she was in spite of the circumstances that brought her there, and like Diana Ross, she had no choice but to do that. To appreciate this literature does not mean to hate our heritage. It does not mean we are trying to forget "home."

Marva Collins (1990) writes about the importance of exposing African American students to cultures other than their own:

> I think it's foolish and hypocritical that many people allow black youths to take on extreme styles and mannerisms under the guise of finding their black identity-without pointing out the social and economic consequences. (p. 141)

I wonder if by not exposing them enough to literature such as the Great Books, do teachers alienate them from engaging in conversation that is more inclusive? What is the human experience? Does it have a color? Can it be discussed and understood in the light of a race that is different? What happens to a student's perception of others by learning about a person's experience who has a different cultural background? Marva Collins (1990) had a desire to see her students become "citizens of the world:"

> I encouraged them to become universal people, citizens of the world…I did not teach black history as a subject apart from American history, emphasize black heroes over white, or preach black consciousness rather than a sense of the larger society. (p. 141)

I remember when I first started this journey into engaging African American students in the Great Books. I had to face a lot of resistance from fellow teachers, students, administrators, parents, and even those in academia. I wonder why there was this resistance? What would happen if the books were just given a try? What would happen, if as a community, varying races read the books, discussed them and shared their common experiences? In Marva Collins (1990), I found that I was not alone in the struggle when I read that she experienced the same resistance:

> My refusal to do so was a sore spot between me and some members of the black community. (p. 142)

Anna Julia Cooper also met the same resistance from the DC school board as she sought to engage the students of the M Street School in classical studies (Johnson, 2000). This battle has been long fought. Yet, I join with these women in continuing to look deeper into their relevancy for African American students. Marva Collins (1990) makes a very bold statement, expressing why she continued to press forward with the struggle:

> I was convinced that English was another barrier confining my students to the ghetto, and I had no intention of letting them be confined. I cautioned my children, "When you don't know the language people are always going to take advantage of you. It's like being a visitor in a foreign country."…Instead of teaching black pride I taught my children self pride. All I wanted was for them to accept themselves….if you have a positive attitude about yourself, then

> no one can put you down for who you are or where you live. (Collins, 1990, pp. 141-142)

Is it necessary for teachers to leave out African American heritage and culture completely? This is the one part where Marva Collins and I do disagree a little. How can students love themselves when their culture is not appreciated in the classroom? My desire is to include their culture in the study of the Great Books. I wonder if by doing this, color lines might be erased, instead of studying these books as "those" books. I wonder if by including our culture in the conversation my students might come to claim them as "their" books—"their" stories—"their" experiences?

Frederick Douglass is an example of seeing things larger. He immersed himself in the literature, without forsaking his heritage. He learned the language and mentality of the culture that enslaved him in order to understand them. Martin Luther King is also an example (as shared in chapter 1). Many of his speeches, essays and other writings cite the authors from the Great Books list. I was so intrigued by the fact that his "Letter from a Birmingham Jail" is based upon the writings of St. Thomas Aquinas. One of my major pedagogical practices of engaging my students in the Great Books is that we first looked up the references of the African American texts that we read. We would then read both the African American texts and then the Great Books texts that were referenced in each. Our discussions would include comparing and contrasting both texts. Raymond revealed how this affected him when he said, "I think the English class impacted me the most… because you had us read African-American literature along with the Great Books. I was able to see the whole story of African-Americans….it made me think differently." I did not get the chance to ask Raymond to explain what he meant by "it made me think differently," but this study pursues such questions with the students of this study.

## The Literacy Struggle Continues

There are a plethora of studies that have been conducted related to this topic, and yet in the area of literacy, "on average, African-American students score at a lower proficiency level than white students" (Flowers, 2007, p. 424). The achievement gap in reading between African-Americans and white students may be narrowing, but there is little evidence to show that it is likely to disappear altogether (Flowers). If we go back to the original African Americans, those slaves who against all odds sought to become literate as a means to gain liberty—can something be learned as to how to understand this problem? In reading about Phillis Wheatley, Frederick Douglass, W.E.B. DuBois, James Baldwin, Lorraine Hansberry, Anna Julia Cooper and others I am able to see one thing they have in common: a reliance on and understanding the Great Books of Western Civilization. As a result, their eyes were opened and they became conscious of their humanity in the society that at one time enslaved them and considered them to be three-fifths human.

## The Great Books: A Door to Cultural Literacy

My experience studying the Great Books at St. John's College, helped to shape the literature program I implemented. Like St. John's, the program was a four year program where high school students (from grade 9 through 12) would spend a full period every day studying the Great Books of Western Civilization for the entire school year. New students were always resistant, but by the end of their first year, they were able to engage. The majority of students who came to our school in the 9th grade came with major literacy deficits. Studying the writings of W.E.B. DuBois and Frederick Douglass offered me inspiration to teach differently. Lisa Delpit's illumination of the dominant discourse provides a palette for my research interest in leading students into focused study of the Great Books of Western Civilization. I share Delpit's view that African American students no longer have to be in the "bottom rung of the social and economic ladder" (Delpit, 2001, p. 301). Becoming literate in the dominant discourse may be a way that they can overcome that. Delpit explains the role of a literacy teacher:

> The teacher's stance can be, "Let me show you how to cheat!" and of course, to cheat is to learn the discourse that would otherwise be used to exclude them from participating in and transforming the mainstream. This is what many Black teachers of the segregated south intended when they, like the teachers of Bill Trent and Clarence Cunningham, told their students…We can again let our students know they can resist a system that seeks to limit them…(Delpit, 2001, p. 301)

The Great Books could be a doorway for my students (and others) that will give them access to the dominant discourse. Engaging in these texts can help to cultivate cultural literacy.

When DuBois (1903/2005) says, "I sit with Shakespeare and he winces not. Across the color line I move arm in arm with Balzac and Dumas, where smiling men and welcoming women glide in gilded halls…" (p. 108), he reveals that he felt that by having access to the

Great Books he somehow gained a key to that dominant discourse. This key, I feel, allows him to speak the language, so that he can "dance in gilded halls" (DuBois) with them and there is no "scorn or condescension" (DuBois). He can call them and they all "come graciously" (DuBois). To be considered equal, to him, was the Promised Land.

The men that Delpit interviewed felt that in some way they made it to the Promised Land or to that place of inclusion into the dominant discourse. I feel that by reading these classic texts, African-Americans can develop their literacy skills, but it is much more than that. They learn how to "say, write, do, be, value and believe" according to the standards of American society (Delpit, 2001, p. 297). So instead of playing "Russian roulette" with the methods for increasing the literacy of our African-American youth, why not go back to the ancestors? These ancestors demonstrated that focused study of the Great Books was a Polaris for them. They were torn from their homeland, forever separated from their family, their roots, and placed in a life that was of the most demoralizing state. If these ancestors were able to take hold of the hands of the Great Books, allowing these texts to pull them from the black hole of slavery and anonymity, then surely it can do something as significant for my students.

## Educators in Cultural Literacy

This journey has been an isolating one, but my experiences with my own students urged me onward. In my loneliness on this quest, I hungered for knowing other educators who also saw the value of the Great Books in the educational program of African American students. I struggled to find many in my life time. I would find an article here or there that discussed an arbitrary lesson or experience that used a classic text, but I could not seem to find an educator who had fully embraced the philosophy behind using the Great Books as a means for providing a quality and equal (equality) education to African American students. However, as I recounted in the previous chapter, I was able to find Anna Julia Cooper and Marva Collins, both educators who used the Great Books as a main educational tool in order to help their students gain access to the dominant discourse.

While Anna Julia Cooper was principal of the M Street School, the students were offered 4 years of classical studies. It was during this time that students were able to read and explain the *Aeneid* in Latin. One observer of Anna Julia Cooper found himself mesmerized as he watched the students inspired by her teachings on Cicero. A student shares her experience in Anna Julia Cooper's class:

> I first knew Dr…Cooper in 1920 when as a student at Dunbar High School, I was a member of her…Latin class…I remember her eyes flashing as she read… She would become Cicero and make us feel his courage…(Johnson, 2000, p. 74)

In the previous chapter, I discussed the stages of classical education. I explained that the school where my class took place was a classical school. When students reach the high school level, they are considered to be in the rhetoric phase, and the reading of the Great Books is considered "rhetoric in action." Anna Julia Cooper, a former slave turned educator, was able to see the relevance of these Western texts to her life, and therefore, was able to pass that belief on to her students. At the M Street School, where she served as principal, students practiced this "rhetoric in action":

> Students were encouraged to reason and think critically about issues rather than depend upon memory. (Johnson, 2000, p. 54)

The Western literature is relevant to every American, whether that person came here by choice or not. Anna Julia Cooper felt and understood that we are an American, and to understand what that means, we must be proficient in the texts that helped to form the American culture, thought and belief system. With this understanding and with great vigor, she engrossed her students in the texts:

> M Street curriculum, however, was dominated by the classical courses. A classical curriculum in a school of African Americans was rare due to the fact that the prevailing viewpoint of dominant society promulgated the philosophy that an industrial education provided the best and appropriate model for educating black students…M Street's college preparatory program would later prove to become problematic and would come under attack by the District's school board; Anna J. Cooper would be in the middle of this controversy. (Johnson, 2000, p. 54)

My question is, as we seek to move to a more culturally relevant pedagogy: are we silencing a discourse that should belong to all? What is the American discourse? And by returning to a more focused study of the Great Books, can room be made for students to include their culture in that discourse, instead of segregating it? Can that come about in an organic way, through the Great Conversations?

By Marva Collins engaging her students in classic works like Shakespeare, she helped them develop a good sense of self-esteem. Marva Collins had her students reading *Macbeth, Twelfth Night, A Midsummer Night's Dream, Hamlet, Romeo and Juliet, King Lear* and many more. She used passages from these texts to teach rhetoric and oration. These students were from the projects of Chicago, many coming from the poorest homes. When they came to Marva from the local public schools, they were way below grade level. Some had been labeled as mentally challenged; however, after being in Marva Collins' class, their academic skills began to improve.

Both Anna Julia Cooper and Marva Collins overcame many obstacles in order to push forward with their educational philosophy. The school districts, fellow teachers and others struggled to believe that African American students, especially those from urban areas could be able to read, understand, appreciate and find relevant the texts from Western Culture. In the face of these obstacles, these two educators continued to put into practice "rhetoric in action" through the reading and discussion of the Great Books of Western Civilization. Most of the students who remained under their educational leadership went on to some of the top colleges in the United States and also pursued their careers post college. I could write for a life time about these two women, and I have found much inspiration from them as I have held their educational philosophy close to my heart.

Like Cooper and Collins, I too, have plowed forward with engaging my students in the Great Books of Western Civilization. I also saw similar results to Anna Julia Cooper and Marva Collins in my students. What do those who went through my Great Books literature class look like? Where are they now? In this year that I am writing this chapter, the last of those students have graduated from high school. I wonder how they would articulate their lived experience being in my class? Did they see what I saw? Did they feel what I felt as I watched them progress through the literature? How did engaging in the texts affect their cultural literacy and their overall world view? How did it affect their sense of self? There are so many aspects I seek to uncover as I provide a rendering of researching their lived experience, and it is my hope and desire that as I share my students' experiences of being in my literature class, that others will find inspiration to implement a similar philosophy also.

**Stars Past and Present**

O'Donohue (1997) says, "Ultimately, light is the mother of life" (p. 5). I am thinking of two of the productions that developed as a result of us engaging in the Great Books texts. There was a play called "Revenge Anonymous" and a play called "The Room." I realize that these books can illumine students' minds in such a way that it can affect the decisions they make. These plays were all student created, and filled with students' feelings about the text. Here is a monologue written by one of the students for the play "Revenge Anonymous":

> I was a young man when I was hit by a car while riding my motorcycle. I was hurt bad. My friend and I decided to retaliate against the person who injured me. After I got out of the hospital, my friend and I hunted the man down. Just before shooting the guy, I remember a sermon I heard in church years ago. I remember the preacher saying that God is the one who should get vengeance and that we should leave all things in his hands. I then drop my gun and walk away.

> My friend, all pumped up with wanting to kill someone continues on and ends up getting shot and killed. It was then that I committed my life to God, became a pastor and started "Revenge Anonymous." (Hamlin, 2013)

A student may be on one path, but these texts can change their way of thinking, their way of being, their way of seeing the world. In effect, a rebirth can take place: "Your birth was first a journey from darkness to light" (O'Donohue, 1997, p. 5)). Like Douglass being exposed for the first time to learning to read and becoming enlightened about where his actual freedom would come from, my students can rethink how they live their lives.

There is a reason why an artist is often called a "star." Actors illuminate the script for the audience through their interaction with the text. Frederick Douglass became a star when he allowed literacy in the Great Books to help him articulate the injustice of enslaving another human being. The slaves became stars, when the songs they created shed light on the stories of the Bible, revealing it as a source of hope and light in the darkness of their lives. Phyllis Wheatley became a star by creating poetry that revealed a connection to the Great Books. My students became stars as well, lighting up the stage with their personal interpretations of the Great Books they read during the school year. Now with the inspiring starlight of educators like Marva Collins and Anna Julia Cooper, I move forward hoping that the retellings of my students might shed some light on **the lived experiences of African American students reading Great Books Literature.**

# CHAPTER 3: ILLUMINATING PHENOMENOLOGY

The Star
Twinkle, twinkle, little star
How I wonder what you are
Up above the world so high
Like a diamond in the sky.

When the blazing sun is set,
And the grass with dew is wet,
Then you show your little light,
Twinkly, twinkle, all the night.

Then the traveler in the dark
Thanks you for your tiny spark,
He could not see where to go
If you did not twinkle so.

In the dark blue sky you keep,
And often through my curtains
peep,
For you never shut your eye
Till the sun is in the sky.

As your bright and tiny spark
Lights the traveler in the dark,
Though I know not what you
are,
Twinkle, twinkle, little star.
(Taylor,
https://www.poets.org/poetsorg/
poem/star)

I can understand how the Magi must have felt as they became captivated by that single star. Maybe no one else noticed. Maybe no one else cared, but to them this one star drew their attention. They were so drawn to it that they had to follow it and follow it and follow it to see where it led. Maybe in following it, they would come to understand its very essence? I can understand how they felt. These were my feelings as year after year I taught the Great Books to my high school students, sometimes using the Bible as one of the Great Books. I saw things happen in my students that I felt needed more than just my testimony to encapsulate clearly what seemed to be transpiring. I wanted to get at the very core of what was happening. However, I could not define that. It was not my experience. I may have seen something happen, but it was not happening to me. I needed to hear from the voices of the students.

When I initially started this PhD journey, I was pursuing a qualitative study in order to articulate what was taking place in my students when they engaged in the Great Books, but as I would share my passion and excitement with others in the department, I was advised to look into phenomenology. Even though I had to take another year in order to complete the classes in this type of research methodology, I found that phenomenology opened new horizons by allowing me to gaze at that which is interesting or beckoning my interest in order to understand it, in order to get a sense of it. Heidegger's short poetic statement is used throughout this paper, because it forms a theme for me: "To think is to confine yourself to a single thought that one day stands still like a star in the world's sky" (Heidegger, 1971, p. 4). As Jane Taylor states in her poem above, whether it is stars or students reading texts outside of their cultural or racial sphere, we are beckoned by those things that cause us to "wonder what you are" and that beckoning compels us to follow our star.

# The Magi's Illumination of Heidegger and Phenomenology

When I first read Heidegger's quote, "To think is to confine yourself to a single thought that one day stands still like a star in the world's sky" (Heidegger, 1971, p. 4), it was Christmas time and I was also taking Phenomenology I. There is no wonder that my mind drifted to thoughts of the holiday season. The various images and scenes from the traditional Christmas story floated in and out of my mind. I imagined the babe lying in a manger. I visualized the animals of the stable. I dreamed about the shepherds kneeling around the manger. But, when I thought of the Magi all kneeling at the manger, presenting their gifts to Him, there developed an intersection of Christmas dreams and the images of those phenomenological philosophers and practitioners that I like to call "The Magi of Phenomenology." I think the catalyst for this merging of holiday visions and phenomenological meditations is the Star that appears to be at the core of the Magi's story. Recalling this star and the intense attention the Magi gave to it seemed to bring Heidegger's short poem to life for me. Maybe if I take apart some of the wording of Heidegger's poem, it will become clear how this phrase facilitated the story of the Magi's illumination of phenomenology.

## The Illumination of the Magi

Magi comes from the Greek word *magos* which refers to the Persian learned and priestly class (Harper, 2010). These men lived to **think**. In addition they devoted their time to studying, meditating, and knowing about the stars, agriculture, philosophy and various phenomena. One of the main areas of interest for the Magi was the study of astrology and astronomy (MacArthur, 1986). Due to their priestly function, spiritual powers, and knowledge of astronomy and astrology they held a position of great political power. They were often used to advise the rulers of the East. It was these men who were consulted by the royalty on most matters regarding the ruling of the kingdom. These men were also responsible for educating the ruling class on astronomy, mathematics, natural history, agriculture, etc. They **confined** themselves to deep study.

Because of their commitment to learning and observing the phenomena around them, they found themselves drawn to an unusual star. When they saw that star, they became consumed by it. I would guess that from the moment they saw the star, it became their primary single **thought**. Their commitment to understanding the star led them on a journey into Bethlehem from the East. Could it be their Deity? Could it be the fulfillment of a prophesy they had once studied? They had to find out, so they followed the star, and what they found was to them a phenomenal discovery. One single **star** shining in the heavens got their attention. No one else seemed to notice it, but these Magi did and they followed it until the culmination of their search lay before them. What they found is not relevant here, but how they went about their discovery is.

I am making connections between two merging thoughts that consumed my mind at the time I read Heidegger's "Star" poem. If I were to dissect the Magi's story and connect it to phenomenology it would be represented in the following way. *The Magi* represent the philosophers and practitioners of phenomenology—those who have committed themselves to the study and practice of phenomenology in order to understand the world in which they live. There are many "Magi" of phenomenology, but there are three that I connect with the most: Martin Heidegger, Hans-Georg Gadamer and Max van Manen.

*The Star* represents phenomenology. It is a research methodology amongst many others, but yet it is different. It catches my attention and I find myself drawn to it, hoping that it will lead me to a deeper understanding of that which interests me. *The Gifts of the Magi* represent what each philosopher has contributed to the further development of phenomenology. Many have speculated that the gifts of the Magi represent some deeper understanding. The philosophers and practitioners of phenomenology, through in-depth engagement in phenomenological study, not only understand the phenomenon in a deeper and more profound way, but they also have come to a more intimate understanding of the process of phenomenology. Each of the philosophers/practitioners I discuss made a specific contribution to phenomenology and I seek to unveil that here. The above components of the Magi's story serve as subheadings for this section. Through telling the Magi's story, I seek to shine a light on the philosophical underpinnings of phenomenology.

**The Star**

> *Now after Jesus was born in Bethlehem of Judea in the days of Herod the king, behold, "magi" from the East came to Jerusalem, saying "Where is he who has been born King of the Jews? For we have seen His* ***star*** *in the East... (Matthew 2:1-2-NKJV)*

The Magi had a fascination with light. Fire was considered sacred to them for it was the manifestation of their god (MacArthur, 1986). They also devoted themselves to the study of the stars. I wonder what could account for this fascination with light? The following passage from *Anam Cara* has captivated me, and even though it was cited earlier in chapter 2, I reiterate it here:

> ...Ultimately, light is the mother of life. Where there is no light, there can be no life. If the angle of the sun were to turn away from the earth, all human animal, and vegetative life...would disappear. Light is the secret presence of the divine...It helps us to glimpse the sacred depths within us. Once human beings began to search for the meaning of life, light became one of the most powerful metaphors to express eternity and depth of life. In its luminosity, the intellect was deemed to be the place of the divine within us. (O'Donohue, 1998, pp. 1-5)

Based upon this passage, it would make sense for me to make the star a metaphor for phenomenology. Stars have always been a source for knowledge and understanding, and phenomenology, too, is a tool used to gain knowledge and understanding of lived experience. The Magi studied astrology, and it was their belief that the stars could be used to help them understand life here on this earth, and so it is with phenomenology. As we research the possible meaning structures of our lived experiences, we come to a fuller grasp of what it means to be in the world (van Manen, 1997).

**Guiding light.** Stars guide our way. I recall a story told in *Getting Back into Place* where the Puluwat of the Caroline Islands in Microneseia demonstrate their ability to chart their course at sea through studying the stars (Casey, 2009). Relating that to phenomenology, I see how it guides us into studying the life world (van Manen, 1997). When the Magi saw the star, they allowed it to lead them to experience something of a wondrous nature. This is why I have chosen phenomenology, because it does the same for me. Phenomenology allows me to think, for myself. Heidegger (1954) states that there is a "call" on us to think. Something compels us to think about that which is most thought-provoking. I am not pressured into taking on the thoughts of someone else for myself, but I am allowed to think about what calls me to think about a phenomenon, just as the Star beckoned for the Magi's attention.

The quote from Heidegger stated at the beginning of this chapter is an anthem for me in my research, because it is a reflection of what happened to me when I chose my phenomenon. I chose my phenomenon before I knew it was one. All I knew is that I had this insatiable desire to look deeper into what happens to my students when they engage in the Great Books of Western Civilization. The thought shined so brightly in my mind that it blinded me from thinking of anything else. I was not looking for this to happen, and according to Heidegger, this is often how it happens for "We never come to thoughts. They come to us" (Heidegger, 1968, p. 365).

When I found phenomenology, and Heidegger's star quote I became perpetually inspired to follow the call of my star. Heidegger tells me that my phenomenon is important and relevant and appreciated simply because my interest lies in the lived experience of African-American students in a Great Books literature class. I can think of an instant when yet another moment in the class, invoked a beckoning for me to follow this star. The students and I had joined an online chat group where we would discuss Great Books with students all over the US. The computers were not that great, and on this particular day, they would not bring us online and time was slipping away. The students frantically pulled out plugs, turned computers on and off, etc. Finally one of the students cries out, "…I'm sick of this?! These computers never work!" That was a big switch from what I encountered when I first took on the class. They used to just lean back in their seats, eat snacks and fool around, but now when the computers would not work, they were frantic about trying to get them on again.

We finally were able to get the computers going and they were excited to share their thoughts on Plato's *Symposium*. They got so involved with the online discussion that they kept talking even after it was over and actually were laughing about how Socrates gets people confused by all of his questions. They were enjoying the literature. THIS beckoned for me to follow. What was THIS? Why was THIS happening? I just wanted to understand, to get a sense of why the transformation happened. Was it the books? Was it me? Was it a combination of those things? Why were they connecting to the books? I wanted to understand why the students, all males, African American, and most from some challenging places in their life, were becoming interested in this literature. What does Plato's *Symposium* have to do with them?

**A different light beckons.** With regards to the Magi who had studied the stars for ages, I can imagine that because of its difference from the other stars they were immediately drawn to it. One main characteristic about the Star was that it moved, almost as if to say "Follow me." It must have said this to them, because that is what they did. They packed up their things, gathered their entourage and followed the Star. I feel that phenomenology said this to me. It must have, because I had finished my coursework, was set to begin the process for heading to my dissertation and when I found phenomenology, I tacked on another year of study so that I could "follow" its teachings. I felt that only phenomenology would deliver me from the stagnating experience of sitting down and researching my topic from an objective outsider view. I was glad to do as Bachelard says: "*A researcher* must forget his learning and break with all his habits of philosophical research, if he wants to study the problems posed by the poetic imagination" (Bachelard, 1958, p. xv).

Research of the type where results can be severed from the means by which the results are obtained (van Manen, 1997) is all too common. With phenomenology this is not so. The two remain linked. The process of researching is directly linked to what is discovered, and together they poetically tell a story. It is like the two dance together, the process of the research and that which is being discovered. It is a symphony. It is a singing of the world (van Manen, 1997). The aim of phenomenology is to transform lived experience into a textual expression of its essence in such a way that the effect of the text is at once a reflexive re-living and reflective appropriation of something meaningful (van Manen, 1997).

**The Sacred Ground of Questioning**

> Now Moses was tending the flock of Jethro his father-in-law, the priest of Midian. And he led the flock to the back of the desert, and came to Horeb, the mountain of God. And the Angel of the LORD appeared to him in a flame of fire from the midst of a bush. So he looked, and behold, the bush was burning with fire, but the bush *was* not consumed. Then Moses said, "I will now turn aside and see this great sight, why the bush does not burn."
>
> So when the LORD saw that he turned aside to look, God called to him from the midst of the bush and said, "Moses, Moses!"
> And he said, "Here I am."
> Then He said, "Do not draw near this place. Take your sandals off your feet, for the place where you stand *is* holy ground."
> Moreover He said, "I *am* the God of your father—the God of Abraham, the God of Isaac, and the God of Jacob." And Moses hid his face, for he was afraid to look upon God. (Exodus 3: 3-5)

Phenomenology is about wonder, words and world (van Manen, 2014). The Old English word for wonder is *wundor*. It has several meanings, but one of them caught my attention: "object of astonishment." I think of Jane Taylor, and her "star," which was an object of astonishment to her. I think of Heidegger's poem, and how he describes when something captivates us, the object stands still in our minds. We are captivated by it, this captivation bringing about questions: "What is that?" "What does that mean?" "Why does it do that?" "Where did that come from?" "I wonder....?" and so on.

As I have reflected on the act of questioning with regards to phenomenology, I find myself drawn to the story of Moses seeing the burning bush. Upon first seeing it, he immediately wanted to carelessly approach it to see why a bush was on fire but not burning up. Then the bush speaks to him, calls his name and tells him to take off his sandals, "for the place where you stand is holy ground." One must take on a special attitude when engaging in questioning. Moses had to get rid of his preconceived notions about what fire is supposed to do and how an object is supposed to respond when it is on fire. He had to take his shoes off and let the "object of astonishment" speak to him.

As stated earlier, that special attitude necessary for approaching the sacred ground of questioning, is humility. Gadamer (1975/1989) says:

> In fact, however, the continual failure of the interlocutor shows that people who think they know better cannot even ask the right questions. In order to be able to ask, one must want to know, and that means knowing that one does not know. (pp. 356-357)

Once Moses stopped pushing forward with trying to make sense of "the object of astonishment," took his shoes off, he could hear it speak to him. Our own deeply held opinions about what *is* deafen our ears, our hearts, our minds from absorbing the very essence of a thing. Once Moses stopped, took off his shoes, the "object of astonishment" identified itself to him and he had to accept it for what it said and what it was. In fact, at the end of Moses' conversation with the burning bush, it identifies itself as I AM.

If I were to take the words *I AM* and analyze their meanings I see that *I* is the first person singular, meaning that I *is* the person. I *is* "the thing itself." *AM* is *to be* or *to remain. AM* means that the person is in the act of being and continuing to be. This may seem rather tedious, but as I go on this journey to look at *I AM,* I recognize that it means only that the thing or the person is being revealed. No other interpretation of someone else or a representation of someone else is present. *I AM,* is. I am going through this for my own self, because in engaging in the work, I frequently struggle with mixing in *myself* with *I AM.* Like God in the burning bush called for Moses to stop looking at the object of astonishment with his own eyes, and told him to take off his shoes and listen, I feel my phenomenon is calling for me to do the same. We have wrestled with this, the phenomenon and I. This calls for the special attitude of humility.

When Moses stopped, took off his shoes and allowed himself to hear *I AM,* he could see who or what it was. An openness came. This is what wonder, which leads to questioning, does. Only when our shoes come off and we get humble can this openness take place. Phenomenology calls for me to retain the wonder of the object of astonishment, but I must release the personal thoughts and assumptions that arise when the wonder begins—like when Moses removed his shoes. A question has been put wrongly when it does not reach the state of openness but precludes reaching it by retaining false suppositions. It pretends to an openness and susceptibility to a decision that it does not have (Gadamer, 1975/1989, p. 357).

Gadamer (1975/1989) explains Socrates' views on questioning:

> There is no such thing as a method of learning to ask questions, of learning to see what is questionable. On the contrary, the example of Socrates teaches that the important thing is the knowledge that one does not know. Hence the Socratic Dialectic---which leads, through its art of confusing the interlocutor, to this knowledge---creates the conditions for the question. All questioning and desire to know presuppose a knowledge that one does not know; so much so, indeed, that a particular lack of knowledge leads to a particular question. (pp. 359)

So often in this process of me preparing for the phenomenological project I embarked on, I was trapped by my convictions, bound by my opinions. It is opinion that suppresses questions (Gadamer, 1975/1989). When I gazed upon the "burning bush" that was my phenomenon, I heard a voice telling me to take off my opinions for this is sacred ground. This is the space where my students had to show me themselves. This is the space where my students spoke to me and I listened.

> Listen (sung by Steve Green)
> I can read your word, but I may not know your mind
> I can think I hear your voice, but I might be running blind
> So I will wait in quiet earnest anticipation
> and I will listen to you
> Listen close
> Listen deep way beyond the silence
> Listen to words you speak (James, Cuesta, & Loeb, 1999)

**Constellating through Question and Answer**

The path of all knowledge leads through the question. To ask a question means to bring into the open (Gadamer, 1975/1989). The best way to extrapolate the essence of a life experience is through questioning, questioning those who are connected to the phenomenon. In traditional social science research there is also questioning, but the questioning is looking for a conclusion, proof or an answer. In phenomenological research, the questioning that should take place has one main goal, and that is understanding the lived experience. In *Being and Time,* Heidegger (1962) writes:

> Our questioning really is a kind of light which casts a certain pattern on the phenomenon, while also filling in our expectation in a way that allows us to formulate further questions, and thus to advance our understanding. (p. 7)

In the end the finished text IS the result, because you are presenting not a conclusion, but an understanding of the lived experience. In phenomenology, I find no competition to unveil the next biggest news, but I do find appreciation for the essence of what interests me, and that interest lies in the experiences of those involved in my study, in order to illuminate my phenomenon of interest.

Every question is a seeking. Questioning is a knowing search for beings in their thatness and whatness (Heidegger, 1962). What guides this questioning is that thing that causes us to wonder. My first year teaching Great Books to just five African American male students revealed some-"thing" that happened in them. This "whatness" has captivated me for so many years, and questioning helped me unpack it. Questioning helped me to shine light on what that experience was like for them.

According to Gadamer (1975/1989), "Thus a person who wants to understand must question what lies behind what is said" (p. 378). One of my favorite seminars at St. John's was "Socratic Dialogues." In this class we spent the entire summer reading Plato's transcripts of Socrates' dialogues. I found myself laughing many times as it seemed that Socrates' questions drew people into total confusion. The dialogue would start with someone asking a question. One question led to another, until the persons found themselves utterly confused. Many rabbit trails would come about. One person wanted to be "right," but Socrates wanted to know truth. He would often say things like, "I myself, am as poor as my fellow citizens in this matter, and I blame myself for my complete ignorance…If I do not know what something is, how could I know what qualities it possesses?" (Grube, 1976, p. 4). The humility demonstrated by Socrates here brings me back to the statement made earlier, "The example of Socrates teaches that the important thing is the knowledge that one doesn't not know. Hence the Socratic dialectic---which leads, through its art of confusing the interlocutor, to this knowledge…" (Gadamer, 1975/1989, p. 359). The questioning and the answering of the questions are what help us to get at the essence of the phenomenon. Using the example of Socrates' dialogues, Gadamer presents a model for us to follow in accomplishing that. But it is not just the act of asking questions. It first begins with the special attitude, recognizing the sacred ground of approaching the phenomenon through questioning.

We approach it with the understanding that we do not know. Once we get to that place, we go through the process of asking questions, allowing the phenomenon to answer our questions and so on.

When we approach the sacred ground of questioning with the understanding that we do not know, and then we engage in the dialectic process to gain understanding, what emerges in its truth is the logos, which is neither mine nor yours, and hence so far transcends the interlocutor's subjective opinions that even the person leading the conversation knows that he does not know (Gadamer, 1975/1989). Truth. Naked truth. Free from my opinions. Free from any suppositions. Just plain and simple truth. I started this journey hoping to show how the Great Books has this really awesome effect on my students. I was hoping to show it as the next wonderful strategy for addressing the literacy struggles of today's African American youth. Yet, I came to realize that my students' answers to the questions I asked should be focused on what each of their lived experiences was like. I had to come to a place of peace with *just* that. As their renderings spoke to me, those who read my study will become enlightened through their retelling and I should not try to control or direct what that enlightenment should be. This is the purpose of my study.

As I constellate the questions and answers between my students and me, a picture is formed, like the Big Dipper or Aquarius or Libra. It represents a work of art that I believe others can appreciate. Gadamer (1975/1989) writes:

> As the art of conducting a conversation, dialectic is also the art of seeing things in the unity of an aspect…it is the art of

> forming concepts through working out the common meaning. What characterizes a dialogue, in contrast with the rigid form of statements that demand to be set down in writing, is precisely this: that in dialogue spoken language---in the process of question and answer, giving and taking, talking at cross purposes and seeing each other's point—performs the communication of meaning that with respect to the written tradition, is the task of hermeneutics. (p. 361)

Even though my students' lived experiences are unique to them, they are not that foreign to others. As the students and I teased out the details of their experiences, aspects came to the surface to which others can relate. Like slaves could look at the Big Dipper and make it relevant to themselves with regards to their freedom, someone can read the constellation of the questions and answers in my study and connect to them. Van Manen (2002) says, "Their experiences could be yours or mine, not because we have all lived through them, but because we are human and nothing human is alien to us" (p. ii).

**Open the Blinds, Let Some Light in**

The essence of the question, is the opening up, and keeping open, of possibilities (Gadamer, 1975). I keep a shoe basket at the door of my home. Some people use it and some just put their shoes by the door. The moment that I see a person take off their shoes, I know they plan to stay a while. I know they plan to rest and visit with me. I know that they plan to let me talk and they will listen and they will share too. We will speak back to each other, enjoying the exchange. All of this comes to my mind when I see the person take their shoes off at the door of my house. When Moses took his shoes off at the burning bush, God wanted him to humble himself, but I wonder if he also just wanted him to stay awhile and listen to what he had to say. I wonder if God was seeking for Moses to open himself up in order to dwell in the wonder of the phenomenon. Van Manen (1997) says, "Even minor phenomenological research projects require that we not simply raise a question and possibly soon drop it again, but rather that we 'live' this question, that we 'become' this question" (p. 43). Like Moses had to dwell in the presence of the burning bush and let it speak to him, the act of taking off our opinions and presuppositions, standing still and dwelling in our question opens up understanding of the phenomenon. Van Manen (1997) writes:

> Is this not the meaning of research: to question something by going back again and again to the things themselves until that which is put to question begins to reveal something of its essential nature? (p. 43)

When a person comes to my home, keeps their shoes, jacket, etc. on and stands in the foyer, I know they have made up their mind about the topic of discussion. They are not there to have an interchange with me. They have come to state their business and move on. But the persons who take off their shoes, their jacket, etc. and come into the family room, sits down and even asks for a snack or something to drink, I know they plan to visit with me and to have a conversation with me. They care about me and want to know me---spend time with me. Some interactions have happened between us that let me know they want to know me. When Moses interacted with the burning bush, he lived in its presence. He engaged in more moments of wonder and conversation there. He experienced the bush. He lived within the wonder of the bush. This reminds me of van Manen's (1997) thoughts when he says, "A phenomenological question must not only be made clear, understood but also 'lived' by the researcher" (p. 44). Throughout my conversations with my students about their lived experiences reading Great Books literature, I invited myself to dwell with them in order that I could hear the phenomenon speak back to me without interrupting through my own presuppositions. Van Manen (1997) writes:

> If we wish to remain responsive to the commitment of phenomenology, then we should try to resist the temptation to develop positivistic schemata, paradigms, models, or other categorical abstractions of knowledge. Instead, we should refer questions of knowledge back to the lifeworld where knowledge speaks through our lived experiences. (p. 46)

Accomplishing the type of openness necessary to get to the essence of a phenomenon is a hard task. We are blinded by what we are familiar with, regarding the phenomenon. I find myself perpetually casting down my hopes, dreams, expectations, and desire to label prematurely what I saw during those years teaching the Great Books class. As Moses prematurely took a step towards the burning bush in order to understand why it was on fire but did not burn, in this process of gaining a phenomenological understanding of my students' lived experiences, I have often stepped forward with my shoes still on and my mind still shaded by what I "think" is taking place. However, I heed the voice of Heidegger, "To think is to confine yourself to a single thought that one stands still like a star in the world's sky." I stand still. I wait. I listen. I take my shoes off. I open the blinds of my mind and let the light of the phenomenon shine in. I do not let the problem of phenomenology plague me, as van Manen warns:

> The problem of phenomenological inquiry is not always that we know too little about the phenomenon we wish to investigate, but that we know too much. Or more accurately, the problem is that our 'common sense' pre-understandings, our suppositions, assumptions, and the existing bodies of scientific knowledge, predispose us to interpret the nature of the phenomenon before we have even come to grips with the significance of the phenomenological question. (p. 46)

My students and I sat down together, took our shoes off, relaxed, and I opened the blinds of my mind in order to let their light shine into my thoughts, as they shared their lived experiences of reading Great Books literature with me.

## Stepping Stars

Star Light, Star Bright
Star light, star bright,
First star I see tonight,
I wish I may, I wish I might,
Have this wish I wish tonight.
(Anonymous)

Stars speak of hope. I wonder if it's because that in the midst of darkness, the specks of light that spangle the black canvas, give a feeling that darkness has not completely taken over? The light continues to shine, even in darkness. This is phenomenology to me. When my phenomenon made its first appearance to me, the wonder of it threw me into a darkness. I did not know what was happening with my students and I did not know why it was happening to them. I could not understand why a student who is a behavior problem, seems to constantly resist the authority figures of the school, will settle down and read Julius Caesar, and then want to argue about how much he hated Brutus. That just made no sense to me! Why did he even care? Yet, that is what happened on numerous occasions. The questions that arose as a result of me taking on the phenomenological mind in my writing, created these "stars" that began to shed some light in the darkness. As I wrote about my phenomenon within class, I found that the phenomenon opened up more and more, little by little, over time. It has not been easy. In his book *Writing in the Dark* (2002), van Manen writes:

> At the more reflective level the difficulty of writing has to do with questions of metaphysics, the phenomenology of meaning, the limits of language, and with the enigmatic nature of words, text, interpretation and truth…Sometimes the words just do not seem to come. Sometimes the text of writing seems to write. Sometimes the writer simply does not know where to turn, what to do next. Indeed, at times it feels as if one is writing in the dark. (p. i)

I write in order to illuminate the phenomenon, even when there is confusion, even when the "awe-ness" of the phenomenon takes my words. Phenomenological writing is my starlight in the darkness of trying to understand **the lived experience of African American high school students reading Great Books literature**.

So like me, when the Magi saw the star, they knew it would lead them to something wonderful. What did it mean? It was moving, but where did it lead? Then began their journey to discovery. As they journeyed they traveled in the light of this magnificent star. Each step in the light brought them closer to the phenomenon, and so it is with phenomenology. There are signposts that light the way, that bring you closer to the phenomenon. I have already discussed the use of questioning (which brings forth conversation). Through questioning and the other means of collecting text, themes develop, that in themselves stand out like stars. These themes are constellated in order to express the understanding.

The other ways of generating text are through observation, connecting appropriate literature (poems, narratives, etc.), biography, diaries, journals, logs, art, phenomenological literature, etc. (van Manen, 1997). Many sources can be used to shed light on the phenomenon, in order to reveal its meaning. Phenomenology allows the researcher to get inside and look at all sides, and therefore, many meanings may become unveiled. In this, however, the real life experience is revealed.

Van Manen (1997) says, "We need to search everywhere in the lifeworld for lived experience material that, upon reflective examination, might yield something of its fundamental nature" (p. 53). In this lifeworld that is created through my study, several horizons are crossed. There is my life and experience with the Great Books, my students' experience with the Great Books, and African Americans of the past (the ancestors) and their experience with the Great Books. Many of those from the past who were connected to the Great Books were former slaves. Because the majority of slaves in America came from West Africa, I have chosen a West African tradition to help me work through the sources of material for my study. The Adinkra symbols help me to name the purpose of each source that I use to collect my lived experience materials.

*Adinkra* means 'goodbye' or 'farewell' in *Twi*, the language of the Akan ethnic group (stlawu.edu/.../education/f/09textiles/adinkra_symbols.pdf). When Africans were captured in West Africa, many would leave the continent from a place that is called "The Door of No Return." This doorway led to the coast, and subsequently, the ships that would take them to their new home and new life as a slave. This is important because to me it reveals a possible reason as to why African Americans connected to the Great Books. George Moses Horton, Frederick Douglass, Anna Julia Cooper and also those slaves, like Phillis Wheatley, that came directly from West Africa, immersed themselves in these texts in order to find their place here, since there was no way to return to their home. The Adinkra symbols to me are a bridge between the ancestors and their struggle to find an identity here, as well as my students and I building our own literacy. Their symbolism provides the wisdom of the ancestors to help me comprehend the purpose behind each source gathered for my lived experience material.

For my study, I gathered my material from the following sources: my personal experience with the Great Books and how the experience affected me; conversations with my students and observing them in our conversations and activities we engaged in to bring the experience back to the light; creative texts (poetry, stories, etc.) that speak to the phenomenon; etymologies of terms that came to the surface during the course of this journey; and the written lives of others who have gone through a similar journey with the Great Books. I think of these sources as "stepping stars" (like stepping stones), leading the lightened path to understanding my phenomenon. Each source connects to the other the essences of my phenomenon that came to light. The Adinkra symbols I assign to each source help to highlight their purpose in my study.

**Personal Experience ( ✠ *Linked Hearts—Akoma Ntoso):* Understanding and Agreement**

In this type of research, I am not on the outside looking in. I am not a computer taking in data about the phenomenon, but I am experiencing the phenomenon and connecting it to my own experiences. Even though I must cast off my own presuppositions, and allow the phenomenon to speak to me, I must be willing to allow myself to be connected to the other's experience. As the author, I must be reminded of the fact that my experiences could probably be someone else's and they reciprocate—their experiences could be mine. I return to Moses and remember how he engaged in conversation with the burning bush, asked it questions, and touched various wonders that the burning bush presented. He revealed his weaknesses and fears, and the burning bush, although a wonder, entertained this interaction. They communed together—related together. My personal experience links to the hearts of my students as I seek to understand their experience of reading Great Books literature.

> In drawing up personal descriptions of lived experiences, the phenomenologist knows that one's own experiences are also the possible experiences of others. (van Manen, 1997, p. 55)

**Etymologies ( 𝄜 Knowledge—*Nea Onnim No Sua A, Ohu-he):* Who Does not Know Can Know from Learning**

What helps me to "Listen close" and "Listen deep" (from the song "Listen" shared earlier) is to allow the words to take me there. Etymology funnels me into the heart of the phenomenon, because when I look up original meanings I find the buried life of the word. These covered over meanings speak life to the phenomenon and bring it to light. My going through the process to look up original meanings of words is my willingness to gain the knowledge necessary to understand my phenomenon.

> Being attentive to the etymological origins of words may sometimes put us in touch with an original form of life where the terms still had living ties to the lived experiences from which they originally sprang. (van Manen, 1997, p. 59)

## Interviewing (ஐ Knowledge/Wisdom—*Mate Masie*): What I Hear I Keep

The thing that drew me into my phenomenological question, **What are the lived experiences of African American highschool students reading Great Books literature,** was that something happened to me. Once I acknowledged how this experience affected me, I then began to wonder if anyone else had the same experience. Through casual conversation and reading, I came across others who have had "something" happen to them when engaging in this literature, but now I have asked those that I taught. Is this just an experience for the older crowd? Is this just an experience for those who love literature? Is this just an experience for the African American in history seeking equality? Or does "something" happen to almost anyone who engages in the literature? I seek to understand what happened to me that first year at St. John's, and I engaged my students who went through a similar process of engaging in these specific texts. I literally found myself shocked when I came to love Aristotle. I could not understand why I fell in love with him. I could not understand why understanding him affected my sense of self. I could not understand why comprehending him gave me a different perspective on life in general. This "something"—the "whatness" revealed glimmers of itself in my students as they engaged in the texts. I sought to name it—to get at its essences. Having conversations with my students and allowing them to tell me their stories illuminated this for me.

An extension of the Adinkra symbol that I use here also says "Deep wisdom comes out of listening and keeping what is heard." This is why it is so important for me to cast off my presuppositions as I listened to my students. If I want to get to the place of getting at the lived experience in its fullest sense, then I must listen to and keep their renderings close to my heart and mind, untainted by my own expectations.

> The point of phenomenological research is to "borrow" other people's experiences and their reflections on their experiences in order to better be able to come to an understanding of the deeper meaning or significance of an aspect of human experience, in the context of the whole of human experience. (van Manen, 1997, p. 62)

### Observing ( Interdependence—*Boa Me Na Me Mmoa Wo):* Help Me and Let Me Help You

The participants in my study were between the ages of 18 and 22. All have graduated from high school and of course are no longer in my class. My study is retrospective. I have some of my journal entries from that time, and I have the memories of my time teaching them. However, observing them in those moments of the past are not possible. In addition to engaging in conversation with my students in order to gain the narrative of their lived experiences, I engaged with the students in various creative activities to bring more memories of those moments in my class to the surface. These were in the form of creative writing, dramatizations, musical representations, Socratic dialogue of a text (in order to relive those moments in my Great Books class), etc. I observed my students closely as they engaged in these activities. For me to get close to the experience of my students, I participated with them in the activities as I observed them. This allowed me to come into their lifeworlds.

*Boa me na me boa wo* represents cooperation and helping one another. I did not come to this study with feelings of mastery. I came humbly, realizing that I did not know. Joining with my students in order for us to gain understanding of the phenomenon cooperatively is the process of taking on that "special attitude" I discussed earlier.

> Close observation involves an attitude of assuming a relation that is as close as possible while retaining a hermeneutic alertness to situations that allows us to constantly step back and reflect on the meaning of those situations. (van Manen, 1997, p. 69)

**Biography ( Return and Get It/Learning from the Past—*Sankofa):* Wisdom, Using Past Experiences to Build the Future**

One source that has been very helpful to me in this journey to understanding my students' and my own lived experiences reading Great Books literature, is biography. The Adinkra symbol Sankofa, means "return and get it." For me to understand the relevance of these texts to my African American students, I had to look at this phenomenon from a historical perspective. I had to "return and get" the significance of these texts from the ancestors who traveled this road before, specifically, those ancestors who came from West Africa through slavery. The Adinkra symbols were derived from Ghana and Cote d'Ivoire and were created in order to share thoughts of wisdom, inspiration and enlightenment. The Sankofa symbol inspires me on this journey because to understand the phenomenon, I had to realize that it was not an isolated thing. The African American's pull towards reading the Great Books has transcended time. Moran (2000) writes:

> Our consciousness of being affected by history belongs to the manner in which we understand everything. When we understand an object, we do not grasp the object as it is in itself, but rather we grasp it through the accumulations of its historical effectiveness what it has evolved into being for us, its…effective history, the 'history of influence' of the object on human communities. (p. 252)

Gadamer's thoughts on history reflected on by Moran above, helped me as the researcher to understand the phenomenon ringing true for my study. It has been a challenge for me not to turn this study into a detailed study of the Great Books being connected to the social uplift of the African American people. Over and over—through every biography, the pattern was the same. There was illiteracy; there were feelings of being "less than;" there was a sense of being lost. The slaves who became literate would discover one of these texts (Frederick Douglass loved to read Cicero), then read another and another until an understanding of their equality (no longer identifying themselves as a slave, or just African, or as three-fifths human) came into place.

History in conjunction with hermeneutics delivers this practice from being too objective. Gadamer (1975/1989) raises the question, "How might hermeneutics, once freed from the ontological obstructions of the scientific concept of objectivity, do justice to the historicity of understanding" (p. 268). Objectivity lends itself to the researcher just standing back and trying to glean understanding of a thing where it is in space and time. However bringing history into the practice of hermeneutics moves us to seek understanding of the thing across time and outside of space. Moran (2000) explains Gadamer's thinking:

> What he wants to oppose is the view that these horizons are mutually exclusive or that our world-views are hermetically sealed. Gadamer wants to emphasize that in fact our horizons are open to other horizons, that they can overlap and indeed are overlapping…Gadamer is emphatic that we can and do reach mutual understanding. This is a process of interpenetration of our horizons, or what Gadamer calls 'fusion of horizons.' (p. 252)

Bringing in history to my study is my practice of "returning" to the ancestors and "getting" an understanding of why they felt the need to read these texts. Writing about these experiences in conjunction with seeking to understand my phenomenon where it is currently, invites the ancestors into the dialogue to gain understanding.

I have read the stories of Frederick Douglass, Martin Luther King, W.E.B. DuBois, Anna Julia Cooper, Phillis Wheatley, Marva Collins, and many others, all so I could get an understanding of the lived experience of African Americans reading Great Books literature. Primarily, I have looked into why historically African Americans have read this collection of literature in connection with their liberation. I recognize that many deem these texts as too culturally distant from my students. There is a concern of students becoming so immersed in these texts that their culture and background are not appreciated. However, reading the biographies of those listed above revealed the opposite to me. Many of the biographies I have read illustrate how reading these texts brought healing to a lost soul. They brought understanding to those living in a world that seemed so foreign. In the midst of this, they embraced their own culture even more but were able to fit it into the context of their new home. They were also able to use this new enlightenment to take the actions necessary to assist in the equality of the African American people in this country. My students are far removed from slavery, so in this day and time, I seek to know how this literature affects them? I also look for understanding of how putting into words, this literature has helped me as well.

> It is not unusual for biographic texts to contain rich ore of lived-experience descriptions for phenomenological analysis or for converting into anecdote or story. (van Manen, 1997, p. 72)

**Art (✻ Spider's Web—*Ananse Ntontan*): Wisdom, Creativity and the Complexities of Life**

Ananse, the spider, is a well-known character in African folktales and this symbol represents a deep connection for me, because of my passion for arts in education. Not only do I use poetry, theatre, and visual art as sources to help me come to an understanding of my phenonomenon (as part of my effort of looking everywhere in the "lifeworld"…), but I also use the art created by my students to help me go through this same process. Aristotle (1941) wrote, "Imitation is natural to man from childhood, one of his advantages over the lower animals being this, that he is the most imitative creature in the world, and learns first by imitation" (p. 1457). This takes me back to when I would use the arts (mainly drama, but sometimes music and visual art) as a part of our class activities. Throughout my class, I would have students use various art forms in order to show their understanding and connection to the texts. When students seek to interpret the literature through artistic means, they are seeking to show understanding of the text, and this is a way of assessing student comprehension of the texts. Gadamer (1975/1989) writes:

> Obviously connected with the fact that interpretation and understanding are bound up with each other is that the concept of interpretation can be applied not only to scholarly interpretation but to artistic reproduction—e.g., musical or dramatic performance. We have shown…that this kind of reproduction is not a second creation re-creating the first; rather, it makes the work of art appear as itself for the first time. It brings to life the signs of the musical or dramatic text. (p. 400)

The creativity displayed during those times of using drama, music or visual arts to interpret the text revealed a wisdom, an understanding of a deeper meaning that connected to my students. When they would graduate from high school and have to give their graduation speeches (each graduate had to give a short speech before getting their diploma), they would always mention the memories of dramatizing the literature in my class. Many times we would create full length films, plays, songs, artwork, etc. all connected to what was read in the class. In this study, then, the opportunity to use the arts to help them conjure back up the lived experience of being in my Great Books class was drawn upon.

My desire to include the arts in this study is essential. As stated earlier, this journey is a personal one for me. Earlier I have talked about Moses and how he approached the wonder of the burning bush. After that encounter, he was inspired to lead his people on a journey out of bondage to a "promised land." Along the way, they would leave stone altars at various points in the journey to serve as a reminder of the experience. This to me is my "stone altar." This is my effort to remember the lived experiences of my students and my students' time to reflect on how those lived experiences affected them. The sharing of artistic representations of those moments helps to feed the conversations about their experiences. Gadamer (1975/1989) writes:

> For players this means that they do not simply fulfill their roles as in any game—rather, they play their roles, they represent them for the audience. The way they participate in the game is no longer determined by the fact that they are completely absorbed in it, but by the fact that they play their role in relation and regard to the whole of the play, in which not they but the audience is to become absorbed. A complete change takes place when play as such becomes a play. It puts the spectator in the place of the player. He—and not the player—is the person for and in whom the play is played. Of course this does not mean that the player is not able to experience the significance of the whole in which he plays his representing role. (p. 110)

The six years I taught the Great Books class shaped my views on teaching and learning. The power of art is that it creates "stone altars" of significant moments in history, and they reveal personal truths to each onlooker—each observer. Even though the work is not equivalent to the time they were created—even though their present meaning may be a bit different, their creation inspires truth in us that the particular moment in history revealed. Heidegger (1971) says:

> The Aegina sculptures in the Munich collection, Sophocles' *Antigone* in the best critical edition, are, as the works they are, torn out of their own native sphere. However high their quality and power of impression, however good their state of preservation, however certain their interpretation, placing them in a collection has withdrawn them from their own world. But even when we make an effort to cancel or avoid such displacement of works—when, for instance, we visit the temple in Paestum at its own site or the Bamberg cathedral on its own square—the world that stands there has perished. (p. 166)

The artistic re-creation of the lived experience of a time gone by should reveal some kind of truth for each student because "art lets truth originate" (Heidegger, 1971, p. 202).

> Because artists are involved in giving shape to their lived experiences, the products of art are, in a sense, lived experiences transformed into transcended configurations. (van Manen, 1997, p. 74)

The two areas that shape who I am as a person are my faith and my culture. In using the Biblical story of Moses to help me process and organize this journey, and in using the Adinkra symbols as wisdom guides along the path, I have allowed some of the essence of who I am to speak to the journey towards becoming enlightened about my phenomenon of **the lived experience of African American students reading Great Books literature.** As stated earlier, phenomenology takes me down many different paths, and other sources come into play as I seek to make sense of my students' lived experiences reading Great Books literature. The above, however, are the main sources of lived experience material that help me to delve into the phenomenon and get at its essence.

## The Magi Revealed

This brings me back to the Magi as they followed the Star. There was more than one Magi; tradition says there were three. If I stay with the traditional story, there were three Magi and three gifts given. I would want to interpret the three different gifts as symbols of how each Magi experienced following the Star to the phenomenon differently. They each had different thoughts along the way, and by the time they were able to experience the phenomenon, they were inspired differently, and thus, the three gave very different gifts. Maybe the phenomenon represented something different to each of them? Either way, the Star led them there, and I would like to suggest that the three gifts reflected their varying response to the whole experience, from seeing the Star, following the Star and then the lived experience of seeing the phenomenon face to face.

So to connect this philosophic trail, phenomenology begins with something calling me to look into it (first seeing the star), and then it involves the journey into discovering the deeper meaning behind that which calls me to look at it (following the star). Seeing phenomenology being a star is appropriate. Portions of the *Anam Cara* passage that I continue to cite within this dissertation, seem to illuminate the phenomenological process: "All your life, your mind lives within the darkness of your body. Every thought that you have is a flint moment, a spark of light from your inner darkness" (O'Donohue, 1998, p. 5). The Magi were in darkness about their phenomenon until the Star shined its light and beckoned for them to follow it. It is the same with me. I was in darkness about my phenomenon until a thought about students' engagement in my Great Books literature class shined for me, beckoning for me to follow it to deeper understanding.

"The soul awakens and lives in light. It helps us to glimpse the sacred depths within us. Once human beings began to search for the meaning of life, light became one of the most powerful metaphors to express eternity and depth of life" (O'Donohue, 1998, p. 5). Once the Magi saw the Star, they were compelled to follow it in order to search for its deeper meaning. It was not just one of the stars that happened to shine extra bright that night. It was different, and for them, the star held a mystery. It is the same with me. My teaching the Great Books is not as simple as teaching students to appreciate literature, but it is much more. I am on a journey to understanding my students' experiences of engaging in these texts.

"In the Western tradition and…Celtic tradition, thought has often been compared to light. In its luminosity, the intellect was deemed to be the place of the divine within us" (O'Donohue, 1998, p. 5). The Star represented what the prophets had foretold and what the Magi had thought about for hundreds of years, something that to them was

Divine. It is the same with me. Once my phenomenon got my attention, its light blinded me from seeing anything else. I could think of nothing else, and I find myself realizing something so incredible, something that even history has revealed about the relationship between the Great Books and African-Americans. Phenomenology is light, and like the Magi I follow this star that I believe will lead me to something great, maybe even something that can shed light on the education of African-American students.

## The Magi and the Gifts They Bring

> *They departed and behold the star which they had seen in the East went before them, till it came and stood over where the young Child was. And when they had opened their treasures, they presented gifts to Him: gold, frankincense , and myrrh. (Matthew 2:9;11-NKJV)*

It is from this verse that many have drawn their conclusions as to who the Magi were. The three gifts determined how many Magi there were, and so in every manger scene three Magi are presented. Some have even gone so far as to use the three gifts as some sort of clue into whom these men were. Who was the one who gave gold? Who was the one who gave frankincense? Who was the one who gave myrrh? There is little concrete evidence as to who these men actually were (or how many there were for that matter). However, since I have chosen to use the story of the Magi, that which many consider a myth, a folktale or a fairytale, I feel it is safe to stay with tradition and adhere to the various beliefs as to who these men were. The purpose of this chapter is not to prove the validity of the

Magi's story, but I am merely using it in a metaphorical sense, whereby I can look deeper into the philosophic foundations of phenomenology. Because of this, I also feel that there is room for me to conjecture as to who these men were, based on the few clues given to me in the Bible.

There were three gifts given, and as mentioned earlier, these three gifts serve to give us a possible clue into the nature of the Magi. There was the one who gave gold, for the phenomenon represented royalty; there was one who gave frankincense for the phenomenon represented the deity; there was one who gave myrrh, for the phenomenon represented wisdom (Roberts, 2005). These three gifts represent the philosophers of phenomenology that I have chosen to highlight.

## Heidegger: The One Who Brought Frankincense

In ancient times, frankincense was considered divine (Johnson, 1991). It was used as a part of the worship of deity. The ancient people burned frankincense, believing that it would carry their prayers to heaven. I have chosen to begin with frankincense, because of its relation to that which is spiritual. In no way do I seek to make this a theological rendering, but I will say that where other research methodologies definitely have a tangible process of engaging in the research, phenomenology seems to bare a spirit within it, and that spirit gives way to a mentality that is necessary when engaging in the work.

**Birth of the phenomenological spirit.** Heidegger first had to have this "spirit" for phenomenological research within him, before he could pass it on to others. This spirit began to develop within him at a young age. He was born in Messkirch, a small town in Germany (Safranski, 1998). The older of two sons he found himself in the shadow of his older brother, who was more of the extrovert, but Heidegger demonstrated intellectual gifting, so much so that the church decided to sponsor his education. This was a great opportunity for him because although his parents were not poor, they could not afford the quality of education needed to nurture the mind of their gifted older son (Safranski, 1998). I'm sure they observed the young Heidegger, noticing his reflective and introspective ways. The community in which he grew up nurtured his meditative nature. Heidegger speaks nostalgically about life as the son of a sexton and young church bell ringer:

> The church feasts, the days of vigil and the passage of the seasons and the morning, midday, and evening hours of each day fitted into each other, so that a continual ringing went through the young hearts, dreams, prayers, and games---it is this, probably, that conceals one of the most magical, most complete and most lasting secrets of the tower. (in Safranski, 1998, p. 7)

On another occasion Heidegger reminisces about when he was a young boy and would make small wooden boats to float in the town fountain:

> The dreamlike quality of such voyages was enveloped in a splendor then hardly visible, which lay on all things. Their realm was encompassed by mother's eye and hand…Those voyages of our games knew nothing yet of wanderings during which all shores were left behind. (in Safranski, 1998, p. 7)

The peaceful atmosphere of his hometown gave way for a bright and creative mind to develop in Heidegger, and when the church realized this, it decided to take an active role in his continued intellectual development.

After junior high and high school, the parish priest suggested to Heidegger's parents that he attend the Catholic seminary, which was a residential institution for young priests (Safranski, 1998). The parish priest also gave Heidegger free Latin lessons and prepared him for advanced work in senior high school. The church worked hard to support Heidegger's progress in school. In fact a grant was obtained on his behalf to attend the Constance Seminary. Heidegger spent his senior high school years also studying at the seminary and continued his advanced studies after high school by studying theology in Freiburg on an Eliner Grant. The church was making this investment in Heidegger's education in order to groom him for service to the church, but little did they know that by exposing him to this advanced training, they would open his mind to thinking for himself.

The seminary at Constance was a part of a larger educational institution, and so the free thinking of the community often collided with the students of the seminary. Some of Heidegger's teachers were quite liberal and often taught against the dogmas of Catholic theology. These teachers affected Heidegger's thinking greatly. In some of his classes, he was able to read and discuss authors and philosophers such as Nietzsche or Ibsen. He was able to learn about atheism or Hartmann's philosophy of the unconscious (Safranski, 1998). It was like Heidegger lived in two worlds, and these two worlds gave rise to an openness of the mind. There was the liberal and free thinking of the community and larger institution, and then there was the dogmatic world of the Catholic church. Heidegger was a citizen of both worlds and this experience helped to shape his philosophy (Safranski, 1998).

Soon, however, Heidegger would have to choose which world in which he would dwell:

> Religious instruction, of all thing aroused
> his interest...He was evidently attracted to

> the intellectually dangerous spheres, where his Messkirch faith would have a difficult time…he was not afraid of intellectual adventure for he still felt firm ground, the ground of faith, beneath his feet….on September 30, 1909, he entered the Society of Jesus as a novice at Tisis near Feldkirch…two weeks later…he was dismissed…Heidegger had complained of heart trouble…and had been sent home for medical reasons…two years later the pains would recur, causing him to discontinue his training as a priest…Perhaps his heart was rebelling against his head. (Safranski, 1998, p. 15)

Heidegger had been on the path for studying theology and eventually to be a priest, but after the heart problems, he took on a new focus, a focus that was taking root in him even as a young man:

> After four semesters I gave up my theological studies and dedicated myself entirely to philosophy. I still attended Carl Braig's lecture course on dogmatics. My interest in speculative theology led me to do this, above all the penetrating kind of thinking which this teacher concretely demonstrated in every lecture hour. (Heidegger, 1962, p. 251)

**Hermeneutic thinking.** Heidegger was drawn to thinking. It was the "penetrating kind of thinking" that drew Heidegger away from his original path. The confinement of the church did not give his mind the freedom to explore thinking. He had to think what was taught in the church. This attraction to thinking was his driving force. His fascination with thinking was the muse behind, "To think is to confine yourself to a single thought that one day stands still like a stary in the world's sky" (Heidegger, 1977/1993, p. 213).

Heidegger speaks of his general orientation in thinking, rather than an exclusive method (Moran, 2000). He says that he had learned to engage in "phenomenological seeing," and the "spirit" behind phenomenology. What is meant by this? Spirit comes from the Old French word *espiri* and the Latin *spiritus* which means "soul, courage, vigor or breath." In 1690 "spirit" took on a non-religious definition which means "essential principle of something" (Harper, 2010). According to Heidegger:

> The question, 'What calls for thinking?' asks for what wants to be thought about in the preeminent sense: it does not just give us something to think about, nor only itself, but it first gives thought and thinking to us, it entrusts thought to us as our essential destiny, and thus first joins and appropriates us to thought. (Heidegger, 1954, p. 391)

The very breath of a philosopher is to have one single deep thought and to struggle constantly to express that deep thought (Moran, 2000). This constant struggle could be likened to what Heidegger calls "the hermeneutic circle." This circle is not vicious, but it is more of a funnel that leads to the truth (Moran, 2000). This tornado of questioning involves the crosswinds of what the researcher knows and the questions of what she does not know. Heidegger writes:

> Is there not, however, a manifest circularity in such an undertaking? If we must first define an entity in its Being, and if we want to formulate the question of Being only on

> this basis, what is this but going in a circle? In working out the question, have we not "presupposed" something which only the answer can bring?" (Heidegger, 1962, p. 237)

**Questioning to understand *Dasein*.** Heidegger's major life work was to single-mindedly attempt to re-examine the question of being (Moran, 2000). Questioning played such an integral part of Heidegger's search for understanding Being. Heidegger says, "Every questioning is a seeking…Questioning is a knowing search for beings in their thatness and whatness…Questioning can come about as a mere 'asking around'" (Heidegger, 1962, p. 45). In his questioning, he uses the term *Dasein*, which speaks to the specific being of the human, the individual, one's essence. This is important to understand when engaging in phenomenology, because it is in phenomenology that the researcher has to appreciate each being's part in the study, but not as a group. I will not conduct this study *on* the group, but *with* each individual's presence in my class in relation to their reading of the Great Books literature. I am interested in the essence of each person and how the essence of a person helps them to have certain perceptions about the experience of being in my class. We have to listen to the story, the experience of each being in the study, because individuals have their own *Dasein*, which results in different perspectives. What they share is "their" reality. Heidegger (1954) articulates:

> Everything we talk about, mean, and are related to in such and such a way is in being. What and how we ourselves are is also in being. Being is found in thatness and whatness, reality, the being at hand of things, substance, validity, existence (Dasein), and in the "there is." (p. 47)

The students that I hope to engage in conversation with about their experiences in my class, will reveal their *Dasein* as they share their experiences. Even though their perception may be different from another student, it is still valid, because their perception reveals their being and understanding. Phenomenology allows me to study beings in different contexts (the context being the Great Books literature class), and how the Beings' essence or *Dasein* helps them to sense the experience.

**The phenomenon's true light.** Heidegger's search to understand being provides guidance for future phenomenologists as they seek to find their truths. Frankincense is a combination of the Old French word *franc* which means noble or true, and the Latin word *incendere* which means set on fire or to set alight. Together I could say that frankincense is "truth set alight or truth set on fire." This constant questioning brings the truth to light, which is what Heidegger meant when he said, "To think is to confine yourself to a single thought that one day stands still like a star in the world's sky" (Heidegger, 2008, p. 213).

> Heidegger reveals the etymology of "phenomenon": The Greek expression *phainomenon*, from which the term "phenomenon' derives, comes from the verb *phainesthai*, meaning "to show itself." Thus *phainomenon* means what shows itself, the self-showing, the manifest. *Phainesthai* itself is a "middle voice" construction of *phaino*, to bring into daylight, to place in brightness. *Phaino* belongs to the root *pha-*, like *phos*, light or brightness, i.e. that within which something can become manifest, visible in itself. Thus the meaning of the expression "phenomenon" is established as what shows

> itself in itself, what is manifest. The *phainomena* "phenomena," are thus the totality of what lies in the light of day or can be brought to the light. (Heidegger, 1954, p. 73)

The above explanation, causes Heidegger's star poem to become even more powerful. The phenomenon captures our attention because of its brightness. It shines; it stands out; it beckons for us to investigate and understand. It causes us to say "Wow! I need to take a closer look at that!" and in so doing we must connect with the beings connected to the phenomenon. This allows us to get to the "whatness" or "thatness" that Heidegger refers to. It allows us to get to the very essence of something as we take a closer look at each being's *Dasein* speaking to the phenomenon.

Heidegger, along with the other phenomenologists I discuss, reminds me of the Magi. The Magi went beyond just sitting and researching the ancient scrolls that told of past prophecies. Yes, they read the scrolls, but they also kept their eyes open (phenomenological seeing) for representations of what they had been researching, and when the need to move deeper into the research arose, they moved. They followed the star to see where it would lead. They must have been engaged in extensive study of the past prophesies, for when they went on the journey to follow the star, they decided to ask the King of that time, Herod: "Where is He who has been born King of the Jews? For we have seen His star in the East and have come to worship Him." This tells me that following the star was not a random act, but it was part of their own "single-minded attempt to re-examine" the prophesies they had been researching (Moran, 2000). One of those Magi brought the gift of frankincense, because he viewed the phenomenon as divine. The word "phenomenon" has its roots in "light" and "light *is* one of the most powerful metaphors to express eternity and depth of life" (O'Donohue, 1998, p. 5). Light is connected to the divine. In fact it is God's divine light that led the Magi to search for the Christ child who in Christian tradition is called "The Light of the World." To the one who brought frankincense, the phenomenon was the very essence of what the prophesies were about.

**Seeing perspectives through "worlding".** So for me to choose Heidegger as the one who brought "frankincense," means that I see him as the one who brings the spirit of phenomenology to light. His "Star" poem captures the spirit of what he is trying to promulgate. His demonstration of *worlding* in the "lectern" lecture is a representation of this spirit:

> …entering the lecture room I see the lectern…What do I see: brown surfaces intersecting at right angles? No, I see something different, a box, moreover a biggish box, with a smaller one built upon it. No, that's not it at all, I see the lectern at which I am to speak. You see the lectern from which you are spoken to…In this experience of the lectern-seeing, something presents itself to me from an immediate environment. This environmental something…these are not things with a definite character of meaning, objects, moreover conceived as meaning this or that, but the significant aspect is the primary experience, which presents itself to me directly…it is all of this world, it is worlding. (as cited in Safranski, 1998, pp. 94-95)

Heidegger also goes on to give an example of what a Senegalese would say if he saw the lectern. Based on his (the Senegalese) background and environment, his perspective on the lectern would be completely different from Heidegger and the other students (Safranski, 1998). The perspectives may all be different, and may even seem disconnected, but by each party looking at the lectern itself and drawing from their own "world" to develop meaning about the lectern, then a larger picture of the full essence of the lectern is revealed. This is worlding. This is the "spirit" of phenomenology that Heidegger seeks to unveil. This is the "star" that Heidegger says will shine in the world's sky. This thought of the lectern now morphs into something so much more than a wooden place to lay the presentation notes and materials. This is the frankincense of phenomenology, the essence of phenomenology, the spirit of phenomenology.

The Magi each brought different gifts and this could be a representation of worlding. They each had their differing perspectives on what the phenomenon represented, and the one who brought frankincense saw something spiritual or divine, an essence, the divine nature of the prophesies. And so it is with Heidegger. His lectures, essays and demonstrations of phenomenological thought reveal the spirit of phenomenology, and he sums it up in his "Star" poem: "To think is to confine yourself to a single thought that one day stand still like a star in the world's sky." What a beautiful poem. So inspiring. It is to me a sweet aroma like that of frankincense.

**A sweet aroma from a controversial life.** The ancients were known to use frankincense in their worship, because the smell of it had such a calming and meditative feel to it. The smell was so calming that it was also used to soothe depression. This calming affect must have served them well in times of worship. It was also used as a fragrance, and it was even used to freshen breath (Johnson, 1991). Unfortunately, Heidegger's life did not "smell" so sweet. He was a controversial figure. This same man, who could inspire his students to take notice of the "things themselves" and to look into their very essence, would also make allegiance with the National Socialist Party. He kept silent on its horrific murder of thousands of people (Moran, 2000). Upon first discovering him, I resisted him, but then I realized that there are many I respect, even with their human failures. Our founding fathers all were slave holders, and yet the beauty of the Constitution cannot be ignored. It is the Constitution that was used to instigate the freedom of the African American people, and it is Heidegger's "Star" poem that inspires me in my phenomenological research, for it is in this simple poem that I am able to embrace the "frankincense" that he has brought, the spirit or essence of engaging in phenomenological research.

**Hans-Georg Gadamer: The One Who Brought Gold**

It is said that the gift of gold represented the royal nature of the phenomenon (Roberts, 2005). "King" has its roots in the Old English word *cynn*, which means "family, race or leader of the people." A synonymous word for "king" is "ruler." A ruler is a person who leads the people. A "ruler" is also a strip used for making straight lines. It is a form of the word "rule." A "rule" is a principle or maxim governing conduct. To "rule" is from the early 13th century and it means to control, guide, direct (Harper, 2010). It is necessary for me to delineate these meanings and origins in order to reveal why I have chosen Gadamer as the Magi who brought gold. The connection to Gadamer that I see is that his "gift" represents the "principles or maxims that govern the conduct" of the way I would like to engage in the work.

**Conversation as text.** The main guiding principle that Gadamer brought to light was his use of conversation as a tool for obtaining meaning:

> Conversation is a process of coming to an understanding. Thus it belongs to every true conversation that each person opens himself to the other, truly accepts his point of view as valid and transposes himself into the other to such an extent that he understands not the particular individual but what he says. (Gadamer, 1975, p. 387)

Gadamer often discusses the meaning of hermeneutics, which was first and foremost the understanding of texts. When applying hermeneutics to conversation he still proposes that conversation is also text, a verbal one. There is a questioning that should happen while reading the text. There should be an engagement with the text in order to seek deeper meaning. Gadamer views conversation as engaging with a verbal text in order to gain understanding, mutual understanding. When using hermeneutics to understand a text, Gadamer (1989) writes:

> The hermeneutical task becomes of itself a questioning of things and is always in part so defined. This places hermeneutical work on a firm basis. A person trying to understand something will not resign himself from the start to relying on his own accidental foremeanings, ignoring as consistently and stubbornly as possible the actual meaning of the text until the latter becomes so persistently audible that it breaks through what the interpreter imagines it to be. Rather a person trying to understand a text is prepared for it to tell him something. (p. 281)

When I engaged in conversation with my former students, I of course brought some preconceived notions about what their experience was, but as we engaged in conversation about their experience in the Great Books literature class, their voices emerged louder than my imagination about their experience. When we talked back and forth in this way, the conversation moved me to direct my gaze to the things themselves, that which actually took place with each individual student, not just what I perceived to have taken place.

So with this in mind, allow me to reflect on the magi who brought gold. Of all the objects that the Magi contributed to their phenomenon, gold was the most significant, because gold was more than a precious metal. The discovery of all of today's medicines comes from the development of gold. Gold is considered one of nature's most perfect substances. This is what caused the ancients to use it in their experiments to find other chemicals. This gave birth to the science of alchemy, which is the precursor to modern medicine (Johnson, 1991). Gold had an amazing healing quality to it. The ancients found it so beautiful that they thought it had supernatural healing powers. To me, this makes it the king of all the earth's natural treasures. It led the early scientists into making discoveries that still benefit us today, and Gadamer's use of conversation has led many phenomenologists into finding deeper meaning in the lived world. Gadamer (1975/1989) believed that understanding takes place through the speaking and interpreting of language.

Gadamer (1994) was a student of Heidegger and he absorbed everything his mentor taught him. Heidegger's lectures were so poignant to Gadamer and touched him deeply. One very important lesson that Gadamer grasped was in Heidegger's seminar style of teaching. Heidegger would allow students to come to an understanding of the texts through questioning (Moran, 2000). Gadamer felt that "The guiding idea of discussion is that the fusion of horizons that takes place in understanding is actually the achievement of language" (Gadamer, 1975, p. 370). When I reflect on Gadamer describing dialogue as a "fusion of horizons" I am reminded of the words of James Risser (2012), when he says:

> As a hermeneutical concern, it would not be at all inappropriate here to describe the formation at issue here through the metaphor of weaving, since discourse, like the nature of every text, has a natural propensity to weave aspects together to form the unity of its particular whole. Accordingly, the formation at issue here can be designated with the metaphor the fabric of life. (p. 60)

**Weaving conversation.** My phenomenological question is the following: **What are the lived experiences of African American students reading Great Books literature?** This question includes the words "African American students" and the word "my." The perspectives of my students woven together with my being in the class as well, brought forward something pretty magical, a full picture of what took place. I envision a fabric of gold because each person's experience articulated through verbal text is golden. It is precious. It is valuable. I recall the story of "Rumpelstiltskin" and the great lengths that the king took to force the young girl to spin gold out of straw, and I think of her ultimate sacrifice (her first born child) in order to keep being able to spin gold out of straw. Weaving together the perspectives of different people, from different backgrounds, who were part of the same experience is a magical occurrence. Like the miller's daughter had to call on the supernatural to help her, the process of weaving together the lived experiences from all types of different people is also a great challenge.

**The pure gold of conversation.** Just as gold is perceived as the most important of all the gifts given, Gadamer felt that language was most essential in finding meaning. Language is where our understanding, our mode of being in the world, comes to realization (Moran, 2000). It is through language that human beings develop communal understanding as well as self-understanding. More specifically, Gadamer felt that language as demonstrated in conversation is the source of finding meaning. He writes:

> When we try to examine the hermeneutical phenomenon through the model of conversation between two persons, the chief thing that these apparently so different situations---understanding a text and reaching an understanding in conversation---have in common is that both are concerned with a subject matter that is placed before them. Just as each interlocutor is trying to reach agreement on some subject with his partner, so also the interpreter is trying to understand…(Gadamer, 1975, p. 370)

Conversation reminds me of the gold, because the work that goes into seeking understanding through conversation reminds me of digging for gold. Conversation reminds me of gold also because it appears to be the main tool for engaging in phenomenological research. In a methodology that is sometimes difficult to grasp, finding Gadamer and his view on conversation makes me feel like I have struck gold. I feel that he presents something valuable that I can hold on to and use in my research. I have seen how conversation can give birth to understanding because of my experience at St. John's College. The seminar was the main manner in which the class was conducted. We sat around a table and had a conversation about the text. We presented our questions and talked through them, until some form of understanding was developed. Seeing the affect this had on me, I then decided to use this same method in the literature class that I taught. I have seen my students come from darkness to light when presenting the classics to them. So Gadamer validates my teaching methodology, and it gives me evidence of the effectiveness of using conversation in my phenomenological study.

Gadamer articulates why conversation truly does bring about understanding:

> Every conversation presupposes a common language, or better, creates a common language. Something is placed in the center…which the partners in dialogue both share, and concerning which they can exchange ideas with one another. Hence reaching an understanding on the subject matter of a conversation necessarily means that a common language must first be worked out in the conversation…in a successful conversation they both come under the influence of truth of the object and are thus bound to one another in a new community. (Gadamer, 1975, p. 371)

Those involved in the "successful" conversation have come together to find meaning. I joined with the participants in my study as we engaged in conversation about what was happening when my African-American high school students read the Great Books of Western Civilization. As a community we sought to understand that. It is not about me "asserting my own point of view" of what I think is happening (Gadamer, 1975, p. 371). There is no truth in that, but it is about my students joining with me, going on a search, and under the light of phenomenology finding the answer.

The word gold comes from the Old English word *gulth* which ultimately means "bright." The idea of conversation that Gadamer presents reminds me of the brightness that illuminated the dark stable once the chest of gold was opened. This gold glimmered and shone a glowing light upon the phenomenon that presented itself to the Magi, and so it is with conversation. Out of all three of the gifts given, it is the only one that glimmers or shines. Gold was given because it was thought that the phenomenon represented royalty or kingship, and it seems that out of all the tools used to engage in phenomenological research, conversation is king. It provides the guiding principle for engaging in the work. As stated earlier, king means "leader of the people." Conversation is what leads me into bringing to light the understanding of my phenomenon.

## Max Van Manen: The One Who Brought Myrrh

The third and final contribution of the Magi was that of myrrh. It is said that they brought myrrh, because they were sages. The word "sage" comes from the Latin word *sapere* which means to "have a taste, have good taste, be wise." The meaning of the word evolved into "man of profound wisdom" in the 1300s (Harper, 2010). Myrrh reveals that the phenomenon represents wisdom. The word *wisdom* comes from the Old English *wisdom* which means "knowledge, learning, experience."

**Defining "lived experience".** Within this final meaning of the word "wisdom" we see the word "experience," which reminds me to think about what my phenomenological question asks. My question does not ask about what the students learned in the class, because that makes assumptions that they actually learned something or that learning something was the most important thing to gain from the study. It does not even ask about how they felt about the class, because that makes assumptions that they actually felt something or that feeling something was the most important thing to gain from the study. It also does not ask how lives were changed in the class, because that makes assumptions that lives were changed or that a changed life was the most important thing to gain from the study. The question is simple but can encompass any of those things and more, simply because I am asking what their lived experience is reading Great Books literature. "Lived experience" is so open and allows us to get at the very essence of something, as opposed to locking our quest for understanding into some type of context. This is the wisdom and understanding that Max van Manen brings to phenomenology, and he brings it forward in laypersons' terms and through practicality. Van Manen (1997) writes:

> But if we wish to remain responsive to the commitment of phenomenology, then we should try to resist the temptation to develop positivistic schemata, paradigms, models, or other categorical abstractions of knowledge. Instead we should refer questions of knowledge back to the lifeworld where knowledge speaks through our lived experiences. (p. 46)

Each participant was able to give whatever perspective they liked. In so doing they allowed me to get at the very essence of the phenomenon of **the lived experiences of African American high school students reading Great Books literature.**

When I wrote about Frederick Douglass in the previous chapters, I could only draw from texts that were written about his experience, and I can only conjecture what his lived experience may have been. But now my opportunity to talk to those who have lived through experiences of engaging in the Great Books, provided a lived understanding of the phenomenon. Van Manen (1997) expresses clearly phenomenology describes:

> To do phenomenological study of any topic , therefore, it is not enough to simply recall experiences I or others may have had with respect to a particular phenomenon. Instead, I must recall the experience in such a way that the essential aspects, the meaning structures of this experience as lived through, are brought back, as it were, and in such a way that we recognize this description as a possible experience, which means as a possible interpretation of that experience. (p. 41)

Again, I did not ask how these books affect them now, but I asked them to take me back in time and to relive the experience of reading, discussing, writing about, and even using the arts to connect to the texts. I asked them to relive the experience of being in the class. This type of understanding cannot come about by a survey or questionnaire, but it involves a special strategy and writing skill, a process that takes me deep into the individual's experience. Van Manen provides the wisdom in engaging in the process of going deep into each individual experience.

**The practice of phenomenology.** The one who brought myrrh (which represents wisdom) was called one of the Wisemen. This particular gift giver was able to look at the phenomenon and see himself. He, along with his companions, were devoted to deep study of the ancient scrolls, nature and of most subject areas. This commitment to study is what gave them the title of "Wise-men" or Magi. Max van Manen is not a philosopher as Heidegger and Gadamer; rather he is more of a practitioner, but it is in his practice of phenomenology that I am able to see his demonstrated wisdom. It is evident that he has devoted his time in deep study of the founding fathers of phenomenology and it is through his writings that I am able to understand even more clearly what phenomenology entails.

In his book, *Writing in the Dark*, van Manen (2002) offers examples of phenomenological writing, and he also discusses the goal of a phenomenologist:

> The phenomenologist does not present the reader with a conclusive argument or with a determinate set of ideas, essence or insights. Instead, he or she aims to be allusive by orienting the reader reflectively to that region of lived experience where the phenomenon dwells in recognizable form. (p. 238)

This to me is a very clear interpretation of what both Heidegger and Gadamer alluded to in their writings. Also in *Writing in the Dark*, van Manen examines the "star" in Heidegger's poem:

> For the person caught up in wonder, what seemed ordinary and common place has now become extraordinary, giving pause to ponder its existence....The gaze of wonder sweeps us up in a state of passivity, or perhaps it is passivity that makes it possible to be swept up in wonder. That is why Plato spoke of wonder as pathos, as something that literally overcomes us, comes over us. And so, a text that induces wonder is a pathic text, evoking the gaze of Orpheus. We are so inclined to convert research into action and usable results that this activism can limit our possibility of understanding, a form of understanding that involves the

> experience of meaningfulness. (2002, pp. 250-251)

I wonder what van Manen means by "The gaze of Orpheus"? Could he be referring to his worship of the sun (the most well-known star)? When I read about Orpheus, I find that he denied all other deity and only worshipped the sun, the rays of its light captivating him so much that it cost him his life. Metaphorically, this can happen to the phenomenological researcher. My being drawn to wonder about **the lived experiences of African American students reading Great Books literature** has consumed my mind, heart and life so much that for these years I have placed life on hold in order to get at its essence. This is what wonder does. It causes us to pause whatever we are doing in order to just meditate, reflect, and investigate that which captivates us.

Jane Taylor found herself in a daze about stars, which compelled her to write the "Star" poem, and in it she says over and over, "How I wonder what you are…" Heidegger also has adopted this hypnotic power of wonder when he says, "To think is to confine yourself to a single thought that one day stands still like a star in the world's sky." When I read the part that says that the thought "stands still," I think of time standing still, life pausing, I am completely enthralled by this phenomenon that calls me.

**Freedom in studying essences.** Merlau Ponty (1962) says, "Phenomenology is the study of essences" (p. vii). In my case it is the study of the essences of these students' experiences, not my experience, and van Manen (1997) reminds me to be mindful of that:

> The problem of phenomenological inquiry is not always that we know too little about the phenomenon we wish to investigate, but that we know too much. Or, more accurately,

> the problem is that our "common sense" pre-understandings, our suppositions, assumptions, and existing bodies of scientific knowledge, predispose us to interpret the nature of the phenomenon before we have even come to grips with the significance of the phenomenological question. (p. 46)

Van Manen is Heidegger and Gadamer personified. His writing comforts me by giving me license to wonder about my phenomenon. Where typical research rushes and pressures you to give a result or to prove something, I am free from that pressure. I can read his writings and realize that I am not just wandering in the wilderness of completing my doctoral studies. I am merely in a prolonged state of wonder, which should happen before the writing. So now I realize that I have been WONDERING around in the wilderness. It is this wonder that shines a light on the darkness of my seeking to get at the essences of my phenomenon. The word "myrrh" means "bitter." Darkness is a bitter place. There are so many thoughts and ideas when a phenomenon first presents itself, and the way to writing about it seems dark, but now I feel myself coming into the light of the phenomenon. The struggle has been intense, but that is all a part of the process as I seek to get at the essences of this lived experience.

**Van Manen's Methodological Process**

Van Manen's practical wisdom for engaging in phenomenological research is found in his book, *Researching Lived Experience* (1997). He offers a delineated process for engaging in the work: 1) Turning to the phenomenon; 2) Investigating experience as we live it; 3) Reflecting on the essential themes; 4) Describing the phenomenon through the art of writing and rewriting; 5)

Maintaining a strong and oriented pedagogical relation to the phenomenon; 6) Balancing the research context by considering parts and whole (pp. 30-34). In the next section I take an in-depth look at this process and connect it to my phenomenon.

**The Turning**

Van Manen (1997) was able to connect the idea of turning to what I have come to adopt as the anthem for my research: "To think is to confine yourself to a single thought that one day stands still like a star in the world's sky" (Heidegger, 1971, p. 4). Engaging in phenomenological research begins with a single thought that so captures you that it literally blinds you from wanting to think about (or research) anything else. The turning expresses the moment that this happens for the researcher. The turning so captivated the Magi that they eventually were inspired to go on a journey to understand the phenomenon deeper. Under a trance, they followed the star.

This has been my experience. The moment those four young men transitioned from not caring about the Great Books class, to frantically trying to get the computers to work so they could do an online chat about the literature, my attention was seized. Over the years the captivation intensified until, like in Heidegger's poem, I found myself confined to the single thought about **the lived experiences of African American high school students reading Great Books literature**.

That moment when I was first called to think about my phenomenon reminds me of what Heidegger says: "We never come to thoughts. They come to us" (1977/1993, p. 365). I was completely puzzled as to what happened. Why did they come to care about engaging in the text? I literally can see them even now, many years later (it was my first time teaching this course) crawling under the computer table, jiggling the cords and wires, saying everything but a curse word (it's a Christian school) in frustration about not getting on line. This puzzling was a spark in the phenomenon, and then the light goes out, because I cannot get a sense of what it is or what is going on here. It withdraws from me like bait on a hook trying to catch a fish, and this withdrawal forces me to follow it. Heidegger (1968) writes:

> What withdraws from us draws us along by its very withdrawal, whether or not we become aware of it immediately, or at all. Once we are drawn into the withdrawal, we are-albeit in a way quite different from that of migratory birds-caught in the draft of what draws, attracts us by its withdrawal. And once we, being so attracted, are drawing toward what draws us, our essential being already bears the stamp of that draft. (p. 374)

When I look into the etymology of the word "turn" I am quite interested in the Old French word *torner* which means to "turn away or around; draw aside, cause to turn; change, transform; turn on a lathe." Particularly the words "draw aside" strike me, because this turning to the phenomenon really does draw us aside from other thoughts, things, even from life in a way. We are captivated by it. We are caught up in a current of wonder. This has been my experience. If you get me talking about it, I will go on a long diatribe about the Great Books and my students' responses to them. I will fuss about the sad state of literacy education. I will go on and on.

The beauty of engaging in phenomenological research is that it allows me to get out of my head. The turning is only the first step in the process, and if I just left it there, I can imagine there would be a sort of mental constipation. My mind would be full and consumed, paralyzed by the wonder of it all. The other steps in the process remind me of when the Magi stopped just gazing at the star and they moved forward. Phenomenological research helps me to get out of my head and into my body, the world around me, and to move forward with making sense of the phenomenon that has drawn me to it.

**Investigating the Experience as We Live it**

After the researcher has given oneself over to a "star" (the turning), then she must then go on a quest to understand the experience of it. Through dwelling in the midst of lived experiences and shared situations, the researcher is able to explore actively every aspect of the lived experience (van Manen, 1997, p. 32). It was not enough for the Magi to continue observing the fascinating star from their observatory. They had to get up, pack up and move. On this journey they met a king, young parents, a child, etc. It was through interacting with these participants of the lived experience that they were able to understand the phenomenon better, all by looking at the phenomenon up close through the participants' experiences.

It is not enough for me just to gaze at the light of my phenomenon. The students arguing across the table over whether or not Dionysius was right or wrong for being angry at Pentheus and his mother, or the re-enactment of the Peloponnesian War, are fascinating to experience, especially when you realize that all of the students are African American and on the surface have no reason to be so interested in the text. The texts for all practical purposes are culturally irrelevant to them. Yet, something happens between them and the text. Writing that statement just now was hard, because I was going to say, "They made a connection" or "The text touched them in some way," but I feel those terms place some type of presupposition on the phenomenon. They need to speak to the "whatness" and "thatness" of the phenomenon. In order to give them that space to speak, I engaged in the phenomenological process of rendering the meaning of each participants' text (verbal and written) that expresses their lived experiences.

There was first "the turning" of my attention to the phenomenon. Then I proceeded to turn "to the things themselves" (Husserl, 1911, p. 80). Gadamer (2013) writes:

> All correct interpretation must be on guard against arbitrary fancies and the limitations imposed by imperceptible habits of thought, and it must direct its gaze "on the things themselves." For the interpreter to let himself be guided by the things themselves is obviously not a matter of a single "conscientious" decision, but is 'the first, last, and constant task." For it is necessary to keep one's gaze fixed on the thing throughout all the constant distractions that originate in the interpreter himself. (pp. 278-279)

Gadamer (2013) goes on to say that "The hermeneutical task becomes itself a questioning of things…a person trying to understand a text is prepared for it to tell him something" (p. 281). Engaging in conversation with my former students allowed them to tell me something about their phenomenon of reading the Great Books. The whole of these conversations was totally focused on them and their experiences, and as we engaged in these conversations and renderings, that understanding of the phenomenon was brought to the light. I think of Gadamer (1989) when he says, "Rather language is the universal medium in which understanding occurs. Understanding occurs in interpreting…Like conversation, interpretation is a circle closed by the dialectic of question and answer" (pp. 390-391).

**Reflecting on Essential Themes**

After turning to the phenomenon (chapter one), and after investigating the lived experience of the phenomenon (chapter two,) my task was to reflect on everything that presents itself to me in the course of the conversations I had with my students. I will drew out themes that somehow constellated meaning for me (van Manen, 1997). I looked forward to what these themes would say to me. I wondered what picture would be drawn for me? As I connected the dots of the essential themes illuminated through our conversations and my interpretation of them, I wondered what the ultimate story would be? In order to be able to express a text's meaning, we must translate it into our own language (Gadamer, 1989).

This causes me to think of constellations. Initially the stars were just specks of light in the sky, but to make sense of how the stars are spread across the sky and to even create a sort of stratospheric map, someone connected the stars and developed constellations. These constellations were given names. In chapter two I discuss Polaris, the big and little dipper, or shall I say "The Drinking Gourd." This picture in the sky symbolized freedom to the slave. This picture of freedom was created for slaves because when they saw "The Drinking Gourd" they knew which direction they should go to get to freedom. When I reviewed my conversations with my students and began to constellate the various themes that came to the surface, a naming takes place through my interpretation of those themes. As I focus on "the things themselves" my interpretations reveal deeper connections. To clarify even more, I share a story about the Pulawatans, from Edward Casey's book *Getting Back into Place* (2009):

> Pulawatans navigate hundreds and sometimes thousands of miles in open ocean without the use of compasses or other navigational instruments and only rarely fail to reach their destination. How is this possible? ...Pulwatans make use of a complicated system of signals from the seascape and the skyscape surrounding them at all times... These unlikely and often seemingly trivial factors constitute veritable 'seamarks.' (pp. 26-27)

Can you imagine the total focus that would be needed to accomplish this? If I could be successful in focusing so much on each student's rendering of the phenomenon, I could notice every single theme that arises! The Pulawatans take all of these signs in nature and are able to develop a meaning as they constellate all of these signs together, that meaning being "how to get to a certain destination." This is an example for me. They viewed every little sign as important to knowing how to reach their destination. I, too, drew from my students' experiences, themes great and small, that helped to bring forward a fuller rendering of the essence of the phenomenon.

It says that after the Magi came face to face with the phenomenon, they saw angels in their dreams, revealing more about the phenomenon. No one else was given these dreams, but this was their revelation. As they rested that night, their minds danced with visions about the phenomenon, and they were able to interpret these visions for themselves. The phenomenological researcher goes through a similar process, by spending time with the participants in the lived experience (as the Pulwatans spent time studying the signs of nature), hearing their thoughts on the experience, paying attention to each element that is shared, interpreting each experience and then by constellating each experience to gain meaning.

**The Art of Writing and Rewriting**

> Revelation by Robert Frost
> We make ourselves a place apart
> Behind light words that tease and flout,
> But oh, the agitated heart
> Till someone find us really out
> 'Tis pity if the case require
> (Or so we say) that in the end
> We speak the literal to inspire
> The understanding of a friend
> But so with all, from babes that play
> At hide-and-seek to God afar,
> So all who hide too well away
> Must speak and tell us where they are
> (http://www.poetrysoup.com/famous/poem/4900/revelation)

This portion of the phenomenological research process is sometimes the most difficult, because now you must take your reflections on the phenomenon and communicate them through language. According to Gadamer, thinking and speaking, rationality and language, derive their modern day meanings from the root word *logos* (Gadamer, 1975, pp. 366-397). *Logos* encompasses conversation, inquiry and questioning, and taking these elements, paint a picture with them (van Manen, 1997). As a phenomenological researcher, I am striving to apply *logos* to understanding and revealing my phenomenon (van Manen, 1997). The challenge is making sure that I stay true to how the phenomenon presented itself to me by the participants in my study.

By far, this deep writing process has been the most challenging for me to write about. To help me work through this difficulty, I turned to my constant source of wisdom, the Bible. In it I found several verses that were a help to me charting my course through this dark space in my writing. Proverbs 4:23 says, "Watch over your heart with all diligence, For from it flows the springs of life." I wanted to continue to look into this concept of words coming from the heart, so I discovered that Matthew 12:34 says, "For the mouth speaks out of that which fills the heart." Also Proverbs 23:7 shined its light on the darkness of trying to articulate this. It says, "For as he thinks within himself, so he is." And finally, Jeremiah 17:9 says, "The heart is more deceitful than all else and is desperately sick; Who can understand it?" This sickness I believe is that it is complex, difficult to understand, and sometimes does not reveal its very essence. When we say we want to get at the "heart" of something, I think of going down deep into some hidden place. I think of going to a dark place where there is no light. All you can use is the sense of your ears to help you navigate through that dark path. Just like our hearts are hidden within our breasts, so are the thoughts and feelings about an experience hidden. The above verses also talk about the mouth speaking to reveal what's in the heart. I recall what Gadamer (1989) says:

> Conversation is a process of coming to an understanding. Thus it belongs to every true conversation that each person opens himself to the other, truly accepts his point of view as valid and transposes himself into the other to such an extent that he understands not the particular individual, but what he says. (p. 387)

So to get at the heart we have to listen, just as we would listen while traveling a dark path in order to get to a certain place, even if the only goal is to just get out of the darkness.

In the above poem, Robert Frost says, "But so with all, from babes that play at hide-and-seek to God afar, so all who hide too well away must speak and tell us where they are." The task of phenomenology is to dig skillfully and carefully, those things up to the light so they can be seen. I believe that this part of the process is so difficult, because the human word is essentially incomplete. No human word can express our mind completely, for the human word is not one but many words (Gadamer, 1989). Herein lies the struggle. It is difficult to think of the words to grasp the meaning of what the participants are trying to say, and at the same time it is hard for me to find the words to express how their words are affecting my perception. It can become such a tangled web, like if we were on that dark path that ends up being multiple paths. We wander around and around until confusion freezes us and we find ourselves paralyzed in a state of confusion, yet wonder. Van Manen (2002) writes how phenomenological writing that addresses itself to the phenomena of everyday life is surprisingly difficult. This is why. We are seeking to navigate through the words of the person and our own.

Frost's above poem also says, "To speak the literal to inspire understanding of a friend." In the course of my research development, a relationship between my participants (earlier students) and me developed. It first developed because of my interest in their experience. This is what we have in common. As a result, the participants became more than just objects in my study, but rather became "friends," and my desire to get to the essence of the phenomenon inspired me truly to understand them more deeply. The word "literal" is rooted in "taking words in their natural meaning" (www.etymonline.com). In that moment when we have a conversation, I must listen to their hearts and try to grasp an understanding of that. This, as said earlier, is not an easy process, and it involves me writing and rewriting their words in order for them to make some sort of sense for me. As I listened and wrote and listened and wrote, the pen or computer keys became a flashlight for me, teasing out their words and organizing them into stepping stones out of the darkness and into the light.

## Maintaining a Strong and Oriented Relation

Staying focused is essential for engaging in this type of research. Although it is a type of qualitative research, because many rabbit trails present themselves in the course of the process, it is tempting to get sidetracked from the phenomenon (van Manen, 1997, p. 33). There is also a tendency to lose sight of how the phenomenon is presenting itself to you. It is imperative that phenomenological researchers allow the phenomenon to speak to them as opposed to placing our own preconceived notions upon it. In addition, we must not allow ourselves to be distracted by what every other theorist, text, belief system, etc. may say or think. The phenomenon must be allowed to speak; we must listen and we must accept what it says.

Van Manen gave an interesting exegesis on the story of Orpheus. However, my perception of it seems quite different. Van Manen, discusses "The Gaze of Orpheus" as an example of how wonder should so captivate us. Orpheus could not help but look at his wife, and in so doing, he lost her forever. If only he could have kept his eyes on where he was trying to go. When I think of my phenomenon, (**the lived experiences of African American high school students reading Great Books literature**), there are at least two paths I could follow. I could get lost in the life stories of each individual, or I could focus on retelling their experiences in my class. Sometimes the two get blurred when I think about bringing the phenomenon forward. I repeat Gadamer (1989) again when he writes:

> Thus it belongs to every true conversation that each person opens himself to the other, truly accepts his point of view as valid and transposes himself into the other to such an extent that he understands not the particular individual, but what he says. (p. 403)

This makes me think of when Orpheus finally was given his wife and he was headed out of the darkness. I'm sure the light was in view, but Orpheus could not help but steal a look at Eurydice. If only he had kept focused on getting to the light, and then he could have beheld her in her true human form. While in the underworld, he was only seeing a shadow of her, not her in reality. If only he kept his head forward, focused on where he was trying to go. This is how I read this story. I don't want to uncover a shadow of the phenomenon, but I want to get at its very essence. The shadow would not satisfy me. No longer would Orpheus feel her touch, the warmth of her embrace, or smell the sweetness of her breath. She was just a vapor, and in an instant she vanished again and forever.

I spent 6 years teaching the Great Books. The school has since closed and the time is quickly becoming a vapor for me in my memory. This is my one last Orpheus attempt to resurrect that dead experience through the retellings of my former students. This is my last and only chance. This is also a personal journey for me, and I am thankful that phenomenology lets it be so. The love I have for this moment in my teaching history is parallel to the love that Orpheus had for Eurydice. I have been inspired to go down into the unknown darkness in order to excavate the essence of that lived experience for my students. The importance of staying focused is crucial to the phenomenological process.

**Considering Parts and the Whole**

Another guideline that is sometimes hard to follow is not allowing yourself to get lost in the research process. I like to think of engaging in the phenomenological research process as cyclical, almost like a tornado. Most research is more linear: you gather the facts and they lead to the conclusion. Phenomenological research has a conversation, and the questioning process can take you round and round until it is quite easy to lose sight of the fact that you must paint a picture of the lived experience. Phenomenological research is about deciphering the "whatness" of something, and it is easy to get buried underneath the process of digging deeper and deeper to excavate that "whatness" (van Manen, 1990, p. 33). Part of the process is going deep. Part of the process is examining every part of that "whatness" in light of the whole that is being revealed, but it is imperative that we not forget to unveil the essences of the lived experience at some point, as opposed to just getting carried away with looking at every aspect of the phenomenon. The Magi did not spend their whole life following the star. At some point they found themselves face to face with the phenomenon.

As I have stated previously, my goal is to get to the very essence of my phenomenon. This is the goal of phenomenology as well. Van Manen (1990) says:

> From a phenomenological point of view, to do research is always to question the way we experience the world, to want to know the world in which we live as human beings. And since to know the world is profoundly to be in the world in a certain way, the act of

> researching-questioning-theorizing is the
> intentional act of attaching ourselves to the
> world, to become more fully part of it, or
> better, to become the world. (p. 5)

This is the process of bringing each person's story together to form an understanding of the whole phenomenon. Questioning my former students is my attempt at searching everywhere in the life world for an understanding of the essences of **the lived experiences of African American high school students reading Great Books literature.**

> Hermeneutic phenomenology is a philosophy of the personal, the individual, which we pursue against the background of an understanding of the evasive (oh so evasive…as discussed earlier) character of the *logos* of *other*, the *whole,* the communal, or the *social*. Much of educational research tends to pulverize life into minute abstracted fragments and particles that are of little use to practitioners…Its particular appeal is that it tries to understand the phenomena of education by maintaining a view of pedagogy as an expression of the whole. (van Manen, 1997, p. 7)

To explain van Manen's quote further, I reference the existential themes he identifies as significant throughout each human life: lived space, lived body, lived time and lived human relation. *Lived Space* is not about a description of the physical space or its measurement, but it is about how space affects human life. How a space may affect the way a person feels is hard to articulate, because few people really meditate on that. However, it is an important part of our very existence and an important part of understanding the human being. *Lived Body* connects to our physical being in the world. Our bodies or physical beings, speak to who we are. *Lived Time* is our personal time as it relates to who we are in the world, whether old or young, happy or sad, relaxed or nervous. It is where we are on the time line of life, and it relates to our feelings and emotions about our location in time. *Lived Human Relation* is about our connectedness to other beings in the world, our world. This relates to how we are in our communities. These existentials shine through in the rendering of the phenomenon.

What I have shared in this section about van Manen's "Magi Gift" to phenomenology demonstrates his gift of wisdom of engaging in the work. His contribution represents the wisdom of how to see the phenomenon, the wisdom of how to engage in phenomenological research, and the wisdom to understand the sometimes bitter process in getting to that place of bringing the essence of the story to light.

## Stepping into The Light: My Process of Engagement

I have discussed the Magi of Phenomenology. Reading their wisdom has been so enlightening for me. Each of their texts was a ray of starlight on my path to opening my phenomenon. Earlier, I shared Raymond's voice, and that gave a tinge of testimony from a student's experience, but his rendering of the experience was merely the first ray of light that drew me to the path of investigating this phenomenon. Now I have gone on a journey in order to go deeper into the phenomenon by hearing from the voices of other students from the Great Books class.

### Selection of Participants

Twenty-two of my former students were invited to participate in the study and only five (all have graduated from high school) were able to participate. These students were all my students for 2 years or more (some for 4 years) at a Christian school that is now closed. I still maintain a connection with most of my former students, as well as their parents. Each participant was sent an invitation (Appendix A) to participate in a weekend retreat where we would talk about the lived experience of being in the Great Books literature class. This invitation was sent through email. Once the students signed up to participate, I held a meeting to explain/introduce the full study and the activities planned to collect the textual accounts I seek. At this meeting the participants were then asked to complete the Participant Consent Form (Appendix B) to officially become a part of the research project. A schedule for the weekend retreat and other project activities was also shared with the participants at the meeting.

**The Process**

> For in six days the Lord made the heavens and the earth, the sea, and all that is in them…Genesis 20:11

In order to develop a representation of the students' lived experiences, it almost involves a creation or recreation of "that" world they were in years ago. It was not something that I could instantly cultivate, but it would take some days, one step at a time to unveil that life-world. In order to accomplish this, I met with the participants during a research retreat in January 2016 during MLK weekend, and during this retreat, I engaged them in a group in a series of activities that helped them to relive and retell their lived experiences. The research retreat took place at a luxury hotel in Northern Virginia. As a way to compensate them for participating, I paid for all rooms, as well as one meal that we shared on Sunday. My husband and I checked in on Friday night in order for us to unpack, unwind, review the weekend's schedule, and to make sure the sound equipment was working, etc. My husband did all the audio recording for this study. The project began on Saturday, January 16 at 4 pm, with the conversations happening over two-hour time slots and a one hour break in between each time slot. Each session had a specific purpose, to allow for a reflective process of getting at the essence of their lived experiences. The study concluded on Sunday, January 17 at 9 pm.

**Dawn of the journey.** At 4 pm on the first day, the participants and I met for our first session together in the hotel conference room. All sessions and conversations happened in the full group. No individual conversations took place for the entire study. During the 4 pm to 6 pm time period, I took the time to explain the schedule of the weekend and to explain again my purpose for engaging in the study. I shared with them that I wanted to know their lived experience of being in my Great Books literature class. After explaining how the weekend would take place, I asked the students to write about their most significant experience of being in the Great Books literature class, and how it affected them. At this first conversation, we began the conversation with each of them reading their descriptive accounts. Thematic paths were then followed from these initial accounts during the rest of the weekend sessions and they helped to guide the discussion.

At 6 pm, the participants were given a one hour break to get some dinner, rest in their room, etc. At 7 pm we reconvened in the hotel conference room and picked up the conversation where we left off. One of the themes that started to form from the first conversation is that they were someone different internally, than who they showed them selves to be in the class. So, at this second session we discussed who their two identities were: their inner person and the persona they presented outwardly in the class. This conversation was rich with the participants revealing some very personal struggles they were having during the years they were in my class. When I realized this, I asked them the question, "Who were you when you took my class those years ago?" We ended this session with them reflecting on that question.

**Solar noon of the journey.** At 1 pm on the second day, the participants and I reconvened in the hotel conference room, and we picked up from when we reflected on who they were while they were in my class. We discussed which books connected to them the most, their personal feelings about the class, their connections to the teacher during the class time, etc. To help them capture these reflections, the participants were asked to create a monologue that they felt expressed their lived experiences as if they were the person they were during the time they took the class. The students ended this session, sharing their monologues (monologues are shared in chapter five).

The remaining two sessions for Sunday (4 pm-6 pm and 7 pm-9 pm) the students and I continued discussions of memories from the class and then the students spent the time working together to create the first draft of a play that would provide a visual representation of their lived experience reading Great Books literature in my class. The monologues helped them to create the play, which they eventually called "The Table." The last two sessions of the weekend research retreat were used to develop and rehearse the play. The monologues turned into actual characters in the play and the monologues were used as part of the script. More about "The Table" will be presented in chapter four.

**Sunset of the journey.** All of the conversations were audio recorded by my husband, and I also kept a journal during the weekend research retreat. This journal was used to record my reflections of each conversation when my husband and I retired to our hotel room. I also took notes during the conversations over the weekend, and during the rehearsals for the play. Transcriptions of each session were completed after the performance of the play. The final "days of creation" for this study took place with two rehearsals after the weekend research retreat for the play at another location, the final dress rehearsal on the day of the performance, and the actual performance of the play on February 13 at St. John's College. The conversations held over the weekend research retreat, the preparation of the play and the performance of the play all contributed to the creation of the life-world of my students who shared their lived experiences of reading Great Books literature.

**Returning to Sacred Ground**

Earlier I spoke of "The Sacred Ground of Questioning." As I approached the time where I met with the students, I came carefully. I came with humility. This special attitude was required in order for me to develop the types of questions that truly get at the person's lived experience, allowing for an openness that invites rather than directs.

Edgar Allan Poe's poem "Evening Star" (1827) evokes an image of what it's like to be in this state of wonder, where I am trying to understand my students' lived experiences. It's an exciting journey, but there is a darkness about it, the darkness being that which I do not see or understand.

from Evening Star
…In thy glory afar,
And dearer thy beam shall be;
For joy to my heart
Is the proud part
Thou bearest in Heav'n at night,
And more I admire

> Thy distant fire,
> Than that colder, lowly light.
> (Poe,
> http://www.eapoe.org/works/poems/estara.ht
> m)

I am in a state of wonder. Like the evening star that brightens the night sky, I asked questions that illuminated my understanding of the lived experiences of the students in my Great Books literature class. Some questions that I asked were the following: "Who were you during the time when you were a part of the Great Books Literature class? Describe your life, who you were/are (your perspective on life, etc.)" "Describe any thoughts and feelings you had about any part of the class." "Talk about any book or text that you most remember. Why is it so memorable?" "Describe your literature class experiences prior to being in this class." "Describe your experience with your teacher (me) in the class?" Of course, many other questions arose as we engaged in the conversations surrounding these questions during the course of the weekend research retreat.

**Textual Analysis**

Upon completion of the textual engagement process, I took the transcriptions, recordings, student monologues, my journal, etc. and carefully unveiled the story of their lived experiences. When I began this journey, I expected to develop a more individualized representation of their lived experiences, hoping to highlight individual themes that expressed the students' lived experiences. Instead, by all of us meeting together, the story became more unified, with each participant sharing the metamorphosis they went through during the course of the years they took the class. Reviewing the transcriptions of the group conversations, I realized that the students all went through several phases that ranged from a struggle to connect to the books, to being fully immersed and influenced by the book. These phases evolved over the time of two or more years that they took the class. My process for extrapolating this understanding, involved three types of processes: the wholistic or sententious approach; the selective or highlighting approach; the detailed or line-by-line approach (van Manen, 1997).

The wholistic or sententious approach is where I looked at all my collected text: the students' written responses to the first question presented the first day of the weekend retreat; the transcriptions of my conversations with them; my reflective journal entries, etc. I then created synthesizing statements that I felt captured the general message of the texts (van Manen, 1997). The selective or highlighting approach is where I read the texts over several times and looked for statements that jumped out at me in relation to the phenomenon. I then highlighted those statements (van Manen, 1997). The detailed or line-by-line approach guides me into taking the texts one line at a time, connecting statements that together speak to a specific aspect of the phenomenon. I also looked for singular statements that spoke to the phenomenon in some way. As I looked at these clusters and singular sentences, I asked myself, "What do these statements illuminate about the phenomenon?" (van Manen, 1997). The hermeneutic interpretive process began to reveal that the students all went through phases within the class. These phases ranged from being uninterested in the Great Books, to being fully engaged with them. Talking together revealed that they all went through this metamorphosis. The themes were titled based upon these phases that the students went through during the years that they took the Great Books class.

**Phenomenology as Modern Art**

As I come to a close here, I think of a conversation I had with one of my former students just before I began this study (I was his literature teacher from 9th to 12th grade). We discussed his participation in the study, which unfortunately he was unable to do. I will never forget his enthusiasm over reading *The Great Gatsby* during the years that he took the class. He is a third or second year art student and we got into discussing modern art. He shared how modern art reveals the interpretation of the artist of the world around him. I cannot explain why, but his words made me think of phenomenology instantly. I decided to look into modern art and what it means. This one definition, I feel captures the heart of phenomenology:

> Modern art is characterized by the artist's intent to portray a subject as it exists in the world, according to his or her unique perspective and is typified by a rejection of accepted or traditional styles and values. (www.theartstory.org)

I think of looking at "the things themselves." I think of searching everywhere in the "lifeworld." I think of modern art when I reflect on phenomenology, because it calls on me to look at the phenomenon through the lens of my students, and my perspective as well. Just as Matisse put together collages of painted paper scraps in his last days in order to formulate the pictures that his perspective revealed to him, I pieced together the themes that arose in the course of my study to create an understanding of the essences of my phenomenon. Just as the modern artist can see any medium as a tool to develop art, I turned to all types of sources in the "lifeworld" in order to create this collage of my students' lived experiences. I do this instead of standing back objectively, collecting data, and forming a theory based on my own presuppositions. In using van Manen's process for collecting text, drawing out themes and connecting those themes, I feel as if I am engaged in the creation of some type of artistic representation of what I have come to understand about the lived experience of African American students reading Great Books literature. Van Manen (1997) says:

> Notice that one of the differences between literary narrative or poetry on the one hand, and phenomenology on the other hand, is that literature or poetry (although based on life) leaves the themes implicit, and focuses on plot or particular incident, whereas phenomenology attempts to systematically develop a certain narrative that explicates themes while remaining true to the universal quality or essence of a certain type of experience. (p. 97)

The end of my journey allowed me to weave these themes of conversations, of stories and of expressions together in order to share **the lived experience of African American students in a Great Books literature class.**

## Star Gazing and Continuing the Journey

I am reminded of the possible perils that were involved with the Magi's journey. They crossed through deserts. They met with the forces of nature. There were possible bandits along the way. Even still they pressed on, guided by one Star. Eventually the Star stopped and it shone above the phenomenon they had come to see. My long arduous journey to this place of writing about my phenomenon has also been filled with hindrances along the way, but I now see that they were all a part of the process of me facing the darkness in my way and allowing my phenomenon to reveal itself. It was in this journey that my "Star" has come to shine even brighter.

Through reading Heidegger, Gadamer and van Manen I see ever so clearly the road ahead. Heidegger brings to my phenomenological study a mentality and a spirit for engaging in the work. Gadamer brings to my phenomenological study the glimmer of gold to light my path and the guiding principle of conversation to help me come to a place of understanding my phenomenon. Van Manen brings the wisdom necessary to understand the philosophers of phenomenology, the wisdom to apply their teachings and the wisdom to see how each part of my journey (the dark places as well as the bright spots) is relevant to the seeing of my phenomenon. I follow my Star and it leads me directly to understanding the very essence of **the lived experiences of African American high school students reading Great Books literature.**

# CHAPTER 4: WHEN ART ILLUMINATES NATURE

From *As You Like It*

All the world's a stage,
And all the men and women merely players;
They have their exits and their entrances,
And one man in his time plays many parts,
(Shakespeare,
http://shakespeare.mit.edu/asyoulikeit/full.html)

## The Stage: A Play is Born

Six years of teaching Great Books literature to African American high school students is a lot of time to unpack. I wanted to make time stand still and capture the moments students would tell me about their lived experiences in my class. In order to capture these moments of students freely sharing their renderings, I decided to have the students and I go away for a weekend, as opposed to interviewing them one at a time over a longer period of time. During this time away they shared openly about their lived experiences of being in the class and there was no interruption. The conversations flowed as students enjoyed an interchange and a walk down memory lane. Everything was fresh. As the questions were asked, students gave the first expressions that came to mind, revealing the authenticity in what they shared. Students were even surprised by each other's personal inner struggles during that time. The lived experiences that were shared that weekend in the transcriptions I read through later, touched me so deeply. The students revealed that they were going through experiences I was not aware of, and they also shared how engaging in the literature helped them to work through some of their inner struggles. I asked the students to write monologues that expressed who they were at the time they were in my class. These monologues revealed internal struggles I never knew were going on at the time I was teaching them.

Eventually, the monologues found their way into a play that we created towards the end of the weekend called *The Table.* The title came out of students remembering how everything within the class happened for them around a table. Years ago, I set my class up with a long table and chairs around it, just like the seminar classes that I enjoyed at St. John's College. *The Table*, is a dramatic demonstration of African American students revealing their lived experiences while sitting around a table, engaging in Socratic Dialogue about a piece of classic literature. The play was developed towards the end of the weekend, after the bulk of the conversations had taken place. To create the play, the students were given excerpts of several classic texts to choose from. They all chose "Character," an essay by Voltaire, because they felt that this essay revealed how they often wore masks that hid their true character when in the class. *The Table* illuminates all of the discoveries (the internal struggles of each student, the process of engaging in Socratic Dialogue with students, and the battle to connect with the students during that time) that took place during the course of the weekend where I conducted the conversations with them.

As a part of this study, the play was performed at St John's College, February 13, 2016. Below is a plot summary written by a UMD grad assistant, for a second presentation at the University of Maryland performance, however, not being a part of the study:

> Though billed as "a play," this performance
> is really a dramatic exploration and
> representation of the power of dialogue

> about literary texts. A group of African American students within a high school literature class engage in dialogue about "Character" by Voltaire and "We Wear the Mask" by Paul Laurence Dunbar. Students, along with their teacher connect the texts to their lives, both as individuals and as African Americans. They also compare and contrast the texts in order to develop a synthesized world view. In so doing, the teacher becomes an equal participant in the search for knowledge and understanding.
>
> Additionally, students share their inner thoughts about their feelings of going through the process...feelings that the teacher was not aware of at the time. These private feelings are shared through individual monologues presented by the students as if they are reading through a private journal. The monologues/journal readings reveal some of the struggles students and teachers face in trying to connect over literature. The monologues also reveal how the dialogue and the literature can chisel away at those internal obstacles. (Groff, 2016)

In order to work through the production of *The Table* and reveal its connection to my study, I have chosen to include excerpts from John Rudlin's *Commedia dell' Arte: An Actor's Handbook. Commedia dell'Arte* was a form of theatre that used masks to depict various characters. I have found that my participants actually reminded me of some of the characters in *Commedia dell' Arte* as shown in the following section. I also draw from Augusto Boal's

*Theatre of the Oppressed*, which addresses how theatre is used as a sort of catharsis for its participants, freeing them from the chains of life struggles that sometimes seek to silence the one who is engaged in the struggle. Both of these texts discuss how art can often times symbolize human nature as well.

### The Metaphoric Plot

Although the production of *The Table* is not the heart and soul of this study, it does provide a framework where I can introduce the participants of the study. This chapter seeks to lay a foundation for them to be understood as I share each of their lived experiences in the proceeding chapters. Also, because the conversations with the students were not conducted individually but in a group, the play helped to synthesize their experiences.

A work of art was created through the oral tradition of stories shared, having deep connections to the story of the slaves' escape to freedom, guided by the North Star. For *The Table* the students and I mainly wanted just to present the lived
experience in dramatic form, to spark conversation from the audience after the performance. We wanted them to look at what happened in the class and to reflect on what it may reveal about teaching, learning, and the relationships between students and teachers. From the active dialogue that took place after the play at St. John's I sense that the audience began the discussion mentally, well before the play ended and the post play discussion began. For example, one audience member noticed that the students in the play seemed to get so into the literature, that they seemed to go into another world. She noticed that whatever distractions they may have had in the real world, they seemed to disappear during the discussion. Her question with regards to this observation was, "What do

students gain by leaving the real world, going into the world of the literature, and then returning to the real world again?"

We discussed how eventually, once the students become more involved with the literature, it is no longer two different worlds, but the two worlds collide, or become one. As students begin to read the literature consistently, something begins to change about their thinking. The audience being able to view this experimental theatre piece, allowed them to visualize the transformative nature of engaging in the literature, and it caused them to wonder. Art is often a silent dialogue between artist and audience (Brackman, 2006, location 169). Van Manen (1997) says, "We might say that hermeneutic phenomenology is a philosophy of the personal, the individual, which we pursue against the background of an understanding of the evasive character of the *logos* of *other*, the *whole*, the *communal,* or the *social*" (p. 7). The drama helped to evoke a conversation that led to a deeper understanding of the **lived experience of African American students reading Great Books literature.**

Throughout this project I have used the star as a metaphor. Returning to it, I think of "The Chained Star," a quilting pattern and how it connects to my study. I see the Great Books as a Polaris for my people during the time when they were not permitted to read or gain literacy by reading the literature of the master. Barbara Brackman (2006) uses poetic license to interpret "The Chained Star" quilting pattern as a way to tell the story of slaves being captured from West Africa and brought to America. The audience viewing *The Table* was given this same "poetic license." As I share this rendering of my students' lived experiences, it is my hope that those who read it will be given the same freedom to interpret the lived experiences of my students for themselves and be able to connect them to their own teaching and learning experiences.

The star in "The Chained Star" pattern is red, set in the backdrop of the chain pattern (any other dark color). Oral tradition states that Africans were lured away from their group by a red cloth that would be hanging in a tree or laying on the ground. Once they went to look at it, a kidnapper would snatch them (most times someone from a rival African tribe) and sell them to those who would take them across the waters. The red represents the heart of the slave and the red cloth that drew them away. The chain pattern represents their loss of freedom. In the first chapter of her book *Facts & Fabrications: Unraveling the History of Quilts & Slavery*, Barbara Brackman places herself under poetic license to interpret the various quilting patterns that she shares. Although there is enough evidence to reveal that slaves did, in fact, quilt, there is no definitive proof that slaves used quilts as symbols to escape to freedom. So, her thoughts on the "The Chained Star" are simply an interpretation.

Like Brackman who chose to interpret the meaning of the "Chained Star" quilt pattern, my students were given freedom to read the literature and to share their interpretation. I recall another question from one of the audience members in the discussion after the play. He wanted to know what caused the masks to come down eventually. He wanted to understand what made the walls between teacher and student finally disappear in the class. Students felt that the masks or walls came down because they could actually talk with a teacher as opposed to being talked to in a condescending way, or as they said, "…as if the teacher feels that they always have to 'teach' us something." They felt that by being allowed to engage in this type of discussion with a teacher, it built their confidence. They also compared their experience of having conversations about the literature with their classmates and myself with the experience of conversations they had with their peers. It made them feel smarter, because they began to see that their peers could not engage in the type of intellectual conversation that they enjoyed in the Great Books class. Having the type of student-teacher relationship we enjoyed in our class, freed them from the mask and allowed them to see value within themselves.

Choosing "The Chained Star" pattern not only connects with my view of what happens with hermeneutic phenomenology and how it connects the pieces of lived experiences to understand the whole, but it brings, again, to the forefront the metaphor of the star in Heidegger's (1971) quote: "To think is to confine yourself to a single thought that one day stands still like a star in the world's star" (p. 4). As the African was drawn away by the red fabric, I am drawn away by my students' lived experiences. The thought glares in my mind like a star, and as my students took their lived experiences reading Great Books literature to the stage, their starlight shined for the audience as well.

Pondering the "Chained Star" quilt pattern, I cannot help but take a brief pause from my star metaphor to think about quilting. Quilting is a physical way to understand constellating. Bringing together the phases my students went through as they were in my class and reflecting on my own personal lived experience remind me of quilting. The definition of quilt is "a warm bed covering made of padding enclosed between layers of fabric and kept in place by lines of stitching, typically applied in a decorative design" (Google). The key words in this definition are "layers" and "decorative design." Quilts take different pieces of fabric and sew them together to make a work of art. Each lived experience may be different, but brought together to tell one story of what it is like for an African American student to read Great Books, it can create a work of art or a "decorative design." Like constellating helps us to draw the pictures in the sky, such as Polaris, Aquarius, Libra and others, the act of quilting helps us to understand how this art can be created. As they each shared their thoughts, feelings, struggles, joys, and pains as they went through the class, an image began to develop. That image was revealed as I pieced together the conversation transcriptions, and it was also revealed in the creation of the play, *The Table.*

The lived experiences shared by my students through conversation and drama are the "layers" to make for a rich and thick retelling. A poem written by Mildred Hatfield expresses how I envision this "quilt" of my students' lived experiences, and for me, it brings me back to the symbolism of the "Chained Star" in how each part of this pattern comes together to tell the slaves' story. The slaves' story is the story of my students. It is a story of freedom and of how a "star"—a Polaris, freed them both.

A Treasure
It's laughter and sorrow,
It's pleasure and pain,
It's small bits and pieces
Of sunshine and rain.
It's a bright panorama
Of scraps of my life –
It's moments of glory,
It's moments of strife.
It's a story I cherish
Of days that have been.
It's a door I can open
To live them again.
Yes, it's more than a cover,
This much-treasured quilt.
It's parts pieced together
Of the life I have built.
(Hatfield, 2016)

In reviewing the transcripts of the conversations, I saw several themes develop. I also call these phases, because it appears that the students went through an evolutionary process as they went through my class. The poem above reveals how a quilt can reveal the phases of a person's life. This is how I see my process of constellating the students' lived experiences. Reading through the transcriptions I was able to identify several phases/themes: The Flickering Light, When the Flame Catches, Being in the Light and The Lived Experience Shining into the Present. ' **The Flickering Light**, speaks to that first step into reading Great Books literature. I think of when night begins to fall and we start to see the stars slowly make their appearance. It seems as if at first they are flickering as they begin to settle into the coming of night. My students flickered when they first started the class. There was a lot of resistance. Sometimes they would complete the reading assignments and sometimes they wouldn't. Sometimes they would participate in the literature discussions and sometimes they wouldn't.

**When the Flame Catches** represents that time when night has fully come and the stars are shining bright. They have settled into the night. The students have settled into the darkness of the book and have begun to let it illumine their consciousness. The books can be a sort of "night time" because they are written in a time and culture that African American students are not familiar with; however, their flickering light starts to settle into the darkness of the book and they begin to shine—they begin to understand and connect to the books. The students start to read more consistently and have something to contribute to the discussion. They even start to read independently, allowing these books to shape their thinking about life and the world around them.

**Being in the Light** is that time in the journey when the students are completely immersed in the books. The books have become a way of life for them, they are thinking more critically and they are starting to see the different quotes and subjects of the books in their current culture and life (i.e. in a movie or song or a quote may be used in their everyday converation).

**The Lived Experience Shining into the Present** reveals how the students shared the way in which the books they read in my class have affected their thinking and way of life currently (several years have passed since they graduated from high school). By engaging in a group conversation, as opposed to having individual conversations, the students talked as one, flowing through the conversation and reminiscing about their shared lived experiences.

## The Players and Their Masks

> Each character is the representative of a social class which, by the act of theatre, becomes the magical incarnation of all its class. (Boso, 1981, p. 9)

*Commedia dell' Arte* is a type of theatre that primarily uses masks to represent human life. Each mask has its own personality and whenever you see the mask you know what character is going to take the stage. Connecting the *Commedia del' Arte* to my project is appropriate, because of the students' decision to make masks an important part of the play they created towards the end of the weekend. Their desire to use masks for their characters came about due to feeling they were hiding behind some type of mask in order to go through their lived experience. The concept of a mask was so strong, that they chose "We Wear the Mask" by Paul Laurence Dunbar as the theme poem for the production. One audience member, during the discussion after the performance, wanted to know why the characters in the play wore a mask. Arthur Scott came forward to answer that question:

> Everyone had their own different reason for wearing the mask. There is no one reason. But let's look at this. Let's think about Batman. He wears a mask because he cannot show who he is to everyone else and that's how we felt when we were in the class.

From this question and Arthur Scott's response, we engaged in a dialogue about why students may sometimes wear masks and how can we as teachers help students come to be liberated from the masks. One of the main reasons we realized that students may wear masks, is because of the fear of not fitting in with their classmates. The masks served a very important part in symbolizing the students' inner struggles while taking the class. Even though in this study I will be using the names my students chose for themselves for the play, I connect them to the various characters of the *Commedia.* As Boso states above, the *Commedia* characters represent the people of society, and my students took on many of the traits of the *Commedia* characters.

During the time that **Sophia** was in my class she had an intense desire to learn and to go deep. She often wrote the most and provided the most dialogue in our class discussions. Her desire was to show me how much she knew. Sophia reminds me of Columbina from the *Commedia*, because it says that Columbina could read and write and went beyond other women by becoming self-educated (Rudlin, 1994, p. 130). Columbina also sought to show others how intellectual she was. Interestingly enough, the name "Sophia" means "wisdom" (although I am not sure she knew the meaning of the name she chose for herself).

Then there was **Zora**, who chose this name in connection with the writings of Zora Neale Hurston, who shaped her sense of self as a young African American woman. Over the course of our discussion for the study, she referenced the amount of "drama" that was going on with her while she was in my class. Like my student, Isabella in *Commedia* was the very heart of the drama. Often times this drama was used to mask her inner turmoil, around her desire to be noticed and significant (Rudlin, 1994). Zora wrestled so much with wanting to fit in with her peers and to be viewed as important, that initially it hindered her from reaching her full potential during the class.

**Arthur Scott**, the third participant in the study, hid behind an air of self-confidence and humor. He chose this name for himself after his maternal grandfather. He also said that he chose this name because Arthur Conan Doyle is his favorite author and Scott Mescudi is his favorite artist. I found that these former students had such wide tastes, spanning from hip hop culture to classic literature. In *Commedia* there is a character that can take several forms called the Zanni (where we get the word "zany" from). He is the comic relief of the play and the star that keeps the plot moving forward. He is the boss and always maintains his status (Rudlin, 1994). He is astute, ready for anything, humorous, quick-witted, and he is capable of intrigue, deceit, making a mockery of the entire world with his mordant, salacious wit (Rudlin, 1994). The Zanni reminded me of Arthur Scott so much, because he always seemed on top of everything and had a humor that entertained all of us, especially as his humor brought to light some of the craziness of the school, the class and the world. We did not realize that this mask was used to hide very deep pain. Like most of the Zanni characters he always appeared relaxed and calm.

**Ray Charles** was the youngest of the students who participated in the project. He'd been skipped forward in school two times and struggled always to fit in with his older classmates. He is like Arlecchino in the *Commedia.* He had a sense of always knowing and he never wanted to be the loser. Arlecchino never simply just "does" anything, but everything was done with a touch of flare. He was also known for using the somersault to complete a task or to get from one place to another (Rudlin, 1994). I found this description interesting because this participant was heavily involved with gymnastics and often did somersaults and back flips at school. He also was a black belt in martial arts and taught classes. Ray Charles hated to be wrong or to fail at anything. He was very smart and many times he and I would go back and forth in debate during class.

There was one student who I feel did not wear a mask and that was **Zeke.** As I listened to him during our discussions, what he revealed to me is what I observed of him myself. In *Commedia,* he connects the most to Pierrot because of this character's somber demeanor. Pierrot also pretended to be mute (http://shane-arts.com/Commedia-Pedrolino.htm). This participant rarely spoke in class, although his mom would often tell me what he was thinking and what he was feeling. Pierrot of *Commedia* was also known for only revealing his true feelings in private (Rudlin, 1994). The one main trait of Pierrot was that he was a very honest character. This was my student. Reflecting on the dialogue I came to wonder if he was the most genuine during the course of the time he was in my class. It was around his senior and fourth year in my class that he became more vocal and more open, but it was always from a genuine place. One more characteristic that I feel connects him to Pierrot is that Pierrot was always sleepy and my student shared that one of the main reasons he struggled with my class was because he was always sleepy. It was hard for him to stay focused on what we were discussing.

These five participants are my window into understanding the **lived experience of African American**

**students reading Great Books literature.** The time we spent over the course of the weekend for the conversations and the time we worked together to create "The Table," was a time of great illumination for me.

**Spotlighting the Table**

That's What I Call a Table
A man filled with the gladness of living
Put his keys on the table,
Put flowers in a copper bowl there.
He put his eggs and milk on the table.
He put there the light that came in through the window,
Sounds of a bicycle, sound of a spinning wheel.
The softness of bread and weather he put there.
On the table the man put
Things that happened in his mind.
What he wanted to do in life,
He put that there.
Those he loved, those he didn't love,
The man put them on the table too.
Three times three make nine:
The man put nine on the table.
He was next to the window next to the sky;
He reached out and placed on the table endlessness.
So many days he had wanted to drink a beer!
He put on the table the pouring of that beer.
He placed there his sleep and his wakefulness;
His hunger and his fullness he placed there.
Now that's what I call a table!

> It didn't complain at all about the load.
> It wobbled once or twice, then stood firm.
> The man kept piling things on.
> (Cansever, 2008)

Years ago, I followed the life journey of a woman named Kara Tippet. I first "met" Kara as I listened to a radio show called Focus on the Family. My husband and I rode together that morning and we listened as she and her husband told her story of dying from cancer as a young wife and mother of 4 school aged children. My heart broke. We were about the same age and her story connected with me. She has since passed away, but I still read her blog that her husband and a lady who was her best friend keep updated. Sometimes they repost her past entries and sometimes they write new posts. Recently they did a repost of one of Kara's blog entries and the topic strangely enough was about the importance of the table in Kara's life. Of course, her thoughts on the importance of a table were related to a family, but I was able to take these views and connect them to a school because a sort of family and community do develop within a school setting. Her blog entry started with a quote from the book *Bread & Wine: A Love Letter to Life Around the Table, with Recipes,* by Shauna Niequist (2013), which is a book she was reading at the time she wrote the entry and the blog entry is based on it:

> The heart of hospitality is about creating space for someone to feel seen and heard and loved. It's about declaring your table a safe zone, a place of warmth and nourishment. (p. 114)

Kara goes on to write in a way that relates to the poem above in how the table is this meeting place to commune together and place our joys and sorrows "on the table." At the time I was listening to Kara's broadcast, I was having my own struggles in life. However, I found inspiration from a woman who was coming to embrace the fact that she was dying soon, and yet was able to find joy through it all. It placed my own life into a better perspective.

Reading her posthumous blog entry about the table and its importance to connecting people sheds a great deal of light on my own journey to me and my students' lived experience of reading and discussing Great Books around a table. Why was this space so important to the students and to me? Kara (2014) says:

> This book is at the very heart of how I want to live, try to live, and hope for my well days to be lived. When we moved into our home I asked Jason to build me an impossibly big table—for the very reasons she mentions in this book. (http://www.mundanefaithfulness.com/home/2014/03/31/bread-and-wine-shauna-niequist)

Her "well" days? Here she is faced with the notion of dying and yet she is focusing on how a table can help her to enjoy the life that she has left. My students revealed how the table became a welcoming space, and the books were instruments for opening their souls up to work through their life struggles. When Arthur Scott blurted out during our weekend conversation "And ya'll, all of her classes happened around a table!" We all agreed that this is what the play should be called, and the stage was set up with only a conference table and chairs around it. Everything happened around the table in the Great Books literature class. I now realize after reflecting on Kara's thoughts about the table that this is maybe how the experience should happen for any student with whom I work. Kara goes on to say:

> But at the heart of wanting the giant table is that I have seen the best of life happen around a table. I am not fancy in any way, but I want my life and love to be met around the table. (http://www.mundanefaithfulness.com/home/2014/03/31/bread-and-wine-shauna-niequist)

We poured out our understanding of the books around the table. I remember in one class years ago, Arthur Scott suddenly got inspired around the table to write a song about how life is all meaningless. All of us were sitting around the table and he just jumped up, ran to the piano and started singing the song. The table is where their minds wrestled with their inner struggles, and the books inspired them to work through those struggles.

We tend to think of a table as only a place to eat and satisfy our appetites, but it is a place to meet others on the life journey and satisfy the longings of our souls. My students revealed longings that they had within: a longing to be heard, understood, accepted, appreciated, and loved. The table is different from desks, because nothing separates us. We are all one around a table. The Great Books, I have come to discover, just as Frederick Douglass did as a slave, also unify us into the realm of our shared humanness. I relate this lived experience of African American students reading Great Books literature to her opus about the table, and its power to draw us into a shared journey through life's ups and downs. Kara ended her blog entry about the table and Shauna Niequist's book with this:

> Her words remind me that the work of the meal isn't the point. Not at all. The point of the meal is the communion of those who are joined around the table. There will be days I can create the intricate meals she includes,

> and there will be days we meet around the table with our favorite bean and cheese burritos from La Casita. It's the meeting, the loving, the time together today that matters. No need to be impressive—just breathing, alive, sharing grace together. That's the meal…Meet around your table and find community and love that you never expected. (http://www.mundanefaithfulness.com/home/2014/03/31/bread-and-wine-shauna-niequist)

To capture the significance of the table in the Great Books class, the students wanted the main staging of the play to happen around a table. As the poem shared at the beginning of this section, the table bore a very heavy burden. Their desire to wear a mask for the play, however revealed a different dynamic. The act of engaging in Socratic dialogue during the class years ago, was an exercise in working through those struggles internally, but the outward dialogue being only focused on the book also prevented me as the teacher, from seeing them go through that process of inner struggle. Ray Charles, in particular, displayed a monologue performance that physically revealed his inner struggle. He literally fights with his mask on the stage, and for his performance he demonstrated how his mask won. The other students provided some type of hope by the end of their monologue, showing that by working through the class, they started to overcome their struggles, but Ray Charles did not win his struggle with his mask. This is interesting because I never felt that I established a connection with him while he was in the class, and I was surprised when he asked if he could participate in the study.

The struggle of Ray Charles and others all happened around the table. It was the burden bearer, a place to come together, a place to struggle through our understandings and questions. Just like the table in the poem above, and just like the table that Kara Tippetts dreams of having and experiencing, our table was a strong place. Sometimes it did actually wobble a bit under the load of books, feet propped up on it, heads leaned down on it, hands banging on it in the midst of a heated discussion, elbows resting on it, bottoms leaning on it, and stacks of essays resting on it written by the students. It still stood strong through the ups and downs of African American students reading Great Books literature.

**Breaking the Chains through Monologue**

> But the theatre can also be a weapon for liberation. (Boal, 1979, p. viii)

The conversations with the students revealed how they were each struggling with their own identity and seeking to build their own "uniqueness." Boal (1979) says, "Art would, then, be a copy of created things" (p. 1). In the book *Childhood's Secrets* I recall the following perspective on the play's use of "masks":

> There exists a paradoxical relation between the need for secrecy and the need for supervision. If we constantly must know what preoccupies the inner life of the child, this could frustrate the development of a unique self. So the question is: When should we try to find out what is going on, and when should we leave children to deal with things in private?...in larger and smaller ways, the tension between privacy and supervision is constantly at work in the lives of children and their parents, teachers or caretakers. (van Manen & Levering, 1996, p. 151)

Through investigating their lived experiences, I am able to get at the essence of each of their inner most thoughts during the course of that journey. The monologues they each created at the first session of our weekend long conversation, created a door into their lived experiences. The monologue is a theatrical element that forces an actor to delve deep into his/her inner self in order to bring out the emotions of the character—without any type of hindrance from another actor on the stage. It is very freeing. There are no other characters to distract you from yourself. The monologue was sort of the ice breaker for the students and from that activity, everything else flowed. Their thoughts about the lived experience began to flow; a play about the lived experience organically developed that they felt symbolized that lived experience; and a world of understanding was created between all of us through the conversation about their lived experiences.

# CHAPTER 5:
# STAR GAZING INTO THE LIVED EXPERIENCES

O star of wonder, star of light,
star with royal beauty bright,
westward leading, still proceeding,
guide us to thy perfect light.
(Hopkins, 1857)

I now count myself as one of the Magi. I am captured by the glare of my star and like the Magi, its light beckons me. During the weekend I spent with my students, our conversations allowed me to take the journey into looking deeper into what my star means. I found myself drawn into its glare through the conversations I engaged in with my students. Gadamer (1975/1989) says:

> …language has its true being only in dialogue, in coming to an understanding…It is a life process in which a community of life is lived out. But human language must be thought of as a special and unique life process since, in linguistic communication, "world" is disclosed. Reaching an understanding in language places a subject matter before those communicating like a disputed object set between them. Thus the world is the common ground, trodden by none and recognized by all, uniting all who talk to one another...For language is by nature the language of conversation; it fully realizes itself only in the process of coming to an understanding. (p. 443)

The weekend time of conversation with my students allowed me to come to an understanding of things I was not aware of as I taught them years ago. They wore masks (and I did too) during that time, but on that weekend, the masks came off as we were so transparent about the lived experience of African American students reading Great Books literature.

There were signs that the experience of reading Great Books literature was having some type of effect on the students, but during the years I was teaching Great Books literature, it was hard to articulate what was taking place. The students would not fully open up to me about how the literature was affecting them during that time. Over the weekend conversation, however, the students talked through how each of their experiences took them through phases. They also discussed how those phases have affected their lives today. As shared in the previous chapter, upon reviewing the transcripts of the conversations with the students, I was able to turn these phases into common themes that connect to the metaphorical light of the star. The phases/themes that surfaced through the discussion were The Flickering Light, When the Flame Catches, Being in the Light and The Lived Experience Shining into the Present, as presented in the previous chapter.

Each student had a different experience or response as he or she traversed each of the phases/themes, and this was revealed as the group talked together and relived their experiences. Although the conversations only happened within a unified group, it is imperative that I bring to the surface the students' individual lived experiences. The group setting helped the students to connect, remember and relive, but in the group conversation there were definite differences in lived experiences accounts. In order to bring the students' individual lived experiences to the surface, as each theme is opened up, a rendering of each student's lived experiences within that theme is given. Each student is given the spotlight, so to speak, within each of the above themes/phases. Within each section, the students' lived experiences are explored in this order: Sophia, Zora, Arthur Scott and Ray Charles.

There is a fifth student whose experience and level of participation in the study was so vastly different from those four that he has been given his own section at the end of chapter five. Initially, I'd thought of not including Zeke in this project because he did not complete his monologue, he talked the least during the conversations and he chose not to participate in the play at the last minute. However, upon careful review of the transcripts, I realized that he contributed some very insightful thoughts during the course of the conversations. His section is entitled **Fragments of Light,** and including Zeke's section reminds me of van Manen's (1997) admonition to look everywhere in the life world for these fragments of light in order that the whole essence of the lived experience may be realized.

I was also able to connect my own personal experiences with the Great Books to these same phases. According to van Manen (1997), my personal experience can also be a part of this study. He says, "In drawing up personal descriptions of lived experiences, the phenomenologist knows that one's own experiences are also the possible experiences of others" (p. 54). I am a part of this journey as well. In our time together we often found out about each other's masks, struggles, etc. Although my students insisted that I did not wear a mask (and they did not want me to wear one for the play), I actually did wear a mask. At the beginning of each year that I taught, I was so unsure of how this process of reading Great Books literature would benefit them, and I often hid my insecurity. As each phase is shared, I also include my own lived experience of taking this journey with my students during the time that we engaged in reading Great Books literature.

In order to constellate each of the phases presented in this chapter, I share excerpts of O'Donohue's (1997) *Anam Cara*, where he reveals how the evolution of light is parallel to the evolution of the intellect. I have used this passage in the previous chapters.These short passages will be at the end of each phase, providing a metaphoric explanation of the journey they went through while in the Great Books class.

**The Flickering Light**

> I summon Aristotle and Aurelius and what soul I will, and they come all graciously with no scorn nor condescension. So, wed with Truth, I dwell above the Veil. (Du Bois, 1903/2005, p. 108)

When W.E.B. DuBois refers to the "Veil" what is he referring to? The word "veil" comes from the Latin word *vela* and one of its meanings is "covering." When the ancestors were an enslaved people, literacy was "veiled" from them. They were not permitted to read, and when it became legal for them to read, the classics were not often made available to them. DuBois recalls this when he takes a stand and summons Aristotle and Aurelius and others. He then goes on to say, "So, wed with truth, I dwell above the Veil." The African American is no longer an enslaved people, and yet, there are still veils present. The veil can be synonymous with mask.

The word "mask" comes from the Middle French word *masque*, which means "covering to hide or guard the face." My students wanting to use the mask as a part of their costume for the play, represented the "veil" or "mask" that they wore during the course of my class. Something was blocking the enLIGHTenment. What were the masks that caused their lights to flicker when they first started the class? The metaphor of the star helped me to understand this, when I looked into why stars flicker. NASA gives a clear explanation as to why stars flicker or twinkle and it directly relates to my students:

> On a clear, dark night, our eyes can see about 6,000 or so stars in the sky. They seem to twinkle, or change their brightness, all the time. In fact, most of the stars are shining with a steady light. The movement of air (sometimes called turbulence) in the atmosphere of Earth causes the starlight to get slightly bent as it travels from the distant star through the atmosphere down to us on the ground. This means that some of the light reaches us directly and some gets bent slightly away. To our eyes, this makes the star seem to twinkle.
>
> You will notice that stars closer to the horizon will appear to twinkle more than other stars. This is because there is a lot more atmosphere between you and a star near the horizon than between you and a star higher in the sky.(https://starchild.gsfc.nasa.gov/docs/StarChild/questions/question26.html)

Stars shine with a steady light, but something stands in the way of the light shining brightly. My students each had their personal reasons for their light being blocked from shining fully. Each student wore a different mask while they were in my class, and I wonder if these masks could be symbolic of some of the "masks" that other teachers see within the classroom?

**Masking a Desire to Learn**

The typical way that Sophia started a class discussion when she was a student, was to seek to refute whatever was being taught or shared. She questioned everything. During the weekend conversation she admits:

> I was just so upset my dad put me in that school. I always felt like I had to challenge what we were reading. I put up arguments and debates with myself. I was just always confrontational. I was trying to prove that I don't need to be here at the school—that I am smarter. I would challenge you too! If you told us to only write a certain amount of pages, I would be like "I'm gonna show you!" and I'd write 20 pages.

I remember the struggle in working with Sophia. Coming across this type of resistance was frustrating at first, but I had to engage her. I resisted fighting her but flowed with the questions that she rapidly would throw at me. According to Sophia, something began to change as a result. She says:

> You will question us in a way to get us excited. We were so busy trying to be cool. You wanted an essay, then I'd give you an essay and all along it was making me a better writer. I just tricked myself.

Sophia was seeking to look as if she was smart enough to be in the class, so she pushed hard at me. I had to let her be in that space and allow her to work through that. This welcomed her to question more, not just with me but with other students:

> Another student and I would go at it for no reason. Like off a pronoun that was put in the wrong place in the King James version. It was more like debates, with so many points to hit on. Some things you might agree on with the other person, but you had a different view. The thing is you never stopped it! We would come to a conclusion together, instead of you stopping it and saying "Let's just move on." You would let us talk it out and you'd ask, "Why do you feel that way? Let's come to a conclusion."

Sophia's desire to question and debate was a flickering light to me. The fact that she was thinking enough about the reading to come up with ways to disagree with the author, me or other classmates was a sign of light in the midst of her resistance and negative feelings about being in the class and at the school. In her monologue, Sophia shared that she did not want to read these books "written by white people":

> Here we go again, this awkward silence waiting for someone to give an intelligent enough answer.
> Mrs. Prather told me I'm always dominating the discussion and making critical remarks. I mean well, I really do! I don't even notice when I do it! I'm not doing it for attention, I just enjoy having something to contribute!

> I spend half the class trying to balance
> between letting her know I got this, but not
> wanting to be a know-it-all, either.
> Look at them, they're not even paying
> attention or remotely interested.
> Got us black kids reading these white folks
> words.
> I already know all this stuff. Why won't she
> let me just take it up a notch?
> I want to ask about this, but don't wanna
> come off too sagacious.
> From the looks of the last assignment, I
> guess my book report was just way too long.
> They tell me I think too deeply into
> everything, but shouldn't I?
> I'm not talking back. I just want to be
> treated as an equal in dialogue, not just
> another student here to learn, but to discuss.
> After all, how do I know she's giving me all
> the information I need to know?
> Doesn't she want me to "engage in
> discussion" with her like she always says.
> And these other kids never have anything to
> say. So maybe I should just sit back and not
> say anything either. (Sophia, 2016)

When Sophia said, "Got us black kids reading this white folks words..." I instantly recalled James Baldwin's thoughts (cited previously) on his connection to Great Books:

> …I brought to Shakespeare, Bach, Rembrandt, to the stones of Paris, to the cathedral at Chartres, and to the Empire State Building, a special attitude. These were not really my creations, they did not contain my history; I might search in them

> in vain forever for any reflection of myself. I was an interloper; this was not my heritage....(Baldwin, 1998, p. 7)

Sophia initially resented me assigning these readings to her. The challenge for me was getting Sophia and the other students to stop seeing these books as "those" books and to see them as "our books." This is what James Baldwin reluctantly had to do or else he felt he would be sort of wandering through life without an identity. He does not just stop at "appropriating these white centuries," however, but he then has to "make them mine." Sophia, not only struggled with the Great Books being "those books," but she also wrestled with making them hers. Initially, her focus was on just showing me her head knowledge with regards to the books and their concepts, but she became frustrated when that was not enough for me. I wanted to see how she was able to appropriate these white centuries and make them hers—as an African American girl in the 21st century.

To "appropriate" comes from the late Latin word *appropriates* which means to "take possession of" or "to make one's own." The word "own" comes from the Germanic word *aigana* which means "possession." "Possess" comes from a 14th century word meaning "to occupy." Sophia's struggle was with keeping the books separate from her very soul. She was able to gain the head knowledge to show me she was smart enough to understand them, but there was another part of the journey that needed to happen and that was the process to occupying the books and allowing the books to occupy or take possession of her. This did not involve her erasing her identity and heritage, but it involved making them a part of who she was. It's the same process Frederick Douglass went through when he read Cicero and says that reading the text helped him to find the words needed to speak against slavery. He did not forget or erase his heritage, but in this foreign land he lived in, the books helped him to navigate his way to understanding his identity as African and American, and it also gave him the literacy to comprehend and communicate that. Sophia was on a similar journey.

In Sophia's journey there was resistance, questioning, debating, etc. Sophia's questioning and debating gave way to wonder and resistance, that in turn, gave way to an earnest search for truth and understanding. This is the power of questioning. Gadamer (1975/2004) says, "…the path to knowledge leads through the question" (p. 357). In her monologue Sophia stated that she "meant well." She was not looking for attention, but she had some earnest questions with which she was wrestling. The flickering light was that she wanted to work through these issues. She had not completely shut me out (as some students have), but she engaged me through her questioning. Socratic dialogue was an instrument for her to wrestle through this. Gadamer (1975/2004) says:

> On the contrary, the example of Socrates teaches that the important thing is the knowledge that one does not know. Hence the Socratic dialectic—which leads, through its art of confusing the interlocutor, to this knowledge—creates the conditions for the question. All questioning and desire to know presuppose a knowledge that one does not know; so much so, indeed, that a particular lack of knowledge leads to a particular question.
>
> Plato shows in an unforgettable way where the difficulty lies in knowing what one does not know. It is the power of opinion against which it is so hard to obtain an admission of

> ignorance. It is opinion that suppresses questions. (p. 359)

Although Sophia began her journey by asking a lot of critical questions, her questions were rooted in some personal opinions and trust issues. By her engaging in the questioning process, she was brought to the same place as those who dialogued with Socrates—a place of realizing that they do not know. Coming to this place of realizing that one does not know is important according to Gadamer (1975/2004):

> In fact, however, the continual failure of the interlocutor shows that people who think they know better cannot even ask the right questions. In order to be able to ask, one must want to know, and that means knowing that one does not know. (p. 357)

In her dialogue Sophia says, "I want to ask about this, but don't wanna come off too sagacious." "Sagacious" comes from the Latin *sagacem* which means "of quick perception." She says, "They tell me I think too deeply into everything, but shouldn't I?" Before coming to the school and becoming a part of the Great Books class, Sophia had been in English/literature classes that did not include reading such challenging literature. At first the Great Books class was intimidating, but she found herself drawn to how the class connected to her natural curiosity. It was hard for her to mask this attraction, but she tried. Sophia worried about trying to come off as being too smart with her peers. This was the constant struggle. Somehow the literature tapped into her intense level of curiosity and sense of wonder, yet she struggled to release herself into that freedom to question and wonder because of her fear of what her classmates may think about her. When she first began the class, she started expressing resistance by asking critical questions about the literature that was discussed in the classroom. Like Columbina in the *Commedia dell'Arte*, who was known for being the rare self-educated woman of that time, Sophia also had a hunger for knowledge. Although negative initially, her way of questioning helped her to work through that curiosity. She read, wrote and discussed furiously in the class. Sophia's lived experience started out from a negative place, as she sought to hide behind her mask of resistance to an insatiable hunger to learn and grow mentally. Her journey began with her critical questions, doubt and even mistrust, but a transition did happen as a result of the class providing a space for her to work through her inner questions and desire to grow intellectually.

**Masking a Desire for Acceptance**

> It is a peculiar sensation, the double-consciousness, this sense of always looking at one's self through the eyes of others, of measuring one's soul by the tape of a world that looks on in amused contempt and pity. One ever feels his twoness—an American, a Negro; two souls, two thoughts, two unreconciled strivings; two warring ideals in one dark body, whose dogged strength alone keeps it from being torn asunder. (DuBois, 2005, p. 7)

It was a challenge to realize Zora's true character in the class. Like Isabella of *Commedia* she often masked her true thoughts and feelings. It is said that Isabella's greatest fear was not being seen as important or becoming unknown. Connecting Zora to Isabella helps me to understand her mask. Isabella's efforts to manipulate the audience or her lover to fall madly in love with her were not for vicious reasons, but she was simply seeking happiness, and that happiness was found in being loved and accepted. For my class, Zora wore a mask of silence. For her friends, she wore a mask of being the "fly" one. Her mask of silence for my class revealed that her desire for acceptance amongst her peers was greater than her desire to do well in the class. Zora's monologue reveals her inner struggle:

> S, Second thoughts, I wanna speak but what if they don't get it, my thoughts, my ideas, my views, my opinions, how will they view me when I'm finished, a know it all, smarty pants. How will I ever fit in if they think that's what I am?
>
> I, Insecurity, am I right or am I wrong, everyday my mind sings this same old song, will they laugh and tease if Mrs. Prather doesn't see, what I'm saying, I don't wanna go too deep, and drown in the ridicule this sea will surely bring.
>
> L, Love, why do I find myself falling in love with these stories, poems and books? Reading in my spare time when no one's around, after my homework's done, I could read until the rising of the sun. These great books touch me in more ways than one.
>
> E, Everyday, my grade is suffering when I don't speak, and Mrs. Prather isn't hesitant about letting me know that. Calling on me when I've been trying to stay low-key, just let everybody else converse and maybe she'll forget about me. But I know that she knows I've got much more going on in this

> head than I let on. She's going to get it out
> one way or the other.
>
> N, No, is what my lips say, but my mind is
> running wild, with answers to these
> questions. I wanna jump out into this
> conversation but I just can't. I'm trying to
> break down this wall of doubt but it just
> won't go away. So for now I'll just write all
> these ideas in the next assignment and turn it
> in. At least I know that'll get me an A.
>
> C, Confidence, reading about women like
> me in this class has boosted my confidence
> in so many ways, but why won't it show
> when I sit in this discussion? An open forum
> to express my mind and my feelings about
> these great books. Mrs. Prather says there's
> no right or wrong but I'd be wrong if I
> disagree with one of my peers and they
> decide not to talk to me for embarrassing
> them in front of the class. This school is too
> small for me to not have any friends. Why
> do I have such a strong need to be liked?
>
> E, Looks like this is the end, I can either
> express my opinion, or go another day with
> a bad discussion grade. I don't wanna seem
> too smart. I just wanna fit in. This is what a
> quiet girl like me wrestles with within.
> (Zora, 2016)

Isabella of *Commedia* was mainly seeking to find a true romantic love. Zora was seeking a different type of love—acceptance from her peers. In her monologue she says, "This school is too small for me to not have any friends. Why do I have such a strong need to be liked?" Initially this was something that she could not seem to get past and so her light flickered instead of shining consistently and brightly.

Zora's monologue reminds me of Zora Neale Hurston's essay, *How It Feels to be Colored Me*. In order not to confuse the two, I will call the author "Zora Neale" and the student will be called "Zora." It was shared in an earlier chapter that Zora chose to name herself this for the study because of how much reading the works of Zora Neale for the Great Books class, shaped her identity as a young African American woman. This short essay was Zora Neale's way of grappling with her identity as well. Zora struggled with two sides of her identity: her intellectual side and the side of her that fit in with her peers. This warring of the two paralyzed her mouth from speaking in the class it seems. Throughout her monologue and even in what she shares in the conversation for the study, she was always warring with two sides of herself. In the first part of her monologue she says, "…I wanna speak but what if they don't get it, my thoughts, my ideas, my views, my opinions, how will they view me when I'm finished…" As a young girl of 13 Zora Neale lost a sense of who she was and she explains this in her essay:

> I left Eatonville, the town of oleanders, as Zora *Neale*. When I disembarked from the river-boat at Jacksonville, she was no more…I was not Zora *Neale* of Orange County any more, I was now a little colored girl. (Hurston, 1928, p.1009)

There was a security Zora Neale felt in her childhood home of Eatonville and when she was placed in a new space, the foundation on which she stood wobbled beneath her.

Zora came into the Great Books class unsure of how to respond to a class structure where students had to think for themselves and voice their opinions. Immediately she was met with fear and uncertainty. Slowly, however, she began to recreate herself independent of what others thought of her, and during this phase of her being in the Great Books class, it seemed to happen as she started to become more involved with the books. Zora's monologue says:

> L, Love, why do I find myself falling in love with these stories, poems and books? Reading in my spare time when no one's around, after my homework's done, I could read until the rising of the sun. These great books touch me in more ways than one.

The books drew her in, and yet she was still becoming involved with the books secretly, afraid to express herself, but then she was introduced to authors outside of the Great Books and she began to reshape her thinking and sense of self. Zora says:

> C, Confidence, reading about women like me in this class has boosted my confidence in so many ways, but why won't it show when I sit in this discussion? An open forum to express my mind and my feelings about these great books. Mrs. Prather says there's no right or wrong but I'd be wrong if I disagree with one of my peers and they decide not to talk to me for embarrassing them in front of the class. This school is too small for me to not have any friends. Why do I have such a strong need to be liked?

Zora's inner person was starting to develop more confidence in her true identity. However, that confidence had not bolstered her strength to speak openly about her thoughts and opinions in the class. She was still so afraid of what people thought. She was so aware of people's supposed perceptions of her.

Zora Neale's biggest struggle is when she left Eatonville, and having to recognize the world was not only African American (as Eatonville was). She says:

> At certain times I have no race, I am me. When I set my hat at a certain angle and saunter down Seventh Avenue, Harlem City, feeling as snooty as the lions in front of the Forty-Second Street Library…Sometimes I feel discriminated against… (Hurston, 1929, p. 1010)

The confidence that Zora was starting to feel while in the class made the struggle greater. Before she could just rest in her silence (the acronym of her monologue), but now she was in a class where she was being challenged to speak her thoughts and feelings, and it stirred up a fight within her. At this point in our discussion I did not know where this fight would lead. I did see, during the years that I taught her, that she did begin to change. Zora Neale, wrestled for a moment as well, but then she eventually decided not to be affected by the opinions of those who sought to oppress her and she says to herself, "How can any deny themselves the pleasure of my company. It's beyond me" (Hurston, 1929, p. 1010).

Zora was one of my first students when I started teaching the Great Books class. At the beginning of my starting to teach this course, I only had students read from the Great Books list compiled by Mortimer Adler and others. While this was taking place, Zora remained very isolated from me, only doing just enough to get a decent grade in the class, and she seldom participated in the literature discussions. However, the next year, I started incorporating more of the arts and African American literature and something began to change in Zora. With her being so silent and withdrawn, I had no idea that artistic expression would be the element that would work its way behind the mask. She shared one of her experiences:

> It was all 5 of us girls and we constructed that play based on something we read and the things you laid in front of us. We struggled, but just being able to stand on your feet and think on the spot of what you would say…you had to put yourself in the shoes of the people you were reading. Weren't we reading the biographies of the slaves at that time? I was feeding off the vibe of how a person would react to certain things.

Even though Zora seemed to come alive with being able to participate in creating a play about slave narratives, she was still wrestling with being a student who was "quiet and wouldn't participate" (Zora).

Incorporating more of the arts into the class, revealed a more dichotomous student in Zora. The Zora of the traditional classroom setting was quiet and somewhat non-responsive, but the one who was given space for artistic expression came alive. Zora's duplicity continued for the following years (I taught her for 4 years), and yet, she was still able to reflect on one of her most memorable experiences:

> My most memorable experience was performing "Raisin in the Sun." This is memorable to me, because at the time I was very quiet and I had to play Ruth. This was big for me because I had to come out of my comfort zone and I was very nervous, but we all came out of our comfort zone. We acted like no one was watching and we all

> got so emotional (the whole group starts talking about how they started crying in one of the scenes). Even though we weren't living back then, we were in high school and not going through anything. We had to go out to the world to be scrutinized by other people…

I finally had found her flickering light. Zora loved the stage. It made her come alive and from behind her mask. In a class setting, she hid behind the darkness of her mask, but on the stage she shined. Zora says:

> Writing the poems, plays, etc. was memorable more so than doing paper assignments and answering questions. It really made you think because you had to make your own opinion of what you're reading. I loved reading the Norton Anthology of African American Literature and I loved turning the classics into plays. Even though I was very shy at the time, I liked that. I liked learning the lines.

Zora was trapped behind a mask that hid her desire for acceptance. The fear of being rejected by her peers or being wrong in class caged her in from expressing her true self, but the theatre being incorporated into the class helped her to break away from the chains of her mask. Augusto Boal (1979) says:

> …theatre is a weapon. A very efficient weapon. For this reason, one must fight for it…the theatre can…be a weapon for liberation. For that, it is necessary to create appropriate theatrical forms. Change is imperative. (p. ix)

"Change is imperative." Zora's shyness and fear of revealing the fullness of who she was to any and everybody was inside, and theatre was one of the main elements of the class that helped her light begin to shine. In addition, seeing herself in the literature that we read by reading African American works, helped her to discover who she was as well.

**Masking Depression**

There was a dark side to Arthur Scott, and the revelations that came to light in our discussion illuminated this darkness. This darkness is not something evil or sinister, but something hidden. In his monologue he unveils the struggle:

> I do not care. I don't care. Do I see the potential of having this knowledge? Sure. But the truth is this info is meaningless to me. My mind is so far from here...But I can't show that. See I have to engage. Not because I want to but because I hide my struggles. And if I don't engage they'll know something's wrong. See I portray a level of transparency to hide my true troubles. No one looks deeper into something that seems shallow. I don't want to be here. And I don't want to be here. (Arthur Scott, 2016)

On the one hand, Arthur Scott was calm and agreeable. He often brought laughter to the class, but he did not seem to let anyone get close to him. He always gave the right answers, which served as a distraction for someone to look deeper. He says, "I don't want to be here. And I don't want to be here." The "here" has two meanings: the class and in the world.

No other student better connects to Dunbar's poem than Arthur Scott:

We Wear the Mask
We wear the mask that grins and lies
It hides our cheeks and shades our eyes,---
This debt we pay to human guile;
With torn and bleeding hearts we smile
And mouth with myriad subtleties

Why should the world be overwise,
In counting all our tears and sighs?
Nay, let them only see us, while
We wear the mask.

We smile, but, O great Christ, our cries
To thee from tortured souls arise.
We sing, but oh the clay is vile
Beneath our feet, and long the mile;
But let the world dream otherwise,
We wear the mask!
(Dunbar, 1895, p. 896)

All of the students had an internal struggle of some kind, but they were wrestling with it—they were not content with keeping their character secret; however, Arthur Scott was different. His monologue acknowledges that his inner character was different from what others see, but he never revealed what his inner character was. He just made it quite clear that he did not want anyone to know it. His monologue is also the shortest—more like a declaration—a statement. Secondly, he revealed his method for hiding his true character. He went through life "cooperating," just doing what others expected of him. But what his actions revealed were directly opposed to what was going on within. Although he was one of my brightest students, always fully engaged with the class, "He did not want to be here."

It took a while for his light to flicker, but the light finally manifested itself when I decided to have the students perform the actual Broadway version of "A Raisin in the Sun." He played the part of Walter in the play. It was a hard character to portray for a young high school student. Throughout teaching him, he rarely showed deep emotion, but somehow he was able to connect to this play and the poem it was based upon. He says:

> A piece of literature I am always constantly reminded of is "A Raisin in the Sun", the original poem by Langston Hughes. I think about it every day and I can recite it to this day, because we did it every day 5 times a day: 'What happens to a dream deferred? Does it dry up like a raisin in the sun? Or fester like a sore—and then run? Does it stink like rotten meat? Or crust and sugar over—like a syrupy sweet? Maybe it just sags like a heavy load. Or does it explode' (Hughes, 1969, p. 21)? As a kid in high school you really don't have that many dreams deferred. You can't really see that from your own perspective, but growing up and experiencing life, you see your dreams do get deferred at times.

This was a flickering light because being a part of this play broke through the mask that he was wearing. It was a hard one to crack. We performed this play in late February and up until that point it was hard to connect to Arthur Scott. However, I remember him literally crying on the stage in one of the scenes. It was totally out of character for him to do so, but he did and all of us were moved by this. He says:

> I was one of the few boys my age and I just remember trying to be "guyish" with there

> being majority girls in the school. I was trying to stay macho, but then you got me doing this play and I was trying to stay chill and cool.

Like Zanni of *Commedia,* Arthur Scott also sought to hide behind being calm and cool, but something about the experience of performing in the play stirred a fire in him. What was it about playing Walter that brought about a connection for him?

Walter was a very troubled character and the play is about breaking Walter so that he can become his true self. It took one main event (losing the down payment to the family's dream house and then being the one to save the house) to break him and to cause him to step into who he was meant to be. Somehow Arthur Scott found a connection with Walter:

> I sort of thought it was shady when you asked me to play this guy…when we first started to do it, I sort of connected with him because he was so cunning. This guy was very cunning. Just seeing how he would work a system or work whatever it is to his benefit. He still ended up taking the L. Just reading his whole character, I felt bad for him. I felt bad for this guy…He was a bad guy. I can sort of relate to him because at the time I'm doing what I'm supposed to do, but why am I not getting what I should get? I'm doing my own work. I was a depressed kid but just didn't show it.

Arthur Scott playing Walter gave him the responsibility of carrying the play. Was it this? Was feeling that sense of responsibility or importance? What broke through to him?

**Reflection: African American Literature in a Great Books Class?**

> …students are less likely to fail in school settings where they feel positive about both their own culture and the majority culture and "are not alienated from their own cultural values." (Cummins, as cited in Ladson-Billings, 1994, p. 11)

This study is about the lived experiences of African American students reading Great Books literature, and yet, I am sharing the experience of engaging my students in "A Raisin in the Sun." In the year prior to this time of reading African American literature, I only had students read from the Great Books list, but I felt like something was missing. The books were "those" books to them, so I eventually began to pull in African American literature that included quotes, etc. from classics. In "A Raisin in the Sun" a line by Walter's sister's boyfriend calls Walter "Prometheus." The students and I then read "Prometheus Bound," an ancient Greek play by Aeschylus. After reading the play, we did a character comparison between Walter and Prometheus to understand why he is referred to as that. Exercises like this caused students to evolve into thinking that ALL of this literature was for them. The masks of each student were strong, and making the literature even more relevant to their cultural background helped the students and I to get beyond the masks in order to bring them to a place of connecting to the Great Books literature. I felt this connection, as did the students, and they began to enter the Great Books in some powerful ways.

**Masking the Fear of Imperfection**

From *The Strange Case of Dr. Jekyll and Mr. Hyde:*

> With every day, and from both sides of my intelligence, the moral and the intellectual, I thus drew steadily nearer to the truth, by whose partial discovery I have been doomed to such a dreadful shipwreck: that man is not truly one, but truly two.
>
> I learned to recognize the thorough and primitive duality of man; I saw that, of the two natures that contended in the field of my consciousness, even if I could rightly be said to be either, it was only because I was radically both. (Stevenson, 2006, pp. 52-53)

Ray Charles was the one student that I failed to see a flickering light appear during the time he was in my class. It took this study for me to see that there was one. One of the main reasons for this is that he took my class for just barely 2 years, and one of those years he was not in the class full time. (Ray Charles was exceptionally gifted academically and the school was transitioning him into skipping, so he took a portion of my class the first year.) The others had me for about 3 to 4 years and so there was time and space for me to see an evolution. During the time that Ray Charles was with me, his mask seemed to be such a strong force that restricted him. This made it difficult to see a flickering light that was apparent at the time.

Ray Charles was complex, like Harelquin in *Commedia*. Rudlin (1994) says that he is never pathetic, always "knows" and is never the loser (p. 79). This was truly Ray Charles. He carried himself with confidence. At just 13 years old he had mastered so much of his martial arts training that he had become a teacher, and like Harlequin, he was also an acrobat. He often did flips around school even in the plays in which he performed. However, little did I know how insecure he was. Deep within, a feeling of inadequacy was thriving. The one clue of his inner struggle, was that it was very difficult for me to pull his thoughts out of him. In my class he was almost frozen in his seat. He says:

> It was a love-hate between me and you. You were like my teacher for only one class and your class was so different from all the other classes. With my math classes and other classes I can just do my studying and get an exact answer or speak out because I could just state the facts. But in your class you had to analyze it and there was not always a set answer. That's why I didn't speak much, because I didn't want to be wrong. I did not want to over analyze or under analyze anything. I just didn't like being wrong and I didn't want someone else coming up with a better point than me.

Unlike the others who revealed a flickering light during the course of me teaching them, Ray Charles did not reveal his flickering light until he became a part of this study. He reveals the struggle with his mask in his monologue:

> Mask: Rule 1, If you're going to be here, you need a mask... Something to let the teacher know you're up to the task of her class, but in reality you must let all the information run right past you…
>
> Ray Charles: But I don't think I…
>
> Mask: Rule 2, in class you, must become this mask... Do not show excitement, interest, or any signs of attention…or you

will be indicted by your peers for operating outside of your predetermined boundaries...

Ray Charles: Wait, wait, I may not seem to like it, but I enjoy the way her class makes me…

Mask: Rule 3, 4 and 5, Do not remove your mask during class ..

Ray Charles: Nah man, listen to...

Mask: Rule 6, Did I mention do not speak? I thought I hinted at that just a moment ago, you don't catch on too quickly do you... Do not speak your mind, as a matter of fact be weak minded…as a matter of fact be meek, be blinded to anything that may remind your mind it can grow... when you wear me your mind is mine...

Ray Charles: My mind is yours huh? Mask, you are just an object that my "mind" has conjured up. Your objective was to help this outcast fit in with the rest of the cast in this show we call life…not to remix and reprise my role... not to fix and compromise my soul… your sole purpose was to help...not to take over my soul's purpose…

Mask: Rule 7…

Ray Charles: Man enough with your rules… your rule is over..

> Mask: Rule 8, This mask gets the last
> laugh.
> (Ray Charles, 2016)

To help me comprehend Ray Charles' inner battle, I turn to those interests in my life that shape me: my religion and my love for super heroes. These may seem odd to use in understanding Ray Charles, but again, van Manen (1997) encourages me even here when he says:

> The ego-logical starting point for phenomenological research is a natural consequence...My own life experiences are immediately accessible to me in a way that no one else's are. However, the phenomenologist does not want to trouble the reader with purely private, autobiographical facticities of one's life. The revealing of private sentiments or private happenings are matters to be shared among friends perhaps, or between lovers, or in the gossip columns of life. In drawing up personal descriptions of lived experiences, the phenomenologist knows that one's own experiences are also the possible experiences of others. (p. 54)

Carefully and without seeking to indoctrinate the reader into my faith, I share a verse from the Bible to somehow mentally embody this battle between Ray Charles and his mask. Romans 7: 21-24 is a verse that has placed this type of inner struggle into some type of understandable context when I am warring within myself. It says:

> So I find this law at work: Although I want to do good, evil is right there with me. For in my inner being I delight in God's law; but I see another law at work in me, waging

> war against the law of my mind and making
> me a prisoner of the law of sin at work
> within me. What a wretched man I am! Who
> will rescue me from this…?

I wonder if books such as *Dr. Jekyll and Mr. Hyde* or super hero comics such as *Two-Face* in the Batman series are ways that creators seek to illustrate this age-old verse shared by the Apostle Paul? Ray Charles' monologue, like the verse reveal how there are these laws set forth by one part of the person, laws that seek to control the desires of the other person. A fight ensues. Ray Charles demonstrated this through his physical fight with his mask when we performed the play. We may not fully understand the war within our souls and what creates these two inner beings. For Two Face in the Batman series, it was a tragic event where he was left with a scarred face on one side. For Dr. Jekyll it was him coming to the realization that he has an uncontrollable evil side and him seeking to oppress that side of himself. For Charles, I learn what caused this battle with his two inner selves, as we enter more into the conversation. I was nervous about Ray Charles participating in the study because I felt that he never enjoyed the class. I found, however, that there actually was a light that was flickering, but it was taking place behind the mask.

> All your life, your mind lives within the
> darkness of your body. Every thought is a
> flint moment, a spark of light from your
> inner darkness. (O'Donohue, 1997, p. 4)

**When the Flame Catches**

> It only takes a spark, to get a fire going and
> soon all those around can warm up in the
> glowing. (Kaiser, 1969)

The words of this old hymn ring true for this lived experience of African American students reading Great Books literature. The lights flickered until they were fanned into a flame. I believe the flame caught when they actually started to finish the reading assignments. Each one began to complete the reading at different times over the course of studying with me, but eventually most of us were reading the literature and enjoying it together.

It is here that I begin to transition away from the role of the mask in this study. *Commedia* has helped me to interpret the inner character of my students, but just like in the play, at some point the masks have to come off. As I stated earlier, *The Table* is used as a way to symbolize and synthesize the students' lived experiences reading Great Books literature. I share glimpses into the play as a way to visualize their lived experiences. For the play, the students wanted the masks to come off after they shared their monologues, because there did come a point and time when they allowed the light to begin to shine through as they went through the class. The flickering light took flame, finally.

## Igniting a Fire through Music

Over the weekend conversation, we discussed Voltaire's essay called "Character." Sophia wrestled with the premise of the essay, especially the part where it says:

> …from the Greek word *impression, engraving*. It is what nature has engraved in us. Can one change one's character? Yes, if one changes one's body….It is a tree that

> produces only degenerate fruit, but the fruit is always of the same nature; it is knotted and covered with moss, it becomes worm-eaten, but it is always an oak or pear tree. (Woolf, 2010, p. 67)

Sophia questioned Voltaire's view on whether character can change, and I feel that her metamorphosis in the class is an example as to how that may not be true. There came a point when the flickering light caught to a flame. I asked the group at what point did a transition (if any) happen for them during the course of the class. Sophia was the first to respond:

> I think it was when it became more personal. You gave us a choice…instead of doing a book report, you can make up a song. I remember one time a student shared a poem (I can't remember his name). One day I was listening to Lauren Hill and thinking "It is almost Monday. What am I going to do for my homework assignment?" So I'm trying to write a poem and I was just going to put this together. I'm listening to Lauren Hill's song. We were reading Animal Farm at the time and then I realize that the song she was singing could relate because it was talking about authority figures. I was thinking, "This song kind of sounds like the book." I presented it to you the next day and you were like, "Yeah! I see it!" I was able to listen to music and relate it to something I had to do for school. I was thinking that was pretty cool.

Sophia came to a place where she realized that *Animal Farm* which was written in 1945 by a man from England connected to her, an African American girl in the 21st century from Maryland in some way. The Lauren Hill song she was listening to was "Mr. Intentional." The lyrics of the song do correspond to the plot of *Animal Farm*:

See the road to hell, is paved with good intentions
Can't you tell, the way they have to mention
How they helped you out, you're such a hopeless victim
Please don't do me any favors, Mr. Intentional
All their talk, is seasoned to perfection
The road they walk, commanding your affection
They need to be needed, deceived by motivation
An opportunity, to further situation
Why they so important, is without explanation
Please don't patrionize me, Mr. Intentional
Oh, ohhh, ohh ohhh
We give rise to ego, by being insecure
The advice that we go, desperatly searching for
The subconscious effort, to support our paramour
To engage in denial, to admit we're immature
Validating lies, Mr. Intentional
Open up yours eyes, Mr. Intentional
Stuck in a system, that seeks to suck your blood
Held emotionally hostage, by what everybody does

> Counting all the money, that you give them
> just because
> Exploiting ignorance, in the name of love
> (Hill, 2002)

*Animal Farm* uses pigs as a metaphor for how a leader can slowly transition from being a public servant to a dictator. As the ego rises and people begin to need the person more, they eventually fall prey to a sense of entitlement and begin to take advantage of those they serve in order to serve their own selfish desires. The amazing thing about Sophia connecting to this book through music is the organic way in which it took place. She is merely listening to music over the weekend and her mind was able to think about the book we were reading for class, naturally connecting it to the music to which she was listening. In our discussion, she was also able to use this moment to understand more about the political systems of the world, something that many high school students do not show interest in or a connection to. The light took flame for her because she was able to see her own interests connect to the literature we were reading. At this point, the literature had worked its way into her daily thinking, as opposed to just memorizing the answers for an essay question to pass the test. She was able to see the literature in the world around her.

**Igniting a Fire through Theatre**

Two of the students in my study were liberated by the theatrical/artistic elements of the class. Zora and Arthur Scott found freedom from their masks by expressing their understanding of the literature through the performing arts. This is in line with Augusto Boal (1979), who gives a historical look at theatre:

> "Theatre" was the people singing freely in
> the open air; the theatrical performance was
> created by and for the people, and could thus

> be called dithyrambic song. It was a celebration in which all could participate freely. (p. ix)

**When stage light frees a voice.** I have chosen to connect Zora's experience with Augusto Boal's *Theatre of the Oppressed*, because of how this concept speaks to the liberating power of the theatre. The etymology of the word "oppress" comes from the Old French word *opresser* which means to "afflict; torment, or smother." Zora's monologue reveals a sense of her inner struggle, the torment she was going through to break free from her shyness and fear of rejection. Asked when the transition happened for her, she shared how theatre and creative freedom helped her to begin to connect to the literature to be able to break free from that affliction. As she remembered her experience acting as Ruth in "Raisin in the Sun" she says, "…we all came out of our comfort zone and acted like no one was watching…"

Boal (1974) speaks about how theatre evolved from being a community of people offering up creative expression for pure enjoyment, to being something governed by politics and societal restrictions. His desire was to create a theatre that tore down all the walls:

> First, the barrier between actors and spectators is destroyed: all must act, all must be protagonists in the necessary transformations of society…the barrier between protagonists and choruses is destroyed: all must be simultaneously chorus and protagonist…thus we arrive at the "poetics of the oppressed", the conquest of the means of theatrical production. (p. x)

Zora talked about the production of "Raisin in the Sun" not as if she was the star of the play (which she was), but she spoke of the sense of community she felt, working together to create the production with her classmates:

> …we all got emotional…in school together…we had to go out to the world to be scrutinized by other people.

She experienced a sense of acceptance in working with her classmates, and this is something she yearned for (as expressed in her monologue). Theatre was instrumental in tearing down those walls she perceived separated her from her classmates and from me (I played an active part in the production as well). This feeling of community is something she needed to experience in the literature portion as well in order to help her flickering light to fan into a flame.

In order for the flame to catch for Zora, some inner struggles had to be addressed. There was an inner rebellion that was taking place, and even though Zora was quiet, there were times when she secretly made poor decisions that affected her academic performance. It took a classmate pulling her aside and talking with her to inspire her to redirect her steps:

> I went through that point between 9th and 11th grades where I was acting out for whatever reason. Still to this day, I look back and think 'What was wrong with you.' I think that I was trying to find myself. So I was acting out and all the crazy stuff that I did…at one point where I was suspended every two weeks…a classmate came to me and was like, 'You are about to graduate. Why are you doing all this? You are about to mess up. Don't you want to get into college?' I was like, 'Maybe she's right.' It wasn't like a teacher was telling me this but someone that was younger. I was like,

> 'Maybe she knows?' I don't know what happened but it made me buckle down.

She mentions, "I think I was trying to find myself." It was so imperative that I included reading African American literature. Zora was having struggles with her identity. She says:

> I'm very creative and I can do things in that nature. I told my father that I wanted to be a hairdresser. He said 'You are going to braid hair all your life. You're not going to make any money.' Every time I tried to do something in my nature, my father was like, 'No, you aren't going to make money.' So what am I going to do? I don't want to be sitting behind a desk. Even if it does make more money, I don't want to do that. So it was like trying to figure out who I wanted to be in the future.

When we started reading the African American literature something began to happen within Zora:

> I love Zora Neale Hurston. Reading her stuff is probably what made me…what helped me develop who I am as a black woman, and black poets really helped me see who I was as an African American woman.

I was able to tap into her personal interest. Zora was "fascinated with African American history" (Zora), and that caused her to become interested in the class. She often found herself reading beyond the reading assignments when we read from African American literature and she sometimes stayed up late into the night to read further. The amazing thing is that this interest caused her to begin to engage with the other literature, as she began to allow the African American literature to help shape her identity. It seems that the African American literature helped her find her voice in the class. By exploring her own experience as an African American woman, she could connect it to the other human experiences in the Great Books:

> The Great Books just isn't this Greek stuff that I'm not into. I can relate it to my life. I went through some of the stories that we didn't read and read them on my own.

Boal (1974) talks about how Bertolt Brecht sought to utilize theatre to bring about an "awakening of critical consciousness" (p. 122). By Zora engaging in plays about African American history that gave her a voice to write the lines and create the production, she was liberated. She was freed from the fear of what her friends thought of her, her father thought of her, etc. She found her voice through obtaining this "critical consciousness" of who she was as an African American woman, through reading and engaging in African American literature. Her passion and interest for African American literature did not isolate her from the Great Books. Instead, this experience freed her to bask in the glow of the flame that was now ignited, and a change had begun to take place.

> …theatre is a weapon. A very efficient weapon. For this reason, one must fight for it…the theatre can…be a weapon for liberation. For that, it is necessary to create appropriate theatrical forms. Change is imperative. (Boal, 1979, p. ix)

**When stage light cuts through darkness.** I remember feeling a sense of relief as I watched Arthur Scott play Walter. Although he was a very engaged student, there were a couple of things that gave me a sign that something else was deep within. Number one, he struggled to meet school expectations in other classes (behaviorally and academically). He often clashed with other teachers, and he was generally in a dark place—he just seemed to see the world from a darker point of view. In my class, however, he laughed, he read, he engaged, he wrote and he participated fully. It was always an enigma to me.

Like Zora, Arthur Scott found freedom from his mask through performing on the stage. This again draws me back to Augusto Boal's *Theatre of the Oppressed.* I find myself fascinated with how two of my students are able to find some type of liberation from the theatre, but not just any theatre. The theatre that was created in my class was such that students created it. They interpreted the literature that it was based on and created ways to present their understandings on the stage. We had all read "A Raisin in the Sun" and to see Arthur Scott interpret the character of Walter was an amazing process. The students set the stage, created the props, and did their own character studies in order to figure out how best to portray the character. *Theatre of the Oppressed,* although created to liberate people who are feeling oppressed within their countries or communities, connects to the type of theatre I used because the techniques I implored are similar. I also feel that the oppression my students may have had within their masks calls for use of this type of theatre. Boal (1994) talks about "Forum Theatre" which has the participants create the drama and then other participants create a resolution to the problem and change the action of the play. We did not perform "Forum Theatre" exactly as Boal describes; however, the concept of allowing the participants to take control of the action or the flow of the performance reminds me of our experience creating drama within my class. Boal (1994) says:

> Forum theatre, as well as these other forms of people's theatre, instead of taking something away from the spectator, evoke in him a desire to practice in reality the act he has rehearsed in the theatre. The practice of these theatrical forms creates a sort of uneasy sense of incompleteness that seeks fulfillment through real action. (p. 142)

In traditional theatre, there is a director, a back stage crew, etc. and the actors wait to be told what to say, where to stand, how to act, etc. They may do some interpreting, but for the most part they are waiting to be directed as to what to do.

Theatre in my class did not happen this way. I gave them a script, but they were allowed to change the lines to something that they felt connected more to how they felt in the action. They chose their own costumes, set, props, etc. The other students were allowed to give their opinions of how their classmate should portray a character. The production became theirs. In fact, they directed me. I was their gopher. Whatever they needed to make their production happen, I would try to help them get it. This freedom of thought and being, aroused something in Arthur Scott that continued to be stirred as he continued in my class for two years.

The flame continued to thrive as Arthur Scott went into another year with me in the Great Books class. Arthur Scott mentioned earlier that he was wrestling with depression. I had no idea until our conversation that he was struggling with this. Arthur Scott shared how writing a song for my class, helped him through his darkest moment:

> I feel comfortable talking about it now because I'm way past it. But when the whole Robin Williams thing happened, I think he hit me weird because Robin

Williams was always happy and everyone thought everything was good with him. He was always cracking jokes and that's how I saw how other people saw me. If something were to happen to me along the lines of what happened to Robin Williams, people would be so blind-sided by that. But that's where I was at the time.

At the time I wasn't cutting myself or anything like that, but I did struggle with thoughts of suicide because I was at a point of—I just wasn't happy. I was like, "Why aren't I happy?" I couldn't put 2 and 2 together. And then making that song "Meaningless", it was almost a relief. It doesn't matter anyway…You shouldn't even stress…Just thinking about how small we are in this humongous world. It just made me think about things. At the time in those classes, I just remember it feeling like a routine that went on and on. And I am like 'What's next?' I just remember thinking, 'I have no idea what's next and I really don't want to.' It's like what some of the others have shared earlier—we knew so much because in comparison to other students we were receiving more information—more analytical stuff. So I felt like I knew so much. I was at a low point in my life. Then I realized everything gets better. I wish I could check up on the 17 year old Arthur Scott and tell him to 'Cheer up.'

Listening to Arthur Scott and his desire to go back in time to talk to his younger self, reminds me of a song called “Dear Younger Me.” I feel it captures the essence of what Arthur Scott was trying to say:

> Dear younger me
> Where do I start
> If I could tell you everything that I have learned so far
> Then you could be
> One step ahead
> Of all the painful memories still running thru my head
> I wonder how much different things would be
> Dear younger me, dear younger me
>
> Dear younger me
> I cannot decide
> Do I give some speech about how to get the most out of your life
> Or do I go deep
> And try to change
> The choices that you’ll make cuz they’re choices that made me
> Even though I love this crazy life
> Sometimes I wish it was a smoother ride
> Dear younger me, dear younger me
>
> If I knew then what I know now
> Condemnation would’ve had no power
> My joy my pain would’ve never been my worth
> If I knew then what I know now
> Would’ve not been hard to figure out
> What I would’ve changed if I had heard

Every mountain every valley
Thru each heartache you will see
Every moment brings you closer
To who you were meant to be

Dear younger me, dear younger me
(Mercy Me, 2015)

Arthur Scott's story gets darker. The oppression of trying to live this double life became almost too much to bear. The effort it took to meet everyone's expectations, while still trying to figure out who he really was, was a challenge, and the adults in his life seemed not to realize (me included) how hard it was to just do what he was told or expected to do. Arthur Scott had a whole other world going on within himself. There are ideas, ambitions, hopes and dreams that he was trying to answer to while also answering to the adults that sought to guide his life path. It was frustrating. Arthur Scott says;

> My whole life people told me I was going to be a lawyer. Then after a few years, I'm like I don't want to be a lawyer anymore, because I did not know what I was going to be. I would just agree with them, but not tell them what I was really feeling. I didn't know what I wanted to be! Just the mixture of not knowing and then thinking that you know too much is just an odd mix. There were days when I would go home and just be so low…so low. And then I would come to class the next day all happy, cracking jokes, like everything was still good. I wasn't trying to hide from anybody, but I really wanted to just hide from myself! I wanted to convince myself that I wasn't some typical depressed kid. I'm

> comfortable talking about this, because I've already talked to others about it. There was a day where I did attempt—didn't try, but I did attempt to hang myself. It just didn't work. Now I'm like 'What were you doing!' I just want to go back to that kid and smack him and say, 'What are you doing? Chill bro! What are you doing? You buggin'!" But the very next day, I'm going over the lines for "A Raisin in the Sun' and my neck is still hurting from…whatever…

Van Manen's (1996) book *Childhood Secrets* takes a phenomenological look at secrecy. Arthur Scott's lived experiences connects to what van Manen says:

> Most people would have little trouble with the idea that each of us possesses a separate and unique "identity" with a more or less stable "inner self" at the center. It is true that over the years our sense of identity may undergo certain changes…Yet we do not doubt that at heart we are still the same person…It is just that we feel we know ourselves better than those people from the town where we used to live. They may not recognize us, but we know ourselves. We know who we are. We know our secret wishes and desires, and we know how some of those wishes and desires may have changed and how these changes may have contributed to our evolving sense of our personal identity and inner self. (p. 98)

Arthur Scott, although young, was clear enough about who he was that he knew he did not want to be a lawyer. He may not have been sure about what his life purpose/goal was, but he knew what he was not. Yet, he recognized that inner self seemed to contradict what others were saying or feeling about him, so he hid behind a mask. The frustration of leading this double life almost caused him to take his life. When Arthur Scott asked, "What is character?" during our discussion of Voltaire's essay over the weekend, I now feel the question revealed his own struggle with revealing his true character. The wonderful thing about Arthur Scott is that he lived through this conflict so that he can now look back at his younger self and say, "Cheer up!"

None of us knew his inner pain and that he had tried to hang himself. The next day after the suicide attempt, he came to school, and he created a song he had written called "Meaningless." At this time, we had been reading *The Count of Monte* Cristo, *Othello* and *Ecclesiastes*, engaging in discussions where we compared the three texts. One of the questions we discussed is whether or not money and power can truly satisfy in this life. By creating "Meaningless" there came liberation for Arthur Scott. Through the discussion he became inspired to write the song, and in that process he received the strength to keep pushing forward in spite of the pain he was feeling. Arthur Scott says that it was through the engagement in the literature class, that he received the insight that maybe he should keep pushing—towards the light.

**The Spark that Later Takes Flame**

With the other participants, as they shared the different times that the light flickered or when the flames caught for them, I could remember along with them. I was able to recall these transitions as they happened for them. The weekend conversation with the students confirmed what I'd suspected. For Ray Charles, I was only able to discover this as he shared it over the weekend we engaged in the study. The mask hid it during the time he took my class. His monologue reveals his struggle to engage in my class, but being overpowered by the mask. According to Ray Charles, the flame caught for him when the school closed and he went on to the school where I became the principal. I count this time in my timeline, because although I was no longer teaching the class, the English teacher and I designed it together, with me creating the list of most of the books to be read during that year he took her class. He talks about the first time a piece of literature drew him in:

> During your class I didn't care too much about the literature. When I was in your class, we read the *Iliad, The Count of Monte Cristo*, and those did not connect with me. But the very next year, we read Richard Wright's, *Black Boy* and *A Raisin in the Sun.* It was the first time I'd read a piece of literature where the author thought like I did. I started getting into it.

As I am writing this, I am beginning to see where the struggle may have been. Ray Charles was also the only male student I had that wore dread locs. He came from a family that was very steeped in the African American culture, and the books I had chosen to read did not resonate with him at all, so it seemed. He felt out of place and struggled to understand the literature because it seemed so far away from him. But the mask would not allow him to let me see the struggle. Instead there was resistance—a wall. Ray Charle's portrayed his resistance to my class during the play by choosing to sit with his back to me the whole time and his mask backwards, on the back of his head. He did not turn to face me until the very end of the play, and this was what I felt when I taught him. I felt he was unreachable. He held on to his mask and as "We Wear the Mask" says, he was intent on me not knowing that he was feeling out of place in the literature. The poem says:

> Why should the world be over-wise,
> In counting all our tears and sighs?
> Nay, let them only see us, while
> We wear the mask. (Dunbar)

He would only let me see him while he wore the mask. I fought against it, however. I tried to push past it. Ray Charles remembers those times:

> I was a contradiction. I was a "know it all" geek/nerd, that really didn't know it all, so I sat back and observed until I thought I was right. Me and you would go back and forth in discussion and I just wanted to be right. I was 13 in the 9th grade and I had so many big books to read for your class. I remember the discussion the most because mainly I couldn't seem to get a higher grade in your class because I would not participate like I should have. I was doing the reading though…

It was not a competition to me. I had no desire to embarrass a student. However, I did want every student to go through a process of realizing that they did not know. Once they got to that place of humbling themselves and accepting that they did not know, then they could ask the question that would lead them into the wonderful journey of self-discovery. I recall Gadamer's (1975/1989) thoughts again:

> …the example of Socrates teaches that the important thing is the knowledge that one does not know. Hence the Socratic dialectic—which leads through its art of confusing the interlocutor to this knowledge—creates the conditions for the question. All questioning and desire to

> know presuppose a knowledge that one does not know; so much so, indeed, that a particular lack of knowledge leads to a particular question. (p. 359)

Ray Charles did not want me to know he did not know. His mask worked hard to hide that from me during the course of my class, but when he went to the new school and read *Black Boy*, the flame caught.

> The miracle of thought is its presence in the night side of your soul; the brilliance of thought is born in darkness. Each day is a journey. We come out of the night into the day. (O'Donohue, 1997, p. 4)

**Being in the Light**

> We are always on a journey from darkness to light. At first we are children of darkness. Your body and your face were formed first in the kind darkness of your mother's womb. Your birth was first a journey from darkness into light. All your life, your mind lives within the darkness of your body. Every thought that you have is a flint moment, a spark of light from your inner darkness. The miracle of thought is its presence in the night side of your soul; the brilliance of thought is born in darkness...Ultimately, light is the mother of life. Where there is no light, there can be no life...It keeps life awake...Light is a nurturing presence...The soul awakens and lives in light...Once human beings began to search for a meaning to life, light became one of the most powerful metaphors to express the eternity

> and depth of life…thought has often been compared to light. In its luminosity, the intellect was deemed to be the place of the divine within us. (O'Donohue, 1997, pp. 4-5)

There came a point in the journey where the students were fully engaged. They were journeying together with me through the literature. There was no more push back—no more resistance. They were now reading on their own and were motivated to do so. I was no longer fighting feelings of discouragement and disillusionment about the process. "Being in the Light" reminds me of the above passage from *Anam Cara*, and when DuBois says, "I dwell above the Veil…" I think of my students. According to the Middle English, "dwell" means to linger. "Being" means to exist. To cultivate the student's mind in this way was a call for them to be or dwell in the light. When they were given freedom to read, question and discover for themselves, they rose above the Veil. Once the light was awakened in their souls and then began to glow all around and through them—once they came to be in the light, they could not return. The effect of being in the light was different for each student, and these differences can possibly reveal the ways individuals respond to "being in the light."

**Dwelling above the Veil**

Sophia's growth in the class revealed a change in her character—a change in her mentality. She says:

> I didn't think there was any way I was going to get through your class. You had to think for yourself. It was more challenging. It was more pressure but before you know it, you are growing and not realizing it.

This expressed Sophia's transition from a place of resistance into a space of joining me in the journey, to engaging in the Great Books and the dialogue surrounding them.

For the class I mixed in African American literature as well as creating a dialogue between the student, a Great Book and African American literature. Throughout the year we rotated through these books. I did this because even though African American authors are not listed on the Great Books list, we are a part of that Great Conversation, and I wanted my students to see that. I wanted them to understand that these texts can be inclusive of them and their cultural background, even though we may have to draw that out through dialogue. Sophia mentioned a book that she really enjoyed called *Abraham's Well,* which was a fictional account of The Trail of Tears. The story is about a family of Black Cherokee (Native and African American) who walked the Trail of Tears with the Cherokee people. She then compared this text to her experience reading *Their Eyes Were Watching God.* Both stories told about a woman seeking to be independent, but also having to rely on men to make it through life. However, for some reason her heart connected more to *Abraham's Well*:

> *Abraham's Well* was the first book that I read and retained. In comparison to *Their Eyes Were Watching God,* I was not able to retain it. I know I read the book, but I can't really remember everything that happened. Whereas *Abraham's Well,* I was able to relate to it and I kept reading it. Just watching her grow up from 8 years old. Even though she was a sharecropper's daughter, she did not realize that she was really a slave to the people who owned the farm. She grew up oblivious to the bad

> world of slavery. But then she ended up on the Trail of Tears. She was living her life as an 8-year-old girl, picking corn on the farm. I related to that because I felt like I came up in the world just doing what my dad does. I'm so used to him just taking me where he goes—going with the flow, and then adversity came. For the girl, they just came along and took her family away, even though she was so young. I kind of related to having to come out of that world where everything is good in life. Everyone has to come to that reality that this is what the world is.

Neither *Abraham's Well* or *Their Eyes Were Watching God* are Great Books, but they both dealt with themes that are found in Great Books telling the human story. I do not feel that the Great Books encourage us to shun other literature, but I do feel they invoke the questions necessary to discovering those books that speak to the human experience. This is why it was not a challenge to transition from reading the above books to something from Aristotle or Shakespeare. The experiences and themes shared in them are what every human goes through. The Great Books make us think about our lives, question our life experiences, relate them to others and hunger to learn more about the lives of those who can relate to our experiences. When I think of what Sophia shared about connecting her life to the literature that she read, I find inspiration in the words of David Townsend (2015):

> What if each American took personal responsibility to read "the transcript" of our civilization"? What if the truth of this *logos* lay alertly and heroically upon every

> American tongue, speaking to the questions, "How to live and What to do?" (p. 19)

Unfortunately, the story of the Trail of Tears or the African American Experience is not included in the transcript of the Great Books, but the students and I inserted it into the dialogue. In doing this, we were able to relate it back to the human experiences that are included in the Great Books. The Great Books are currently the only organized transcript for this civilization.

By being in the light of this experience, Sophia also came to gain a better understanding of our political system. This understanding caused her to think about politics and how her childhood literature experiences helped her to relate to the allegory of *Animal Farm*:

> For me *Animal Farm* still sticks out to me because of how it was an allegory. It was hard not to see things in a certain way...My brain goes back to how it is in the jungle. You have the lion who is king of the jungle. I related to that because I grew up reading animal tales and so even though animal stories are childish, I can relate to *Animal Farm* because of that experience reading animal stories. Animal Farm is not a kid's tale or a regular metaphor, it is actually about a political system! You have animals talking so it's like it's a kiddy book, but you see the transition. I'm a teenager reading about this and experiencing this!

Orwell's skill in drawing us into thinking about politics in this way was brilliant and it helped my students gain access to knowledge to which they otherwise would be oblivious.

Sophia felt pride in being able to not only read the literature, but she understood it and could speak of it. Her resistance at the beginning gave way to a desire to read more and to pursue her personal questions more. She began to realize that she had been given access to something most of her peers had not been given. This access caused her to understand references made in the media, news and other outlets:

> Even though we didn't really connect to those Greek classical readings, when it is mentioned in the media, we know it. We are not on the outside. We are not like African American kids who say, "I don't know what you're talking about." We are in on the joke.

Sophia relished the fact that she had knowledge that her peers did not have. Her initial entrance into my class was one of resistance, but as she began to be in the light, that resistance began to bolster her rebel spirit in a way that no longer fought against me. She became hungry for what my class had to offer her, as she realized that this set her apart from her peers. I return again to DuBois' (2005) "ode" to the Great Books, specifically to the part that speaks to rising above being under the "Veil": "So, wed with Truth, I dwell above the Veil" (p. 108). Sophia came to be in the light, her rebel spirit drawn to this light for the same reasons to which DuBois speaks. She, like DuBois, found pride in being able to rise above the shadows of not understanding the transcript of this civilization.

**Liberated by Light**

Augusto Boal (1974) expresses the objective of *Theatre of the Oppressed*:

> …one must keep in mind its main objective: to change the people—"spectators," passive beings in the theatrical phenomenon—into subjects, into actors, transformers of the dramatic action. I hope that the differences

> remain clear…the spectator delegates no power to the character (or actor) either to act or to think in his place; on the contrary, he himself assumes the protagonic role, changes the dramatic action, tries out solutions, discusses plans for change—in short, trains himself for real action…Theatre is a weapon, and it is the people who should wield it.

The main objective of *Theatre of the Oppressed* is to "change the people" (Boal). This change comes about as more power and authority is given to the people to write the script and create the action for the production. The actors and audience work together as a community to create the action and that action speaks to that which is going on in the world around them. Theatre becomes their voice, their weapon to fight for their place in society. This was Zora's journey in her lived experience. Theatre cut away the mask that oppressed her through the first half of her high school years. Once that mask was removed, her eyes were opened and she could see the light—she could be in the light.

Zora went beyond obtaining the "critical consciousness" (Morrell) of who she was as an African American woman, but she began to write the script of her life. She causes me to think of Lorraine Hansberry (1969) when she says in her posthumous autobiography *To Be Young Gifted and Black*: "For some time now—I think since I was a child—I have been possessed of the desire to put down the stuff of my life" (p. 17). Although Zora did not literally write her story, through action and theatre as her catalyst, she began to "write the stuff of her life" by forging her own path. The talk with the classmate jarred her into wanting to make a change, but she didn't know where to begin. There was a fight within her to figure out who she was as a student and as a creative being, beyond what her father wanted for her or that which she felt her friends would approve. The literature helped her to sort through this, specifically African American literature. Embracing her heritage through reading the literature that spoke to that experience now freed her to engage in dialogue about the Great Books, and their transcription of the Western culture she finds herself living in. She had found her voice to contribute to the Great Conversation, as an African American woman.

Suppressing her character had been Zora's way of coping up to this point. This suppression of Zora's true character as a high school student, was also an oppression. Zora's hiding what she really wanted for herself caused her outward pain and turmoil. It leaked out in her impulsive negative choices and created a dissatisfaction with her life. Change happened when she had the conversation with her classmate, when she began to engage in theatre performances and when she started to read African American literature. Her lived experience in my class began to be just one of fulfilling a duty to me. Zora says:

> …in the mornings my brother and I would get to school early because my mom taught there, so my brother and I would read the books so we could know at least something for the class discussion…we knew that if we did not do the reading you were going to make sure we did it at some point…you might say, 'Oh you didn't read? Ok, then you're going to have to read through the summer!'

She also did the readings out of a sense of duty to her classmates and out of a desire to feel included:

> For me, it was seeing my peers actually reading the book. I did not want to sit there and not know the answers. You asked a lot

> of questions to make sure we read, not about the book, but how we related to the book. I didn't want to be sitting there like, 'Okay, I don't know what she's talking about.' I wanted to be in the loop. I didn't want to do the work, but I didn't want to sit there and everyone else is giving the intellectual answers. I didn't want to be sitting there and all I could say was, 'Yeah, it was a good book.' Because then I'd look stupid! Everyone else did the work and I did not want to look lazy.

As Boal's (1994) objective for *Theatre of the Oppressed* was to "change the people," Zora needed change from within, and most of that change happened as a result of being in my class. Reflecting on her lived experience, I was reminded of the book of Gloria Ladson-Billings (1994), *The Dreamkeepers: Successful Teachers of African American Children.* Zora's rendering of her lived experience resonates with me because it gives a very explicit look into why culturally relevant strategies are a necessity when teaching in culturally diverse settings. Zora speaks to me of the importance of teachers incorporating culturally relevant materials and strategies when teaching African American students (and students of other races and cultures as well). Research shows that students are less likely to fail in school settings where they feel positive about both their own culture and the majority culture and are not alienated from their own cultural values (Cummins, 1986). The Great Books class sought to connect the African American experience with the experience of Western Culture transcribed in the Great books. This marriage fostered a change of character in Zora.

I have looked at Zora's experience in light of the characteristics of teachers who have successfully taught African American students, as shared by Ladson-Billings. Zora's account reveals why these characteristics displayed in my class, helped her to be in the light. These characteristics are outlined in the book *The Dreamkeepers*.

**Culture matters.** Initially, the school where I worked required us to go through a certain list of Great Books each year. On the surface it appeared that there would not be time to read from African American literature. However, to make room for this, I mainly used the *Norton Anthology of African American Literature* and we read short excerpts of the literature. I just felt that if we could get a taste of it, something would spark for the students. We would read a short excerpt of African American literature and then connect it to a larger piece of literature from the Great Books list. As the years progressed, I was able to include full texts into our Great Books reading list and we got to the point where there was an equal amount of both texts on the list. Zora developed a connection with Zora Neale Hurston and others during this time, and even though we were only reading short excerpts in the class, she would go home and read from more African American texts on her own. My class wet her appetite for more. She shared earlier that this helped to develop her identity as an African American woman. Before doing this, she had no interest in the Great Books, because she could not see herself at first, but incorporating the texts that reflected her culture created a bridge for her to the Great Books. Ladson-Billings (1994) says:

> Thus culturally relevant teaching uses student culture in order to maintain it and to transcend the negative effects of the dominant culture. The negative effects are brought about, for example by not seeing one's history, culture or background

represented in the textbook or
curriculum…(p. 17)

**The fallacy of color blindness**. I believe that Zora's struggle with her identity may have come from her background. She had been going through her life not quite being conscious of her racial and cultural identity. She was not one who was raised to look down on her race, but she had not come to a place of fully embracing it. She was dwelling in a space of color blindness. Ladson-Billings (1994) recalls what some teachers say when working in diverse settings: "…some teachers make such statements as 'I don't really see color, I just see children' or 'I don't care if they're red, green or polka dot, I just treat them all like children'" (Ladson-Billings, 1994, p. 31). However, these attempts at color blindness mask a "dysconscious racism," an "uncritical habit of mind" that justifies inequity and exploitation by accepting the existing order of things as given (King, 1991, pp. 31-32).

Earlier I discussed that by Zora being given the opportunity to engage with African American literature, she was able to develop a "critical consciousness" (Boal, 1994) about who she was as a black woman. She came in not knowing who she was, but the literature helped her to her to sort through that. By me supplying the literature to her, she was also made to feel that her culture mattered and that her teacher did not feel this curriculum was the absolute source of knowledge and understanding. I communicated to her that her voice mattered as well as the voices of the African American people overall. These voices were just as important as even the voice of Shakespeare or Aristotle.

**Creating a learning community.** Zora discussed her experience developing the production of *A Raisin in the Sun* and she expressed how working together with her peers to create the production was her most memorable moment.

Zora also shared about how she enjoyed the dialogue that took place in the class:

> …we could talk to each other. More so then you talking at us and we respond. We were talking to each other and that enhances the experience. Instead of you telling us what the book was about or what we should have learned, you were asking us questions to have us think on our own. We got our thoughts from our classmates, our opinions were formed by what they said, and you too. And we would talk about it amongst ourselves so that gave us different opinions too. We saw how other people think.

Ladson-Billings' research on those characteristics that make successful teachers of African American students revealed that those teachers created a more cooperative learning environment within their classroom. She says:

> Cooperative learning is premised on the notion that students can and should learn together and from one another…the underlying ideology that informs their use of these strategies is to prepare their students for collective growth and liberation. Rather than elevate the importance of individual achievement, the teachers encourage their students to work within a collective structure and reward group efforts more often than individual ones. (Ladson-Billings, 1994, p. 60)

As stated earlier, I know that when I first say the term "Great Books of Western Civilization," a wave of controversy arises. So much has been attributed to these texts, and one notion is that these books are "The Tree of

Knowledge" for all education. It is my hope that this study has revealed that in no way do I feel that way. However, I do recognize their importance in teaching all children, but especially those often excluded from them—the African American student.

Zora said that we all learned from each other and this was true for me as well. I learned from my students, the Great Books, my faith and many other places. I do not see knowledge as coming from one place, but I visualize an ocean full of sources that I was able to pull from in this journey to educating Zora and her classmates. There was my faith, first and foremost. I found so much wisdom in the writings of the Bible in order to reach my students. I reflected on the compassionate and inclusive way that Jesus taught and tried to incorporate that into my teaching. Acts 10: 34 states that "God is no respecter of persons." Zora recalled where this was true in my class:

> Every child had a special way of learning, you had to work with them at their individual level and learn how they do. You had 9th graders with 12th graders and everything was the same. You had to learn how to master how to communicate with an 18-year-old and a 14-year-old…and the different struggles that they have.

Our school was small and so many times the classes functioned like a one room school house. Many years I had 8th-12th in one literature class, but somehow it worked quite well. I really tried to emulate the way Jesus did not seem to care about the background of his followers and friends. They all just walked together, talked together, learned together and everything was equal. He saw them as individuals and sought to relate to them based on how they were created. Ladson-Billings (1994) says:

> In recent years there has been debate about conflicts between what has been regarded as the literary canon and what is historical fact. We now ask if the canon represents a culturally specific set of understandings or objective truths. For example, was the ancient Egyptian civilization black? And did Columbus discover, or conquer, or contact? These kinds of questions should present exciting challenges and learning opportunities. Instead they have lead to vitriolic debates and accusations from all sides about both our educational system and western civilization. (p. 79)

My desire to teach the Great Books class was not rooted in feeling that this collection of books was by any means a main source of knowledge or superior, but rather the books represent a catalyst to engage students in some critical discussions that need to take place with them regarding the culture in which they live. They also serve as a reference point as we seek to construct our own interpretations about the world in which we live. The questions that Ladson-Billings raised in the above text reveals the discussions my students and I had many times within our class. My class sort of had a "face-off" with these texts as we sought to construct our own understanding of human life. Zora eventually came to see value in these controversial texts:

> That is why it is called a "Great Book" because it has a meaning and a take away. It is just not a story like a children's book that you read. A lot of children's books do have meaning, but these books have some type of take away that you can keep. When you talk to someone about it you have something to

> say. A Great Book is a classic because it is timeless. It is not a fad of whatever is popular in that date, but it will reflect every generation and what they are going through.

This is said from a girl who at the beginning of the journey felt isolated from the texts, but then once connecting to African American literature, was able to read the texts with new eyes. The text began to speak to her. The discussions in class allowed her to explore those topics that raised questions for her, and then she was able to re-write the text so that it had meaning for her as an African American woman.

**When the Light Lifts You from a Dark Place**

The students began to dwell in the light of the literature. I call it "light of the literature," because each student came to a place of enlightenment about themselves through one or more pieces of literature that we read and discussed in the class. For Arthur Scott, he came to be in the light after writing the song "Meaningless" which was his way of synthesizing the meaning of Ecclesiastes, *The Count of Monte Cristo* and *Othello*. Evidence of him being in the light can be seen in his reading his first book on his own (without Spark Notes or being pressed by a teacher or parent). He says:

> For me it was *The Count of Monte Cristo*. That book was so big! I started out reading "Spark Notes" because there was no way I was going to read that whole book. In the "Spark Notes" it started saying some crazy stuff and I was like 'He did what? Hold on let me read this.' The right kind of literature

> will grab you and make you want to read more.

When Arthur Scott started the class, he was not really that interested, but just participated to cooperate with what was required of him. He said:

> I would participate and I could engage in the conversations and not have read the assignments the night before. I'd just be making stuff up and everybody would be just agreeing.

However, after the suicide attempt and writing the song "Meaningless," his perspective on the experience began to change. Once Arthur Scott came to see the value of this learning experience he interpreted the assignments and activities of the class differently:

> This class wasn't a bunch of desks speaking to a teacher saying 'Yes madam, no madam.' It was an engagement. The whole year was a long conversation. We had debates and discussions and it wasn't about 'You're right and you're wrong.' It was more of 'Let me show you my point of view' and the other person can also say, 'Let me show you my point of view.' We may clash on some points, but at least we come to see a bigger picture.

As he began to read the literature and become more engaged with the dialogue that took place around the literature, he developed a sense of duty to completing the assignments. He says:

> I saw it as more of a competition, but it wasn't with each other, because it was such a small group we were in. It felt more like

> we were all on the same team. If we didn't read up or do the proper reading it was like we were letting the team down because we could not contribute to the conversation if we didn't read. So it sort of pushed me to engage and do all the reading.

Reflecting on Arthur Scott's retelling of his lived experience and the evolution that began to take place with him as he began to be in the light, causes me to think of the journey that Marva Collins went through to inspire her students to love learning. She was also met with resistance, but through her persistence she was able to see students' attitudes about learning change. She says:

> After the children had filed out the door, Marva found his homework papers on the floor under his desk. This boy had to change his priorities, but she wasn't going to force him. Eventually, with lots of praise and lots of hugging, his defensiveness would melt. The one thing all children wanted was to be accepted for themselves, to feel some self-worth. Once they felt it, children became addicted to learning, and they had the desire to learn forever. (Collins, 1990, p. 92)

Arthur Scott reveals that a fire was born in him through being in the class and that flame was connected to the self-esteem that was developed in him. He says:

> I felt like an educated snob. People would reference a Great Book, and I'm like, 'I read that.' Typical kids our age aren't going to bring up Great Books in a conversation. But because we took the books to a level of analytical examination, we can bring them

> up because we know them so in-depth. It's not like we just read the book, but we know the book because we analyzed every chapter, and had conversation about every chapter. We became fluent in it. I use the word fluency because it literally flows from us. It's not something that we have to work up. I saw the benefits of it. If I just brought up something in a conversation that we read in the Great Books class, it would make me feel more intelligent.

Arthur Scott's self-esteem was increasing as he gained more knowledge. Somehow the process awakened in him a thirst to know. He mentioned that "it literally flows from us." This is how our class was designed. We read literature and then we casually explored the literature through conversation. Many times a student would reference another book that connected to what we were currently reading and that would bring students to looking fervently through past notes and books to contribute more to the conversation. Marva Collins (1990) talks about this when she says, "I hit upon it (knowledge) in a generalized way. I wanted to get my students to see the flow of knowledge" (p. 148). This was not done just to make students feel smarter than others, but I wanted them to see how the literature speaks to the human experience, and that's why they can relate to it. Arthur Scott talks about why he was able to connect to books like *The Peloponnesian War*:

> Reading the Peloponnesian War and all the prequels to Rome was kinda cool because we could look at what was going on in the media and understand. At the time we read that, "300" had just come out. All of the movies coming out at that time, we could

> understand the back story of them. It was like a fad or something. We understood Greek mythology. Reading the actual facts and the actual history in the literature was so cool. It was also cool to be able to go to those movies and be like, 'This movie is totally inaccurate." because I knew the facts about the story.

This to me is how a student is able to take this literature and make it relevant to where they are in society and the culture. Arthur Scott was so excited to be able to have a deeper understanding of the movies that were popular at the time. My belief is that if I just gave them access to this literature, engaged them in conversation about it, then they would be able to connect it to their own lives. In connecting it to their lives, they could add their own perspective to the Great Conversation. Maybe, just maybe, they could desegregate the Great Books?

Marva Collins (1990) resonates with me when she says:

> Many educators and publishers seemed to think that children should not be reading Shakespeare or, for that matter, any other great works of literature. The prevailing thought among the curriculum experts was that the best way to teach inner-city children to read, was through 'realistic' story content…All that 'relevance' undermines the purpose of an education. It doesn't expand the children's horizons or encourage inventiveness or curiosity. Instead, it limits perspectives to the grim scenes they see every day. (pp. 155-156)

The literature provided a way for my students to exercise their minds. Writing about the literature gave them opportunities to explore their own thinking. A student doing this over and over for 1 to 4 years developed an openness of mind that Arthur Scott still has to this day. He says:

> I had writer's block a lot. And having so many assignments where we had to come up with our own stuff was not easy. It wasn't like fill in the blank. There were never worksheets…ever…in that class. Every single thing we ever wrote was from our own mind to a blank sheet of paper. One frustrating thing was just always having writer's block. 'What am I going to write?' It was frustrating at first but I would figure out where I would start. It was always so much content. You never read anything and were like, 'This is this and that is that.' Whatever we read you would allow us to come at it 5 and 12 different angles, so that was hard…Our job was to create our own summary and not use someone else's analysis. You would always talk about having our own writer's voice. I remember someone getting in trouble for that. You could hear our writer's voice in everything we wrote and when we wrote someone else's voice (like Spark Notes), you always knew.

The experience that Arthur Scott had within my class seems to have affected the path he chose for his life currently, and this was the objective of the class—to create lifelong learners. After years of being in the light of my class, he was able to create a life for himself where the skills he developed in the class influenced his current life.

**Fighting to See the Light**

Probably caterpillar thinks it can
Decide which way

It wants to go—to fly or die,
By simply taking an oath and dreaming

Of having the loveliness
Of, say, the male-crow butterfly

Or having the stripes
Of the tiger butterfly

Or maybe stay in the chrysalis stage
Or become a friar butterfly

Caterpillar is a dreamer
And a natural schemer

In this changing light where
Cuticle-shaped drops of fluid

Glow and glow
Like red nectar

Changing itself
As it hangs from the bottom
(Major, 1936)

Earlier in the rendering of this study, I shared a portion of the poem, "On Watching a Caterpillar Become a Butterfly" in reference to Raymond, my very first Great

Books student. In this second portion of the poem, I am struck by the artistic way the author, Clarence Major, unveils the struggle of the caterpillar to break into the light from the chrysalis. Although I was not able to see Ray Charles come into the light while he was in my class, his participation in the study reveals how some students may not come to see the light a teacher is seeking to impart until much later in life.

In our discussions, Ray Charles was able to reveal some retrospective thoughts he had during the time he was in my class. These thoughts revealed a secret process of seeking the higher purpose for the class. Ray Charles says:

> When I was in the class, I honestly did not understand why I was reading these books, but I felt that it was for some reason, so I went ahead and read the books. I understood that I was missing something in the books. I couldn't put my finger on it. I knew that these books had a greater purpose, but at the time I did not know what it was.

This is the reason why I want students to do at least 2 years in this course, preferably 4. There were some preconceived notions he had about the literature. He could only see that they were not written by African American authors. He was not able to see how this literature speaks of the human experience. So, if this was his struggle for him, how much more of a struggle would it be for another student, forced to read only literature that is culturally irrelevant. In *Dreamkeepers* Gloria Ladson-Billings (1994) shares insight from Bernardo M. Ferdman:

> …in a multiethnic society the "cultural framework" for literacy must be considered. Being literate has always referred to having mastery over the processes by means of which culturally significant information is

> coded. In a culturally heterogeneous society, literacy ceases to be a characteristic inherent solely in the individual. It becomes an interactive process that is constantly redefined and renegotiated, as the individual transacts with the socioculturally fluid surroundings. (Ferdman, 1990, pp. 181-204)

It is not just enough to read the Great Books, but it is imperative that there is an equal exchange between this collection of literature and the literature that represents the reader's cultural background. Students must be able to pull their heritage into the dialogue with these books. Ray Charles did not have enough time with me to get the fullness of the mix of Great Books and African American literature. He did not have enough time in the class to appreciate the dialogue they had with each other.

Ray Charles mentioned the one book that he really got into in my class was "Othello." Back when he was in the class, he was instantly connected to the fact that Shakespeare portrayed Othello as a black man. The thing that I also realize is that one day (in college, on a job, etc.) he was going to have to read literature that did not connect to his heritage, and he had to exercise his mind to be able to work through that literature. We are not just citizens of the African American culture, but as Socrates says, we are global citizens. The mix of literature is important, allowing the various cultures and races of America to speak to each other within the Great Conversation.

The class seemed to be torture for Ray Charles. His monologue and how he performed it, revealed as much. He literally fights with his mask during the performance, eventually flinging it on to the floor and trying to walk away. Then, the power of the mask pulls him—drags him back to it. Through a fight between Ray Charles and the mask, the mask takes its place back on his face. He walks back to his seat with heavy feet and head down. The last stanza of "We Wear the Mask" illuminates Ray Charles' struggle to me:

> We smile, but, O great Christ, our cries
> To thee from tortured souls arise.
> We sing, but oh the clay is vile
> Beneath our feet, and long the mile;
> But let the world dream otherwise,
> We wear the mask!

Ray Charles wrestled within. He fought within. He could sense the importance of the class, but the mask would not set him free and he could not free himself. The light for him was connecting to "Othello" and coming to a realization that there is a greater purpose for the Great Books class. It would take Ray Charles until college to discover what that purpose was.

> Ultimately, light is the mother of life. Where there is no light, there can be no life. If the angle of the sun were to turn away from the earth, all human, animal and vegetative life, as we know it, would disappear. Light is the secret presence of the divine. It keeps life awake…the soul awakens and lives in light. It helps us to glimpse the sacred depths within us. (O'Donohue, 1997, p. 5)

**The Lived Experience Shining into the Present**

> The question, 'What calls for thinking?' asks for what wants to be thought about in the preeminent sense: it does not just give us something to think about, nor only itself, but it first gives thought and thinking to us, it entrusts thought to us as our essential

> destiny, and thus first joins and appropriates us to thought. (Heidegger, 1954, p. 391)

The students revealed to me over the course of our weekend conversation that students are actually hungry for freedom—freedom to think and ponder what comes to mind. Maybe it's because this is instinctive for every human? As shared earlier, the school these students belonged to, where the Great Books class was taught, eventually closed down. The students talked about how much they missed the school when it closed. It affected them greatly, and even now they find themselves yearning for this type of space to read, think, question, and discuss. They missed it in some of the schools they had to attend when it closed (only 2 of them actually graduated from the school). They missed it when they went to college, and they miss this type of learning experience in their everyday life. They have all graduated from high school now. Some are finishing college and some are just beginning their college journey. Even still, they miss this space to think and dialogue with others who have the same appreciation for classic literature and critical thought.

**Living a Life of Thought**

In this study each participant has a different story of how the lived experience of reading Great Books literature has affected them after leaving my class and the school where I taught. Sophia's story is very unique because she left the school for a year and then came back for her senior year. Although this section seeks to discuss how the lived experience of reading Great Books literature has affected her currently, I feel it is necessary to start at the point when she left the school, and then work up to where she is presently. Sophia shared this about leaving the school:

> At times I was like "Oh God, why do we have to read these Great Books. When I went to another school or even when I went to PG Community College we had to bring that stuff back up and I am like "I already know about this." Other students would say, "I don't want to read this 300 page book. It was nothing to us because we did already. We read Shakespeare plays like "King Lear" and you had us write our own plays and sonnets. It helped with creativity and built confidence.

Sophia came back to the school for her senior year and she had to complete a thesis. For my class, the thesis was required for all high schoolers to complete each year from 9th-12th grade. Most schools only require a senior thesis, but I felt that African American students need more opportunities to practice this skill as they prepare for college and beyond, so I required it for all 4 years. I made different requirements for each grade level, but they all had to do it. Sophia's senior thesis was more involved than the other high school students, but she was up for the challenge and she reflected on that experience:

> When we were writing the thesis, you made us prove our point. We had to come from the point of view that someone might argue. We had to refute the argument that someone else might have. Now I think before I put a person on blast. I think of how they might come at it. I do it in life without even thinking about it…I just got into a debate with a guy in a car. He had the nerve to say that black men had it worse than black women. So I throw his points back at him. I

> feel that's what we learned in the Great
> Books class.

To hear Sophia speak of how engaging in the Great Books affected her ability to debate and discuss with others in her everyday life, was so revealing. I think of how the Great Books are rhetoric in action (Wise & Wise-Bauer, 1999). She continued to express how her lived experience has affected her current life:

> …reading the Great Books kind of made
> you think about certain things in a certain
> way and then when I went to another school,
> they're like, 'Oh Sophia, you're
> overthinking things or thinking about things
> in an analytical way.' Okay, but this is how
> I've been taught to think about these things.
> I don't see nothing wrong with this, but with
> people it is a turn-off and it's hard to build
> friendships. They're like, 'Why do you
> always have to think like this?' Sorry I
> think.

I was so eager to open students' minds to a new way of learning, that I failed to realize how much of a minority they were. It was not until the students like Sophia told me how their friends and students from other schools they attended were not having these same school experiences, that I realized that maybe this experience was also isolating them.

Realizing this isolation that Sophia expressed made me think of Socrates. He was often isolated as people thought him so strange for spending so much time in thought. Heidegger (1968) expresses how this isolation occurs:

> Once we are so related and drawn to what
> withdraws, we are drawing into what

> withdraws, into the enigmatic and therefore mutable nearness of its appeal. Whenever man is properly drawing that way, he is thinking—even though he may still be far away from what withdraws, even though the withdrawal may remain as veiled as ever. All through his life and right into his death, Socrates did nothing else than place himself into a draft, this current, and maintain himself in it. This is why he is the purest thinker of the West. This is why he wrote nothing. (pp. 381-382)

Sophia's curiosity had been aroused so much that just about any question or topic that was raised drew her along like an entranced rabbit to a carrot on a string into a current of wonder. As the thought presents itself to her, she is pulled along to explore it, as it withdraws from her. This withdrawal to me is that unanswered question. The theme of this study and my inspiration has been Heidegger's short poem, "To think is to confine yourself to a single thought that one day stands still like a star in the world's sky." I see this happening for Sophia as she engages in her daily life. That sense of wonder was stirred in her and although to me it is a beautiful thing to see, it has isolated her. She is willing to take the time to follow the withdrawal to explore it, while others may not be so interested in going on that journey. Because of this isolation, she does have some personal struggles:

> I started thinking, 'What is wrong with me?' Everyone else is into other things, but I overthink stuff. I'd rather think about the necessities of life and enlightenment…it made me lower myself…Now I find myself going to a party. Not to fit in, but to feel close to somebody. If you are up here all

> the time and the party is happening down here, you are like, 'Let me come down here a little bit.' That's what I'm struggling with. I'm trying to remember that I don't have to be ignorant, but I can bring them to where I am. I guess that is where I falter.

On the other hand, this sense of wonder and in-depth thinking and her ability to follow it through to gain knowledge and understanding, has affected her performance on her job and in school. She is able to share in the staff meetings or even help her older sister with her college assignments. She gave an example of this:

> When we sit around the table at Fannie Mae, they want you to contribute something…before you know it they are like, 'That's very interesting…' Back then, we were like, 'Why can't we just get the answers? Why can't we just do a worksheet? Why we gotta do all that?' But it really helps your work ethic. Because I'm so used to all this heavy work, so when the teacher gives me a little somethin'-somethin', everyone is complaining and I am done. I finished it and it is done. My older sister was in college and was like, 'I gotta write a 15 page paper.' I was like, 'I can help you with that.'

So currently, even though there is that personal struggle of knowing how to balance her sense of wonder with how to fit in with her peers and their common interests, she is still able to see the benefit of her lived experience to her overall life. One of her final statements to me really expresses how her lived experience is lighting her present life: "You lit a torch to a path."

> "Every thought that you have is a flint moment, a spark of light from your inner darkness…" (O'Donohue, 1997, p. 4)

**Finally Free to Think**

Currently Zora is working for Navy Federal and completing her accounting degree at the University of Maryland. Her plan is to open her own boutique. She chose to go into accounting so that she would know how to run it. She has come a long way from that inner struggle of wanting to know what to do with her creative self. The struggle that Zora went through while being in my class was not something she went through alone. I struggled with her. It is something that she misses now while she is in school. She says:

> You don't have someone literally being on the verge of tears because you're not doing what you're supposed to do. It's not that important to them. They're like, 'I want to give you a grade.' And that's it. But you were like, 'You are going to get an A in this class. You can do it.' Having that I didn't really realize it back then…You're sitting there with tears in your eyes and I'm trying not to cry too. But now I can see that it definitely helped and it is missing in college. You don't get that. The role you played with me, I have to play that with myself in college. It taught me to think about the consequences of not doing well in school.

Zora's way of thinking that was developed through engaging in my class also affects her social life (as it did with Sophia). I think of how she thought critically about what to major in for college (accounting), so that she could run her own fashion boutique, and I realize that she is different from her peers. Over the years she has worked for banks and in the accounting departments of various businesses in order to stay in constant practice of how to manage money. At just 22 years of age she already has a very full resume and loads of experience on how to manage a company's finances. She recognizes that she is different as well:

> I think this came from you teaching us how to think independently, on our own…learning how to do things on our own and thinking and asking questions. And once you start doing that you start thinking a whole different way. Me and my friends, we think completely different, especially the ones that went to public schools and I am not saying there aren't any good public schools, but the way they think and the way I think is like we are on two different pedestals. I don't think that I'm better than anyone else, but I just think in a whole different way. It is sometimes hard for me to understand why they don't think that way. How could they not think this way?

She sees the positive influence of being in a class like this. Even though we were discussing literature and expressing our understanding through discussion, creative writing and theatre, the skills developed in this class flowed into her current life as she charted her career path. She is thinking. She is "critically conscious" (Boal, 1994). This all came about as she regularly read, discussed, wrote plays, and collaborated to create productions. We consistently and ferociously pursued the act of thinking, and this practice spilled into her current life. Boal (1994) says:

> While he rehearses throwing a bomb on stage, he is concretely rehearsing the way a bomb is thrown; acting out his attempt to organize a strike, he is concretely organizing a strike. Within its fictitious limits, the experience is a concrete one...Forum theatre, as well as these other forms of a people's theatre, instead of taking something away from the spectator, evoke in him a desire to practice in reality the act he has rehearsed in the theatre. The practice of these theatrical forms creates a sort of uneasy sense of incompleteness that seeks fulfillment through real action. (pp.141-142)

When the students did theatre, I did not come with a script and director's notes ready and just tell students how to create the production. I had them create it all themselves. This is the kind of theatre that Boal created with his participants. Of course he was referring to politicial emancipation, but I connect it to my students—to Zora and her journey to being emancipated to think for herself.

In creating the plays, my only stipulation for the students creating the plays, was that the play had to be connected to what they were reading in my class. So they were not only thinking as they read; they were not only thinking as they worked on their essays. But, they had to think in order to create a production that reflected understanding of what was read. My whole program was a practice in perpetual thinking. As Boal seeks to explain above, when you are constantly acting out a certain process, it eventually becomes reality. The class was a crucible for developing thinkers who would go out into society, be able to thrive and hopefully make an impact. Zora has revealed this to me in my journey to capturing her lived experience.

Unfortunately, Zora has the same struggles as Sophia in her social life. She says:

> I think it is a struggle for most of us. Especially when it comes to guys or girls. It's like we are not on the same level. Especially if they did not come up the same way we did. Conversations are like…like with a boyfriend…you want to be able to have conversations with them about everything. And if you want to talk to them about something that has to do with Great Books or something on a different level and they want to talk about shoes. I don't mind talking about shoes, but I also want to talk about poetry. I like to go in depth on stuff like that. It's hard because there's not a lot of kids that came up like this.

This makes me want to pick up where we left off. So far two of the students have expressed feeling isolated from their peers because of how their mind works. They have attributed their thinking to their experience being in my class. It makes me wonder if there should be some way to continue to nurture this within them, to provide an outlet for connection and comradery with others who feel the same way about thinking, literature, etc. I think they feel alone because they are African American and have this interest in still engaging in the Great Books within their cultural context. It is rare to find African American students who have been through this process. For Zora there is the interest in African American literature, but there is also still that desire to connect her cultural transcript to other texts that may not reflect her race and culture. It appears the impact on Zora was great, and although the light of her lived experiences continues to shine through into her present, she is left in this lonely state of wonder.

**The EnLIGHTened Man**

"Of the Training of Black Men" has formed a foundation for my research, and several excerpts from that text have been sprinkled throughout this study. Arthur Scott, I feel is an embodiment of what Du Bois was looking for in the education of the African American people, specifically African American men. Reflecting on Arthur Scott has brought this essay back to the forefront of my mind, especially when I connect Arthur Scott's thoughts on his lived experience to this particular part of the essay:

> Hampton is still a high school, while Fisk University started her college in 1871, and Spelman Seminary about 1896. In all cases the aim was identical—to maintain the standards of the lower training by giving teachers and leaders the best practicable training; and above all, to furnish the black world with adequate standards of human culture and lofty ideals of life. It was not enough that the teachers of teachers should be trained in technical normal methods; they must also, so far as possible, be broad-minded, cultured men and women, to scatter civilization among a people whose ignorance was not simply of letters, but of life itself. (Du Bois, 2005, pp. 97-98)

As Arthur Scott shared how engaging in these texts opened his mind to the life and culture in which he lived, his lived experience expresses the fullness of what I had hoped would happen for my students through reading Great Books literature.

I understand that Du Bois is from many years ago and so, I have sought to find another source or example that could serve as a reflection of what I saw develop in Arthur Scott. Surprisingly, I found that reflection in Barak Obama. Just recently a dear friend of mine sent me several articles about Barak Obama and his "reading list." She thought I would be interested in what the article had to say. I almost flew to the stars as I read these articles. Obama says, "I love traditional books." And then he goes on to list some of his favorites: T*reasure Island, Of Mice and Men, The Great Gatsby, Self Reliance, Moby Dick*, Shakespeare's Tragedies, and many more (Lerner, 2015). In another article, however, I was able to get even more details of his comprehensive reading list, and the list revealed his habit of including the works of African American authors such as James Baldwin, Ralph Ellison, Langston Hughes, Richard Wright and W. E. B. Du Bois (Kakutani, 2009). He read these texts as a teenager in order to come to terms with his racial identity. Then while he was in college, he read the works of Nietzsche and St. Augustine in a spiritual-intellectual search to figure out what he truly believed (Kakutani). Obama's broad acceptance of literature and refusing to allow color lines to segregate him from the ancient authors has contributed to how he has been able to communicate to the American people and the world. He tends to take a magpie approach to reading — ruminating upon writers' ideas and picking and choosing those that flesh out his vision of the world or open promising new avenues of inquiry (Kakutani, 2009).

I wonder if Arthur Scott will have a similar impact on the culture because of how he allowed the Great Books to help shape his thinking, especially as he made personal and cultural connections with the literature? I ask this because of how Arthur Scott articulated his current goals and interests. He says:

> Currently I am interested in broadcast journalism. I really want to do film, but there are not a lot of strong film programs

> out there. When I told my dad I was going to do film, he said that I was not going to make a lot of money. No one thinks I can make good money with film, so I have to show them that I can make good money with film. The reason why I want to do film so bad is because I see the influence that it has on our society and our culture. The way we talk, what we wear, our fashion, our dialect, etc. is influenced by the media and film. I've always wanted to be a leader. I've wanted to have influence over a lot of people. I see that film has the real leaders of the world, because they program us and they program what we're supposed to be thinking. I remember reading through "Othello" and I thought about it as I have been pursuing doing film. Othello showed how characters are developed. All characters fit a character model. How Othello and Iago, those iconic characters, were portrayed is what we see in everyday movies and TV. They are the original of that.

Unfortunately, Arthur Scott was the only one of the participants that I did not graduate. The school where my class was held closed the summer before his senior year. When the school closed, I was hired as the head of school for a DC Christian school and most of my students followed me there. Arthur Scott could not come because he was so far advanced in his classes. His senior schedule could not fit into the program, so he had to go to another school. This school also had a program that studied Great Books (although the philosophy was quite different, not using discussion and the arts to engage the students), so my students were able to continue their studies of the Great Books on some level. I was not the English teacher, but the teacher and I worked together to design the reading list. When Arthur Scott went on to another school, I believe that is when he came to really miss the class. He shared the following thoughts about this transition to a new school:

> The difference between your class and the new school I went to is that I could not cheat in your class. At the new school, everybody was cheating, and I'm like, 'Why are you all cheating? What are you doing?' It was just a normal thing! And then I graduated and went on to college and ALL of them are cheaters! Every last student was cheating. They actually said at one exam, 'We pass together, we fail together. If you got the answers, slide them back.' What? That's unheard of! But for your class, there are not clear cut answers. There was no 'This is right and this is wrong.' It was all about what you took away from it. Our educational system involves herding the masses. We are just trying to put a bunch of kids in the system. Cook it up. All right next kids come in. But in your class and at the school where we were, there is a total difference. We were like it was with Socrates and his students, being taught one on one or in small groups. And we learned through having a relationship and understanding with each other.

Arthur Scott shared some of the same struggles as Zora and Sophia, such as developing meaningful relationships (platonic and romantic). It has been hard for him to develop relationships that allow for him to engage in deep conversation and reflection as he enjoyed in the class. Like Sophia and Zora, he sometimes feels that he has to dumb himself down in order to have some type of connection with others. I do not think these students mean to feel superior to others, but they recognize that many of their peers are just not into the type of conversations they would like to have about literature, human nature, culture and society. Another struggle for Arthur Scott was getting used to more structure and meeting deadlines in a more traditional school setting. He says:

> When I made the transition to another school from doing all the reading, I noticed the more structured the new class was. The Great Books class was very open and very conversational. If you did not get a chance to complete the reading assignments in your class, you would just give us more time. You did that because you wanted to make sure everyone got the information before moving forward and so we could all engage in the conversation. Sometimes you would just let us all read in class and that would set us back about a week. Then I transferred to another school and if I missed an assignment there were consequences.

So, although the class impacted Arthur Scott in a positive way, there were some negative points to the relaxed structure of the class. I desire to make learning an enjoyable experience for students; however, the relaxed nature of it did not quite prepare them for a different school with more structure, or even for college. I seemed to "mother" the students a bit too much and that was also something Arthur Scott missed when he went to college:

> When I went to college and I would think about how your voice would sound so

> disappointed in us when we didn't do our work. In college, we don't have someone to do that but we still have a memory of that. I would say to myself, 'Let me go ahead and get these grades right so that I can come home and not have anyone mad at me or disappointed in me.'

On the other hand, the connection that was developed from being in the class gave Arthur Scott and the others a sense of duty. This sense of duty motivated them to do what was needed to succeed eventually, even though the school and class structure were different from that which they were accustomed.

Arthur Scott's lived experience revealed so many ways where the light of his experience shone into the present. It affected the career path he chose for himself. It affected his inner battle with depression. It affected his sense of duty as he moved on to other educational institutions. It also affected his overall mindset as he learned to engage with the society and culture in which he lived.

**Retrospective Light Shining Forward**

At the time this study was done, Ray Charles was a sophomore at a local university. He had just changed his major to kinesiology. He was also a gymnast for an acrobatics group, where his group performs for local high schools in Maryland. He was a very different person. In fact, when I saw him for the first time (it had been several years), I hardly recognized him. He seemed at peace with himself. I used to notice the "wall" that the mask created between him and me. During the question and answer period after "The Table," I mentioned to the audience that there would be times where a teacher may not reach a student, but you cannot let it discourage you. Immediately, Ray Charles interrupted my comment and shared how I in fact did impact him. It just didn't become apparent until later.

Ray Charles talks about how he and I were able to have discussions with each other that took him out of his comfort zone. This experience gave him courage in college:

> Your class really helped me be more assertive with my thoughts. Even now, when I go in for an interview or an internship, I don't hesitate to ask questions I need to ask. In the gymnast club, I will approach the coach and discuss any of my routines.

In no way did I expect that the students' lived experience would affect them in this way, especially a student who remained so resistant through the entire time he took my class. I find so much inspiration in Marva Collins. I have shared an excerpt earlier about one of her students who also resisted her teaching. I find Marva Collins inspiring because her skill was no magic trick. She just simply demonstrated patience, persistence, kindness and respect for the student. She talks about her student again:

> As the weeks passed, Gary found it difficult to remain hostile. No matter how many times he shouted to me, "I hate you and I'm not going to do the work," I always answered, "I love you all the time, even when you behave like this." I guess it took the fun out of fighting. A fair fight was one thing; taking swipes at someone who wasn't fighting back was quite another. Gradually

> Gary began to do the work. (Collins, 1990, p. 99)

The students talked about how my relaxed format made it a bit of a challenge to adjust to a more structured educational setting, and so I asked them how I could include better preparation for that within my class structure. Arthur Scott felt that the class prepared them to be able to know how to think and make the adjustments on their own. Ray Charles agreed:

> I agree. The university I attend is huge and predominately white. When I started to struggle with my grades, I was able to go visit the teachers during their office hours. I was able to take the initiative to talk to them. It's up to the student to get the help that they need.

Ray Charles seems to take me away from just the books being "great." Because he connected more with the skills that he obtained as opposed to appreciating the literature, I am seeing another aspect to the class. What did the students gain from the class with regards to skills that could help them in other facets of their life? Ray Charles gave another example of how being in the class taught him how to think and strategize in order to figure out how to get his grades up when he fell into academic probation:

> For all the first semester it was terrible. Grade-wise I really wasn't doing anything. My martial arts I really wasn't doing that. I was getting caught up in other things to do. Just wasting my time. When I fell into academic probation, I recognized it wasn't for no reason. I said to myself, 'Let me take a step back and see what is going on here.' I could see a trend of getting involved with

> things that did not build me up. So I sat down and picked apart ways I can build myself up. I want to be great. I don't care about being known, but I want to have something I can do that I can say I am great. I just picked apart what I could do to accomplish that. I looked at what I needed to take out of my life and went from there.

He gave another example of how the process of learning to think in my class, helped him to chart out his career path:

> At first my major was business. The school I was in, is one of the top business schools in the nation. It's all about trying to turn a profit. It's true that a business needs to turn a profit to survive, but they are teaching that it should be done by any means necessary. I want to help people. This is why I started looking into doing some type of therapy. I want to help people in a gym train in martial arts. I want to help them get into their craft, so they can make their own craft. The business school I was in was teaching me to not care about people. The first business class I took, I was taught that I should invest in cigarette companies because their stocks are always rising. I don't like that! I've learned what I need to know from the books and those things will help me be an entrepreneur, but I needed to get out of that atmosphere and put myself inside of one that's about helping people.

Ray Charles also shared that his interest in forming a gym for stunt and martial arts training started when he had to do stunts for the plays at the school. The play where he was used to do stunts was "The Room" based upon "Othello" and "The Count of Monte Cristo." Ray Charles developed the courage to let his voice be heard. This was his greatest struggle in my class. He also wrestled with connecting to literature that was not connected to his culture, but he also shared that in being exposed to this literature he learned to articulate his thoughts and feelings in a way where his voice can be heard no matter what race he is speaking to. In an earlier chapter I write about this where I quote Lisa Delpit (2001):

> They also seek to teach students about those who have taken the language born in Europe and transformed it into an emancipatory vehicle. In the mouths and pens of Bill Trent, Clarence Cunningham, bell hooks, Henry Louis Gates, Paul Lawrence Dunbar and countless others, the "language of the master" has been used for liberatory ends. Students can learn of that rich legacy, and they can also learn that they are its inheritors and rightful heirs. (p. 301)

I am also reminded of when Frederick Douglass spoke of how reading Cicero and others of the Great Books gave him the words to speak against slavery in a language that all men—all races—could receive.

It was important for me to include a student in my study that I felt I had failed. This is the reality of this journey. We may seem not to win them all, but with persistence, patience, kindness and respect, you never know how your teaching will affect a student down the road. This has been one of my greatest lessons in this journey. As Ray Charles shared how the light of my class shines into his present, I realize that the sun may be hidden behind a cloud for a while, but eventually the rays will burst forth, breaking through the cloud to reveal its light.

> Once human beings began to search for a meaning to life, light became one of the most powerful metaphors to express the eternity and depth of life…In the Western tradition…thought has often been compared to light. In its luminosity, the intellect was deemed to be the place of the divine within us. (O'Donohue, 1997, p. 5)

## Other Light Sources

It was imperative that I search through all the sources of light available to me, in seeking to get at the essence of the lived experience. I had to look at each student who agreed to participate, regardless of how much or little they contributed to the conversation and the project overall. I had to look within myself as well, to gain another source of light for understanding the lived experience.

### Fragments of Light

Every Star is Different

Ev'ry star is diff'rent,
And so is ev'ry child.
Some are bright and happy,
And some are meek and mild.
Ev'ry one is needed
For just what he can do.
You're the only person
Who ever can be you.
(Cameron, 1951)

There was one more participant in my study, and I had initially considered not including him in this rendering. He did not talk as much or as openly as the others, and he chose not to participate in the play at the last minute. I felt that he would not offer as much illumination of the lived experience as the others. However, upon reviewing the transcriptions, I was able to see glimmers of light that would open up yet another perspective on the lived experience. Van Manen (1997) says:

> Hermeneutic phenomenology is a philosophy of the personal, the individual, which we pursue against the background of an understanding of the evasive (oh so evasive…as discussed earlier) character of the *logos* of *other*, the *whole,* the communal, or the *social*. Much of educational research tends to pulverize life into minute abstracted fragments and particles that are of little use to practitioners…Its particular appeal is that it tries to understand the phenomena of education by maintaining a view of pedagogy as an expression of the whole. (p. 7)

The whole concept of constellating involves someone looking at a group of stars—different stars and connecting the dots to form one whole image. It doesn't matter how bright the star shines, or its shape, or its color. Connecting each star together creates an image. The image I am seeking to create should reveal a wholistic look into the lived experience of African American students reading Great Books literature, with varying attributes contributed by the individuals who have taken this journey to discovery with me. I must leave no stone unturned, no fragment of light ignored. Van Manen (1997) says, "We need to search everywhere in the lifeworld for lived experience material that, upon reflective examination, might yield something of its fundamental nature" (p. 53). So, I decided to include Zeke. I also realized that by including Zeke a very clear and straightforward evolution can be articulated.

When I first reviewed the transcriptions, there were very few moments when Zeke spoke in the discussion. It was hard to place his words within the study as the rest of the participants, and yet, the few words he spoke were powerful. He revealed his determination not to participate in the class discussions. He says:

> Throughout your classes, I would not say anything. I was determined not to say anything.

This was a constant battle between Zeke and me. I met with his parents about it. I met with him about it, and yet he would not open up until he was ready. I asked Zeke what caused him to begin to open up more and he shared with me his turning point:

> I got more comfortable. I read more and I had more I could say. Maybe in the beginning I didn't read the full books all the way through…*1984* for me was the turning point. I don't like to read books, but that one was kind of interesting. It made me want to read the whole thing. That world that they were in made me think.

*1984* was a turning point for Zeke because it gave him confidence that he could read and enjoy a book. He says:

> *1984* was the most memorable book to me because it is the first book in your class that I read in its entirety. The way I took a book in your class is that I would read the first

> several pages and say 'I'm not reading this…Spark Notes!' But that one I started reading it and I couldn't stop reading it or go to Spark Notes because I just wanted to keep going. It was an interesting story to me and I just wanted to keep going back. After reading it, I thought, 'I can do it now.' Before that, I thought the books were too long and not exciting. I didn't think that I could go through a full book. Now I felt that I could read books and they would be interesting.

There is something in finishing a book. It is a powerful moment, and I can identify because I recall the feeling of accomplishment I had when I read my first book without having to be forced. It unlocked a passion in me for the written word. For Zeke it was the catalyst to becoming an actual reader, and that transition also motivated him to begin to open up in the class discussions.

Zeke's frustration with school seemed to relate to how his natural instinct of thinking was interrupted. Heidegger (1968) says that thought is our "essential destiny." Thinking called for him—pulled at him, and school interfered with him heeding the call of thought. Because of this constant interruption, Zeke did not like school, and his dislike for school affected his attitude about the class:

> All throughout high school I did not like school at all. I really hated it. If someone were to ask me, I would say, 'No I'm not ready to go back to school.' It was because of that I didn't do well as I could have done. I didn't work that hard in school. I liked to do stuff on my own. All my work, I never asked for help and it's the same now in

> college. When I started to play the piano, I taught myself. I didn't take lessons, but I just taught myself. At that time I just liked to do a lot of stuff on my own…learn stuff by myself and just try to make it on my own through school.

One of the last comments that Zeke made to me that I felt really spoke volumes, was when he connected his experience in my class with his current performance now studying computer engineering in college:

> In school, in class, with computer technology my professor will give us an assignment and you have to figure out how to do it on your own. Last semester, my whole class would come to me for help in trying to figure stuff out. I didn't know why they couldn't see what I was seeing. They couldn't break stuff down and figure it out on their own. They just didn't think the way I did about everything.

Zeke felt that the readings and discussions of the class helped to exercise and develop this ability within him. His thoughts are significant because it speaks to those moments when teachers have a student that they feel is unreachable. The walls that they have up seem impenetrable, but with persistence, it is possible to break through somehow, and you may not realize it until much later. He developed an interest in reading more, and he began to engage in more discussion and writing. The skills he developed within this class gave him the critical thinking skills he needed to perform well in his computer engineering courses. This account drew me to the following haiku:

> A seed is planted
> In the warm darkness, it grows

Heading to the sky
(Pancoon, 2014)

Hearing Zeke share with me was so inspiring because it spoke to those dark moments we often have as teachers when faced with a student that seems unreachable. However, if we remain strong for the course, never giving up, remaining consistent, the light will break forth and the "Zekes" of our classes will finally speak.

**Behind My Mask**

I think one major part of this study that revealed how much these students had benefited from their lived experience of being in the class, is when they participated in the discussion after the performance of "The Table" at St. Johns. In chapter four I shared how my students stepped up to respond to those questions and they surprised me by wanting to answer the audience's questions. I was prepared to respond, but they all came forward and asked if they could answer the questions instead. It was amazing to see these former students of mine articulate what happened in the class and what they felt the purpose of the class was, especially since we had not spoken about the class since they graduated years before. I stood there in awe, reflecting on the struggle of getting these same students to want to read and engage, reflecting on the insecurity and uncertainty I felt in going through that process. They had no idea how difficult it was for me back then.

During our weekend conversation, the participants said that they did not think I wore a mask; however, I did wear a mask. There was so much uncertainty and insecurity along this path. These feelings often gave way to fear and frustration. Many times, I would cry at night with my husband, unsure if this passion I had for these students to read these texts was worth pursuing. I had no idea that it was their own inner struggles that were making it hard for me to move them forward into the books initially. I felt this wall between us in the class. Even though the literature was having an effect on them, they somehow kept it from me. I was only able to see small glimmers of light along the journey. These glimmers, however, became my Polaris, drawing me into wondering about the possibilities of what this lived experience could entail. Now I understand that the wall between was a mask, and that mask was being infiltrated by engaging in the books through reading and discussion. The power of these pages, the words of these Great Books cutting through their fears, insecurities, and inner wars, became so apparent that weekend where we all came together to share about the **lived experiences of African American students reading Great Books literature.** The power of these pages brought about this epiphany over that weekend, and also opened my eyes to new perspectives on literacy education, and my future in education overall.

In These Pages
There is so much to glean from the ancient folk
There is so much to learn from those who spoke
Centuries ago.
It is different for every person
How the books connect to your soul
But they will if you let them
And it may take time to reflect them
Doesn't matter the color of your skin
Look deep inside you will find that you are in
The pages spoken of by the sages of your humanity
It's plain to see and if you can't
I understand
You see others have struggled too

But we all had to invite Hurston, DuBois,
Woodson or Wheatley
To speak for us, so let them guide you
Let them ask the questions that reveal
How these books speak what's true
About your humanness
Let the process cultivate your mind
To be able to know beyond what's read
between the lines
Talk about it, with a friend
or not
Draw close to a stranger of a different shade
Or not
but is of the same specie—
Woman or man the whole lot
Of humanity
Can be found in these pages
(Prather, 2016)

# CHAPTER 6:
# FREEDOM'S LIGHT

From "The Caged Bird"

The caged bird sings
with a fearful trill
of things unknown
but longed for still
and his tune is heard
on the distant hill
for the caged bird
sings of freedom…

But a caged bird stands on the grave of
dreams
his shadow shouts on a nightmare scream
his wings are clipped and his feet are tied
so he opens his throat to sing.
(Angelou,
http://www.poetryfoundation.org/poem/178
948)

What does it mean to be free? What does it mean to set something or someone free? The most ancient root of the word "free" means "beloved, friend, to love." In this journey to exploring the lived experiences of my students I discovered that they all felt that at the very root of what I was giving them was my love for them. It was my love for them that inspired me to want to free them. When I started the journey, I did not realize that is what I was doing, nor did I realize that my love for the students is what was driving me. What was I freeing them from?

When I review their writing I see a common thread. I asked the question at the very beginning of the weekend we were together: "What is the most memorable thing to you about the class?" They were then asked to write it down. I gave them some time to work through their responses and then we shared them. One of the most common phrases they each said in their written responses was "…leaving or coming out of my comfort zone." Who would ever think that someone would need freeing from a place that brings comfort? The word comfort means a "feeling of relief" and the word zone means "to gird." These two words almost have opposing messages. One expresses some sort of release and the other expresses tension or tightening. In Zora's monologue, she expressed how she always had so much to say in her mind, but was afraid to express it. When I would turn to her and ask "So what are you thinking?" it always frustrated her. It was so much easier for her to stay in her mind. Yet, once she was able to release what she was thinking and feeling about the text, there came a sense of freedom. So what do I understand to be freedom? What is this place of freedom?

### Freedom as an Illumined Space

> Reading is not equivalent to living. Nevertheless, to live free, you must learn to read as you have never read before: "Those who have not learned to read the ancient classics in the language in which they are written must have a very imperfect knowledge of the history of the human race; for it is remarkable that no transcript has ever been made of them in any modern tongue, unless our civilization itself may be regarded as such a transcript." Walden summons us to "our" true citizenship one reader at a time. What if each American took personal responsibility to read "the

> transcript" of "our civilization"? What if the truth of this logos lay alertly and heroically upon every American tongue, speaking to the questions, "How to live and What to do?" (Townsend, 2015, p. 19)

To illuminate an understanding of freedom, I draw upon "Freedom upon an Achillean Shore" by David Townsend (2015) to help make the connection to the Great Books classroom. The article reveals the author's connection to Henry David Thoreau's *Walden,* and I connect to his writing because of his practice of in-depth reading and quiet, yet intense reflection. *Walden* was based upon his written reflections as he lived in a simple cabin he built on Walden Pond (located on the property of Ralph Waldo Emerson). He resided there for two years in order to "…not live cheaply, nor to live dearly there, but to transact some private business with the fewest obstacles" (Atkinson, 1992, p. vi). Thoreau intended for *Walden* to be the fullest expression of his philosophy (Atkinson, 1992, p. vi), wherein he wrote: "Be a Columbus to whole new continents and worlds within you, opening new channels, not of trade, but of thought" (in Atkinson, p. vi). I will also connect passages of O'Donohue's *Anam Cara* to the phenomenon.

**The Circle of Freedom**

> We are lonely and lost in our hungry transparency. We desperately need a new and gentle light where the soul can shelter and reveal its ancient belonging. (O'Donohue, 1997, p. 4)

When my students and I embarked on the journey of reading the "transcripts of our civilization" (Townsend,

2015), freedom stripped us of our skin color, our cultural backgrounds, and even our socio-economic status. All we were left with was a text and sitting around a table in what I like to call a Circle of Freedom. While dwelling there, we allowed the light of the texts, our lives and personal experiences to unveil new places of understanding. No papers, no worksheets, no red pens to mark answers right or wrong. There was only "us" and the texts and we did as Townsend (2015) implores us to do in his tribute to Thoreaux's *Walden*, "…to live free, you must learn to read as you have never read before" (p. 19).

By abiding in our Circle of Freedom, we bonded together, a bond, that has remained even after graduation. The bond is so meaningful that the participants in the study even have struggled with feeling alone because there are no peers with whom to enjoy the same type of dialogue. The Circle of Freedom is powerful like that. We became as O'Donohue (1997) has said, each other's *Anam Cara*—"soul friend." This passage from O'Donohue describes the illumined transformation that happened between the group of "soul friends" in this study as we all engaged together around the literature years ago:

> When the human mind began to consider the next greatest mystery of life, the mystery of love, light was also always used as a metaphor for its power and presence. When love awakens in your life, in the night of your heart, it is like the dawn breaking within you. Where before there was anonymity, now there was intimacy; where before there was fear, now there is courage; where before in your life there was awkwardness, now there is a rhythm of grace and gracefulness; where before you used to be jagged… (p. 6)

As we traversed the books, questioned them, questioned ourselves and questioned each other, an intimacy grew between us, that freed us to explore the truth about ourselves. I recall Sophia having doubts about Christianity. She mentioned this in the study and how she realized I was giving her the space to go through that process. She was allowed to voice these questionings in our discussions, in a Christian school sitting around a table, discussing a text (many times the Bible), in the Circle of Freedom. The bond that was forged has remained over the years so that when her mom died suddenly after she graduated, when she saw me at the funeral, she hugged me tightly, held my hand and we stood together to view the body. The Circle of Freedom does this to those who allow themselves to dwell there. It draws us closer together, students and teacher, in an *Anam Cara* relationship, as we explore our humanity through the humans who have gone before us and written about their human experience.

The word "circle" originally comes from the Latin *circul* which means "a group of persons surrounding a certain interest." Our interest was exploring the Great Books together and seeing how those texts speak into our lives today. Although it initially was a required class, students found themselves reading the texts sometimes in the privacy of their bedrooms, outside of the assigned readings. They came in to class ready to ask a question or to talk about a perspective they gained in reading. This brought us together and soon it did not seem like a class to me or to them. It evolved into our Circle of Freedom, a free space to become illumined within ourselves. Henry David Thoreau, expresses my thoughts on this when he says,

> Direct your eye right inward, and you'll find
> A thousand regions in your mind
> Yet undiscovered. Travel them, and be
> Expert in home-cosmography.

(Thoreau, 1954/1992, p. 300)

When we came together in the Circle of Freedom, the questioning that is shared in the dialogue around the Great Books, causes each of us to explore not just the perspectives of the authors, or others taking part in the Circle of Freedom, but it causes us to look inward at our own personal perspectives. In doing this, we develop this reciprocal sharing with ourselves, those in the Circle and the authors of these texts. Maybe in doing this we learned to open our hearts to new perspectives. Maybe we became confirmed in what we held to be true and drew others into what we each believed. Maybe we learned tolerance of others who may not share our perspectives. As O'Donohoe (1990) says, "We are always on a journey from darkness to light…" and doing this inner search through reading the Great Books, dialogue and self-introspection—this process of home-cosmography—maybe drew us into the light.

**Freedom within a Cultural Space**

> Resist giving away your life to those who would dominate and master you, and your rewards will be great. In Thoreau's parable, the artist's "Singleness of purpose and resolution, and his elevated piety endowed him, without his knowledge, with perennial youth."…But you are no one's disciple. Not even Thoreau's. Never, never, never surrender your own life in order to live someone else's. (Townsend, 2015, p. 18)

At the start of this journey to understanding my students' lived experiences reading Great Books literature, I called upon the life of Frederick Douglass as a blue print for the African American's journey to reading the Great

Books. I revealed how he first became free in his mind before ever obtaining physical freedom. He had a "singleness of purpose and resolution" in moving forward to liberation. His study of the classics (Cicero being one of his favorite authors), aided him in that process. The master told him he could not ever learn to read, but as a 6 year old boy, he determined that he had to do it at any cost. I identify with Douglass in that I often have been told that this literature is not for me, my students, or any other African American, but I refused to let the boundary line of skin color deter me from finding the beauty and relevance of these texts to myself or my students. I may be Black, with kinky hair and have graduated from Howard University, but this was my life, my choice, my path and these books have beckoned for me. I am not my skin color. I am not the texture of my hair. I am not Howard University. I am merely human and these books reflect my humanness, the humanness of my students and the humanness of any who read them.

The same realization has happened with my students. There was resistance at first. They realized that the books were mostly written by authors outside of their race. The initial thought was that these books held nothing for them, but the walls soon crumbled down and they realized that they had to take this journey for themselves. They mentioned how none of their friends read books like these and how it sometimes made them feel isolated, but then they felt "smart." The texts opened up a whole new world for them as it did for W.E.B. DuBois. They were free of color lines and restrictions because of a slave mentality or a Jim Crow identity that says "You can only go here." As I write this, I again recall DuBois' thoughts on this, "…I sit with Shakespeare and he winces not. Across the color line I move arm in arm with Balzac and Dumas…" (Du Bois, 1903/2005, p. 108).

The Promised Land. The Land of Freedom. For the slave this was north, away from the chains of the South, away from the restrictions placed upon the African American people to gain the same knowledge held by those who enslaved them. Even though slavery ended hundreds of years ago, I sometimes wonder if African American students still have a slave mentality—a segregated mentality when it comes to their education. For me and for my students there was a different understanding. We had the same intellect as any other race. We had the same human experiences as other races. Therefore, we could appreciate the same contributions to our understanding that these books provided. We also felt that we had the freedom to connect the content of these texts to our cultural experiences. We felt the freedom to insert ourselves in the age-old conversation that discusses the human experience, even though most of the authors did not look like us.

When I think of freedom, I think of freedom from segregated education. I think of the freedom I have to learn what I want and what I need to learn, no matter the cultural context. Henry David Thoreau understood this for himself, in writing *Civil Disobedience* (a text that formed the basis for the work of Martin Luther King), and *A Plea for Captain John Brown.* In a time where slavery and the mistreatment of African Americans was common, he stood against it. It did not matter to him that he, himself, was white. In his own reflective process, he determined that slavery was wrong. In fact, he spent a night in jail in 1846 as a protest against slavery (refusing to pay a tax that he owed), and later explained his reasons in the essay *Civil Disobedience.* This was how he lived free of the boundaries and lines we humans construct to divide ourselves. He did not live his life to be accepted by the traditions of the white majority, but he freed himself to stand for the justice of all human beings. In his reading and reflecting he developed a better understanding of the human race and was able to see the flaws in the current system.

## I Have Seen a Star

> …for we have seen his star…and, lo, the star, which they saw in the east, went before them, till it came and stood over where the young child was.
> When they saw the star, they rejoiced with exceeding great joy. (Matthew 2:2, 9)

I began this journey with the short poem that has haunted me from the day I started learning about phenomenology:

> To think is to confine yourself to a single thought that one day stands still like a star in the world's sky. (Heidegger, 1971, p. 4)

I feel like the Magi who years prior to Jesus being born, saw a star that captivated them. It took them a long time to discover what the star was about, but they never took their eyes off of it. They stood in wonder, followed it, and rejoiced as the star illuminated the phenomenon. From that moment when my first student (Raymond) began to show a real interest in the Great Books, I could not stop looking at and wondering about my "star." It seems to be never-ending, as if now that I have allowed the star to draw me into its light, everywhere I turn I see these texts affecting the lives of another African American.

### I am a Magi

Because I have had a realization that engaging in these texts can bring about a freedom of thought, speech and expression in students, like the Magi, I seek to understand the power of this moment of discovery in a broader sense. I have discovered that sweet light of freedom and that freedom has led me to apply this understanding to how I carry out education now in my current school, as well as how I would envision my future career. I took a huge step of faith in September 2015 and decided to open my own school that incorporates reading the Great Books. As a part of their day, students participate in literature groups where they engage in Socratic Dialogue about classic and rich texts with staff members. There are no worksheets or comprehension exams, but just relaxed discussion about the texts. The reason I felt it was imperative to include the Great Books in the school's program is because the participants expressed how reading the literature and discussing it, developed their global understanding as a young student.

I can see the predecessors of African Americans reading Great Books literature, who allowed their global understanding to impact America. I can see this play out in Frederick Douglass who was able to meet with Abraham Lincoln on behalf of the African American people. The language and literacy he obtained in reading the Great Books helped to create that bridge to freedom for him. There is also Mary McLeod Bethune, a daughter of illiterate slaves, who learned to read from one of the most ancient Great Books—the Bible, so she could teach her family to read. She then grew up to work alongside Franklin and Eleanor Roosevelt for the cause of the African American people. Then there is Martin Luther King who was able to meet with President Lyndon B. Johnson in promoting civil rights. Finally, there is our first African American president, Barak Obama who found himself connecting to this literature as well, as he sought to shape his own personal philosophies and identity (especially since he was of a mixed race and needed to sort through where his true identity lay). These great leaders crossed boundaries that no other African American has been able to cross. They did not achieve this by forgetting their race. They did not achieve this through militancy and hatred towards the oppressor either. They did not achieve this by refusing to read the books of those written by European Americans, deeming them as culturally irrelevant. They achieved it by embracing their heritage, while at the same time becoming well-versed in the literature of the master, so that they could speak the master's language and bridge that intensely wide gap between the races. Since I am serving primarily African American students, I felt it was necessary to encourage their engagement with these texts to broaden their understandings so that maybe, just maybe they, too, can contribute to the progress of American society in some way.

Engaging in this work has prepared me for this moment. It gave me the evidence that allowing students to express themselves in their own way and giving them freedom to learn for themselves, develops active, happy learners. Thinking is a natural process and it does not have to be taught or forced. Heidegger (1968) says:

> Yet man is called the being who can think, and rightly so. Man, is the rational animal…Being the rational animal man must be capable of thinking if he really wants to. (p. 369)

Just as my class removed the desks, the worksheets, the busy work and left the students with the freedom to read, understand and express for themselves, the school I opened provides this in a broader sense. Students must have the freedom to think or else we are going against their instinct. A bird must be free to fly or it will sing frantically within a cage, disturbing all that can hear it. A human being—a child—a student, must be free to think, to go wherever his mind takes him, or he, too, will sing a song of oppression until he is set loose to sing a sweet song of freedom.

**Constellations Leading to Freedom**

> What is meant by non-interference of the school in learning?...*It means* granting students the full freedom to avail themselves of teaching that answers their needs, and that they want, only to the extent that they need and want it; and it means not forcing them to learn what they do not need or want…I doubt whether *the kind of school I am discussing* will become common for another century. It is not likely…that schools based on students' freedom of choice will be established even a hundred years from now. (Tolstoy, 1904, pp. 143-151)

When Heidegger (1971) writes, "To think is to confine yourself to a single thought that one day stands still like a star in the world's sky" (p. 4), I can visualize myself looking up into the night sky in order to see the constellations. As shared in an earlier chapter, constellations are often used to lead sojourners on their path to a certain destination. The slaves, for example, used the Big Dipper or Drinking Gourd as a way to guide themselves north to Canada in order to obtain freedom. So, what have my guiding constellations been? What starlight images help me to visualize how the phenomenon is opening for me? Lyra, Aquila and Leo draw my attention to the elements in my journey that have illuminated the **lived experiences of African American students reading Great Books literature.**

**Lyra: The sweet music of freedom.** Martin Luther King called us to free ourselves from a slave mentality in this well-known call to freedom: "…And when this happens, when we allow freedom to ring, when we let it ring from every village and hamlet, from every state and every city, we will be able to speed up that day when all of God's children, black men and white men, Jews and Gentiles, Protestants and Catholics, will be able to join hands and sing in the words of the old Negro spiritual, "Free at last! Free at last! Thank God almighty, we're free at last!" (King, 1963). When I first heard the "I Have a Dream" speech, I internalized it as being an anthem for my race, but reflecting on when he says, "black men, and white men, Jews and Gentiles…" I understand that he is calling for all of us to come to that place of freedom where we open our minds to the oneness of humanity. We have been segregated so long. I now see freedom as a universal concept—one that can be applied to the kind of education I give my students. Reading the literature of the Great Books, pulls my African American students out of just knowing their culture, but it also draws them into understanding the foundational culture of American society, and in doing that, they become more a part of it. In reading these texts, my students can find the literacy to communicate with all races and cultures so that maybe they can be the catalyst for bringing racial unity in today's society.

**Aquila: So students may be free as the eagle.**

John F. Kennedy once wrote to the Audubon Society:

> The Founding Fathers made an appropriate choice when they selected the bald eagle as the emblem of the nation. The fierce beauty and proud independence of this great bird aptly symbolizes the strength and freedom of America. (http://www.va.gov/opa/publications/celebrate/eagle.pdf)

Freedom forms the very essence of our Declaration of Independence when it says, "…That they are endowed by their Creator with certain unalienable rights, that among these are Life, LIBERTY, and the Pursuit of Happiness" (http://www.archives.gov/exhibits/charters/declaration_transcript.html). It was an amazing experience for me to hear a student share their perspective on "A Mid-Summer Nights Dream" and actually appreciate it, even if the perspective was different from mine. If Heidegger says that thinking is our "essential destiny," then giving students the freedom to think for themselves with regards to what the ancient philosophers and others have said, cultivates that instinct. As the eagle flies, so does a human think and wonder. I have had the wonderful opportunity to watch these 5 students grow as independent thinkers from grades 9 to 12 and beyond, through just one class (even though the rest of the school functioned in a more traditional way). Their nature allowed for them to get what they needed from my one class to soar towards their personal goals outside of the class.

**Leo: My little lion leading me.** On this journey to understanding the lived experiences of my students reading Great Books literature, there have been some interruptions along the way. One of the "interruptions" on the journey was the birth of my oldest son. I specifically chose to name him Dillon—the exact spelling (as opposed to Dylan), because it meant "Like a lion." He truly lives up to the meaning of his name. Dillon has taught me a great deal about what my students came to experience by being in my class. Dillon is a unique child. He is very intelligent, but wants to learn in his own way and at his own pace. When he turned 5 I began to look for schools that would accommodate his way of learning and could find none. He felt so unhappy and confined. His varying interests and desire to wonder were often interrupted by teachers, scopes and sequence, assessments and this brought about frustration. Taking time to observe his early entrance into the world of education, also shined a light on the lived experiences of my students. The same freedom I gave my students in exploring Great Books literature, I began to apply to my son as he developed as an early learner. I freed his mind to wonder. One of the main aspects of my class that Zeke enjoyed was, "…us being able to do whatever we wanted." Zeke hated school, but he enjoyed my class. Although the Great Books class was a self-contained class, teaching in a way that frees the students' minds to think and wonder for themselves, drew me into having a better understanding of how best to educate my son. I realize that my students and my son are the same in that they are human with the essential being to think, and it is my job to nurture that. My journey into finding a way to help my son work through his early learning frustration, awakened in me an understanding of why my students may have thrived in the class.

**Constellating the Stars on the Journey**

If you look up the etymology for the word "school" it means "leisure or leisure for learning." In ancient times, schooling took place in the context of relaxing with friends and discussing topics in a leisurely manner—topics of personal interest. There was usually an adult there to guide the discussion without too much interference in the students' thought process. The Platonic Dialogues (the transcriptions of Socrates' conversations), reveal this type of teaching. Reviewing these dialogues also reminds me of my faith, which also plays a big part in lighting my path. This is the way Jesus taught. There was no classroom and very little work in a text or book. In discussing the ancient scrolls, He rarely told them straightforward what he believed, but he questioned them and they questioned him and they freely discussed their understanding. Jesus and his disciples spent most of their time living, talking, questioning, and connecting their understandings with nature and other such things. He used storytelling and hands-on experiments many times to get his point across. The disciples and other students were not forced to sit and listen to him, but they could come and go as they pleased, sort of "grazing" on what he was sharing. Learning was a very natural and organic occurrence that took place through the journey of living together with friends—in a space of unity.

**Let There be Light**

> Darwin knew a century and a half ago that the Encyclopaeida had it backward—that it wasn't a "highly developed brain" that gave us language…and abstract thought, but language that gave us abstract thought and a highly developed brain. (Bickerton, 2009, p. 5)

When Gadamer (1975/1989) says, "Language always presupposes a common world…" (p. 407), I think of the very beginning. My lived experience draws me to the Biblical history of language. St. John chapter 1 says, "in the beginning was the Word." The book of Genesis says that the Word was used to speak creation into existence. Initially, this Word was used as a way for the Creator to commune with his creation, but even He did not feel this was enough. He recognized the importance of humankind to have communion with others like himself. Therefore, he created two humans to commune together. Together they named the various elements of creation. They were soul mates. They were *Anam Cara* communing together, working together, dwelling together. The beginning of the human use of language was two *Anam Cara* working together to "name." Gadamer says, "Greek mythology more or less began with the insight that a word is only a name" (p. 406). So, this power through the Word—through naming, drew human beings into an Anam Cara relationship as they worked together, communed together and named the world around them in order to create a common space of understanding. Darwin understood that the Word came first and from that all else was birthed into being.

When humans come together under the same language and understanding, *Anam Cara* relationships are formed. According to the Anam Cara Therapy Center in Berkley, CA, Anam Cara can be defined as the following:

> Anam Cara means "Soul Friend." Anam is the Gaelic word for soul and Cara is the word for friend. In Celtic tradition, an Anam Cara is a teacher, companion or spiritual guide. With the Anam Cara you can share your innermost self to reveal the hidden intimacies of your life, your mind and your heart. This friendship cuts across all convention to create an act of recognition and belonging that joins souls in an ancient and eternal way. (http://www.anamcaratherapycenter.com)

So, going back to the Creator's initial work of creation, where he established the first Anam Cara relationship, I wonder if within every human being there is a need to enter into this type of relationship. Some would say that Anam Cara relationships are formed with certain individuals that a person feels a special connectedness to, but I wonder if all humans were meant to be in Anam Cara relationships with each other? This is a far stretch, I know, but when I think of my students and how our ages, backgrounds, and interests dimmed into the background as we moved into engaging in the books together and a connection began, is an Anam Cara relationship possible for any person, when some type of common language is shared? When I think of the Anam Cara relationships that were formed with my fellow "Johnnies" (St. Johns graduates) and I, even though our races and backgrounds were different, I wonder if once a group finds a common language can this Anam Cara relationship develop with anyone? For my Great Books class, our common language was the Great Books. What made these books our common language was that we are all American and we share that cultural background with our founding mothers and fathers and the other authors who have paved their way into American culture.

Another example of when common language drew people to work together is in the building of the Tower of Babel. Again, this Biblical account I found in the book of Genesis: "In the beginning was the Word," but in the beginning, was also humankind in close relationship, communing together around common language. Seeking Anam Cara is innate within us and it occurs around a common language. As the first humans could work together in order to accomplish the daunting task of naming creation—using words that they had in common, those who built the Tower of Babel, spoke one language. It says in Genesis 11:

> Now the whole world had one language and a common speech. As people moved eastward, they found a plain in Shinar and settled there. They said to each other, "Come, let's make bricks and bake them thoroughly." They used brick instead of stone, and tar for mortar. Then they said, "Come, let us build ourselves a city, with a tower that reaches to the heavens, so that we may make a name for ourselves; otherwise we will be scattered over the face of the whole earth."

"Now the whole world had one language and a common speech…" is how it all began. I am careful not to suggest that these books help African Americans to assimilate, because the definition of assimilation is the process by which a person or persons acquire the social and psychological characteristics of a group. I am not interested in my African American students' identity disappearing, nor in condensing all languages into one. Like the Creator, who at the building of the Tower of Babel decided to mix up the languages so that they could not finish, I want students to maintain their unique identity. Somehow, the Creator saw something dangerous in this unity without differences being appreciated. Yes, they were accomplishing a great task of building the tower; however, the Great Books can aide in facilitating students finding an intersecting point where they can share their unique cultural and life backgrounds within the Great Conversation, and accomplish something great. Most importantly, they can develop Anam Cara as their instinct would have them do.

One of the first words spoken by the Creator is "Let there be light." O'Donohue (1997) says, "When love awakens in your life, in the night of your heart, it is like the dawn breaking within you. Where before there was anonymity, now there is intimacy" (p. 6). Those who were building the tower of Babel were not individuals, they were each anonymous. When the Creator split them up through giving them different languages, they were made known to each other and were forced to learn how to communicate together even with their differences. The light shined on each of them as an individual, this light being spoken into existence by a Word. Some could not come together or they resisted coming to that intersecting point where their different languages could be shared in order to bring unity. So, they had to separate, but those who freed themselves to come to the intersecting place of sharing their "words" with each other and sought understanding, bonded together. Even though humankind is now separate through different colors, races, cultures, languages, etc. there is still that instinct to draw close to others. Coming together at the intersection of words—of languages (even if they are different), helps to facilitate the formation of Anam Cara relationships. Gadamer (1975/1989) says:

> Something is placed in the center, as the Greeks say, which the partners in dialogue both share, and concerning which they can exchange ideas with one another…in a successful conversation they both come under the influence of the truth of the object and are thus bound to one another in a new community. To reach an understanding in a dialogue is not merely a matter of putting oneself forward and successfully asserting one's own point of view, but being transformed into a communion in which we do not remain what we were. (p. 371)

If the Great Books can be considered an intersecting point for all who allow themselves to join in the Great Conversation, could Anam Cara relationships be forged with students, teachers, individuals of different cultural backgrounds, races, socio-economic statuses? As Gadamer says, if we place these texts at the "center" of our Circle of Freedom to be talked about, shared and connected to our own cultural experiences, can Anam Cara relationships be formed with all of those who engage with them? Can the divine light, coming from the written and spoken word of the ancients, the contemporaries, students, teachers, and anyone who frees themselves to engage, shine among us and bind us together?

**Wondering into the Light**

W.E.B. DuBois, in his speech, "Galileo Galilei" encourages the graduates of Fisk University to consider more intellectual/academic schooling as opposed to the vocational training encouraged by Booker T. Washington. He used Galileo as an example of what is possible for any human, black or white, to accomplish if they simply open their minds to wonder. He said:

> But it is in such half-finished biography that men do mischief in the world and blind the eyes of young men and women like these graduates here. It sweeps dust in their eyes and discord in their ears, and to the eternal thunder of questioning, "How?" it returns only the answer to the answered question, "What?" Easy it is to tell what men have done in this world—Lincoln, and Hamilton made us a nation. But—How? Ask the men who will do. Stars there are; them we see and know, but—How do men reach them?—What of the Way, the Power, and the Opposition?
>
> …From the time of Dante in the thirteenth up to the blossoming of Petrarch in the fifteenth century, Italy had been seeing life anew. Galileo was a child of this awakening. The impulse behind him was the Wonder of an open mind at the mechanism of the universe. (DuBois, 1908, p. 37)

DuBois implored the graduates to choose this path of wonder and the possibilities of what they might discover and accomplish could be limitless, just like it was for Galileo. I read this and I imagine that DuBois is talking to me—he is talking to my students and my son! In an age where one could only look at the sky above to see a star, Galileo's impulse to wonder gave him the wisdom to invent the telescope, discover the law of falling bodies, discover the moons of Jupiter, explain the reflected lights of the planets, set the laws of cohesion, apply the law of the pendulum to the creation of the clock, and most of all revealed that the sun was the center of the universe (Dubois, 1908). With wonder anything is possible. With freedom wonder becomes possible for anyone. Through the Great Books we are incited to wonder more about our shared humanity and to share that experience together. My journey into the Great Books has incited me to wonder about my identity as an African American woman, as a teacher and as a facilitator of engaging others in the Great Books.

**Wondering about "who" we are.** Upon deciding on the title for this study I wrestled with how to name the racial identity of my students. I understand that there are stirring reasons as to why we (my students, myself and others) should be called "Black." I understand the struggle. It is hard to identify ourselves with a country that once enslaved us, counted us as no more important than cattle, and still struggle to find a "place" for us here. It is also hard to identify ourselves with a country that is hundreds of years removed from us and across the waters—Africa. Baldwin revealed this same struggle when he said, "At the same time I had no other heritage which I could possibly hope to use--I had certainly been unfitted for the jungle or the tribe" (Baldwin, 1998, p. 7). Yet, it has been through reading this literature of Western culture that I was more compelled to name myself and my students by the space that most reflects some type of cultural root, as flimsy a root it may be. As the great great grandchild of slaves, I felt drawn to Africa. When I reflect on my personal history and how I was raised, my first and middle name being Yoruba and having been raised to embrace my West African roots as much as possible, it is very difficult for me to not name myself "African." Also, the school where I taught these students even went so far as to have students wear uniforms made from African material. For this particular study, those of us who participated in it, share a connection with Africa. This is one of the reasons their parents chose this school as well. However, we were all born in America and live within the American culture. So, we approach these texts as a person of African descent and as an American. Regardless of how we got here and what that naming may mean with regards to our history, it is how we see ourselves.

Now that the study has ended, I realize that anyone can approach these books, regardless of how they name themselves. If they identify more with being Black, connecting mainly to the struggle and power associated with finding our space here in America, a person can see oneself in these texts. If people identify with being a Person of Color or Asian or Hispanic or Jewish—these books tell the human story, but it is up to individual persons to decipher how these books speak to them and the name they call themselves. This process of bringing our personal selves to the Great Conversation gives us the freedom to name ourselves and to insert that perspective into the Conversation. As we find ourselves at the intersection of these books, we are invited to wonder as Socrates compelled us to do, and in wondering together we become unified as the human race, yet we retain our individual selves. What would happen if there were a school or a classroom or a class session where students of all races and backgrounds could come together to share their personal identities with this literature of ancient times? I wonder…

**Wondering about teaching.** I have changed as a teacher. From the time I started teaching many years ago, I evolved from one who depended on curricula, scope and sequence, assessments, etc., to one who depends on the dialogue shared with my students and myself as a way to assess learning. I also have evolved from feeling that I am the master of knowledge to being a partner in this learning journey with my students. We have a reciprocal learning experience as well: I learn from my students and they learn from me. This wondering about my evolution as a teacher also makes me wonder what are the implications of what I have learned about myself. Can other teachers find themselves at this same space where they rely less on plan books, tests, text books, etc. and just read, discuss, and listen to each other? Can students actually learn this way? In order to test this wondering I started a school where this is mainly what the students and I do. It is two years old now and already one of my 11th graders is taking classes at the local community college, with the other college students. She came to me unable to focus and get much out of school just a year ago, and she already has become a very different being. By students being given the freedom to wonder, they learn more about themselves and the goals they want to reach. By taking away testing, they are free from the apprehension of scoring at a certain level. At the same time, when the above student decided to enter community college early, she had to take a proficiency test, since she was so young. She asked me to tutor her for the test and she passed. She still learned how to take a test, but more importantly, she developed her own educational goals. The students from this study all talk about how my giving them freedom to read and learn for themselves, gave them the intellectual tools necessary to just sort of figure life out for themselves, regardless if they are taking computer engineering, accounting or film-making. They felt equipped because they were cultivated to think.

Liberal education is the art of apprehending, understanding and knowing (Nelson, 2001). This is "free" education. Could we as teachers possible develop those who could be the next Steve Jobs, Bill Gates or Barak Obama if students were given more freedom in their educational journey, simply because students are given time and freedom to explore wherever their minds take them? Even if teachers are within a school compelled more by a planned curriculum (my school is a school that practices the Sudbury model), they can build in small spaces of time for students to practice free thinking. Here are some possible ways that this can take place, no matter what type of teaching/learning model the school a teacher finds themselves may practice: hold a book club during a lunch hour or recess, where they read and discuss shorter Great Books texts; have an after-school program where teachers and students engage in dialogue about rich literature; assign a Great Books text once a quarter or once a month, and invite students to present arts based/creative interpretations of the texts at various "free pockets" during the school year. How would this freedom affect the rest of their learning and school life? I wonder…

**Wondering about my future in the Great Books.**

With all of the racial unrest and division that now plagues this country, I have often wondered, "What would happen if we all sat around a table with a Great Book and just talked?" When I first said this to my husband, he questioned my boldness, but I really do wonder this. I wonder this because of my experience at St. John's. Often times being the only African American, I felt the walls dissipate. I even felt that those who may have had one view of African Americans changed as a result of my presence and participation there. The reason for this is because we had to stick with discussing what was in the book and our personal truths. Doing this guided us into opening our minds to another's perspective, yet while understanding our own. This process also led us into changing faulty perspectives we may have held. We were challenged to really think our perspectives through. This is what Townsend (2015) meant when he said, "Resist giving away your life to those who would dominate and master you, and your rewards will be great. Never, never, never, never surrender your own life in order to live someone else's" (p. 18).

I reflect on when I first started this journey and how I was questioned about why I would engage African American students in reading these texts by "dead white men." I truly understand the controversy, but as my historical account and the lived experiences of my students have revealed, it is not so much about whether African American students should or should not read these texts, but it is about how we read these texts and insert ourselves (our life, experiences, race, cultural background, etc.) in the Great Conversation. This is one of the perspectives that Leon Forrest (1990), shares. He discusses the Great Books list and how Mortimer Adler and his colleagues failed to include the many African American authors who have cited these texts in their works, such as Ralph Ellison (*Invisible Man)* and others. Forrest explains how he reads the Great Books AND the works of African American authors, synthesizing the two. The African American people, since coming out of slavery, have actively inserted themselves into the Great Conversation. Reading these texts, did not make them want to forget their race or even to assimilate into the American culture. By the example revealed in Frederick Douglass and the many others I have shared about in this study, they did anything but that. We have a unique story. Our "double-consciousness" as DuBois (2005) has said, makes us an amazing people, having thrived and survived through the perils of the Middle

Passage in both Western, American and African culture. Since there was an attempt to strip us of our identity (as Kunte was renamed Toby in *Roots*), there had to be a re-establishment of that identity, now infused with two other cultures. Instead of it erasing that heritage, it caused them to re-discover their actual identity as a free human, with the intellect equal to the master, now well rounded because of the many cultures that have been grafted in them. The African American people, through all of their trials, became a "Citizen of the World" (https://www.goodreads.com/quotes/28389-i-am-not-an-athenian-or-a-greek-but-a).

In light of the above wonderings, I do often think about opening a center where Great Books discussions take place, inviting all races and backgrounds together to share in the texts. What kind of unity could be forged? Could Anam Cara relationships be formed with complete strangers, even if their race, religion or socio-economic status were different? What would happen if this center were created and educators of all kinds could come together to dialogue not just about great and rich literature, but also about providing a more liberal education through the Great Books wherever they are teaching? I wonder…

I am surrounded by stars and I freely embrace each one as they enlighten me for the journey. There are the Great Books constellated with me and my students' life experiences, my faith, the ancestors, my son, the school I have just begun, my mom and dad—these are my stars. Through their connected light God has allowed me to see my future in education. I am free from the darkness of stifling thought within my students and within myself. Our minds are free and open to the starlight, that we may do as Socrates said, begin our journey as Anam Caras seeking wisdom together through a life of wonder.

# REFERENCES

Adler, M. (1993). The great conversation revisited. In M. Adler (Ed.), *The great conversation* (p. 28). Chicago, IL: Encyclopedia Britannica, Inc.

Angelou, M. (1999). Human family. Retrieved from http://www.afropoets.net/mayaangelou12.html

Angelou, M. (1983). The caged bird. Retrieved from http://www.poetryfoundation.org/poem/178948

Atkinson, B. (2000). *Walden and other writings.* New York, NY: The Modern Library.

Baby Names World ( 2011). *Raymond.* Retrieved from http://babynamesworld.parentsconnect.com/search.php?p=qsearch&s_gender=1&s_copt=2&i_search=Raymond

Baldwin, J. (1998). Autobiographical notes. In J. Baldwin *Baldwin: Collected essays. (*pp. 5-9). New York, NY: Literary Classics of the United States Inc.

Barr, S. (1968). *Notes on dialogue.* Annapolis, MD: St. John's College.

Bickerton, D. (2010). *Adam's tongue: How humans made language, how language Made Humans.* New York, NY: Hill and Wang

Boal, A. (1994). *Theatre of the oppressed.* New York, NY: Theatre Communications Group.

Boso, C. (1981). Contre la mort sucree. In *Bouffonneries*, 3, 9

Brackman, B. (2006). *Facts and fabrications Facts & Fabrications-Unraveling the History of Quilts & Slavery.* Lafayetter, CA: C & T Publications.

Cameron, J.C. (1951). Every star is different. Church of Jesus Christ of Latter Day Saints. Retrieved from https://www.lds.org/music/library/childrens-songbook/every-star-is-different?lang=eng

Casey, E.S. (2009). *Getting back into place: Toward a renewed understanding of the place world.* Bloomington, IN: Indiana University Press.

Collins, M., & Tamarkin, C. (1982). *Marva Collins' way.* New York, NY: Penguin Putnam, Inc.

Cohn, S., & Fain, S. (1953). You can fly. Walt Disney Music Publishing Company.

"Comico" Retrieved from www.shane-arts.com/Commedia-Comico.htm

Cooper. A. J. (1988). Has America a race problem; If so, how can it best be solved?
In A. J. Cooper *A voice from the south* (pp.149-174). New York, NY: Oxford University Press.

Cummins, J. (1986). Empowering minority students. *Harvard Educational Review,* 17(4),
15.

Declaration of Independence. (1776). Retrieved from https://www.archives.gov/founding-docs/declaration-transcript

Definition of modern art. Retrieved from www.theartstory.org

Delpit, L. (2001). Acquisition of literate discourse: Bowing before the master? *Theory into Practice*, 31, 296-302.

Douglass, F. (1845). *Narrative of the life of Frederick Douglass.* New York, NY: Dover Publications.

DuBois, W. (2005). Of the training of black men. In C. Johnson (Ed.) *The souls of black folk* (pp. 89-108). New York, NY: Simon & Schuster.

DuBois, W. (1908). Galileo Galilei. In H. Aptheker (Ed.), *The education of black people* (pp. 33-48). New York, NY: Monthly Review Press.

Dunbar, P. L. (1895). We wear the mask. In H.L. Gates & N. Y. McKay (Ed.), *The Norton anthology: African American literature* (p. 896). New York, NY: W.W. Norton & Company.

Ferdman, B. M. (1990). Literacy and cultural identity. *Harvard Educational Review,* 60, 181-204.

Flowers, L. (2007). Recommendations for research to improve reading achievement for African American students. *Reading Research Quarterly,* 42, 424-428.

Forrest, L. (1990). Mortimer Adler's invisible writers. Retrieved from http://articles.chicagotribune.com/1990-12-03/news/9004090924_1_black-boy-invisible-man-great-books,

Fox, W. (1997). Beacon for the black press. *Editor and Publisher Magazine,* p. *14*

Frost, R. (1921). The road not taken. In Henry Holt and Company (Ed.), *Mountain Interval* (pp. 9-10). New York, NY: Henry Holt and Company.

Frost, R. (1913). Revelation. Retrieved from http://www.poetrysoup.com/famous/poem/4900/rev elation

Gadamer, H.G. (1975). *Truth and method* (Joel Weinsheimer and D. G. Marshall, Trans.). New York, NY: Continuum.

Gadamer, H.G. (1989). Elements of a theory of hermeneutic experience. In D. Moran & T. Mooney (Eds.), *The phenomenology reader* (pp. 309-337). New York, NY: Routledge.

Gadamer, H.G. (2013). *Truth and method.* (Joel Weinsheimer and D. G. Marshall, Trans.). New York, NY: Bloomsbury Academic.

Ganter, G. (1997). The active virtue of the Columbian orator. *The New England Quarterly, 70, 463-476*

Groves, S. (2005). Fly. Music Services Inc.
Hatfield, M. Retrieved from http://www.with-heart-and-hands.com/2016/09/quilting-poems-sayings-superstitions.html

Ferdman, B. (1990) Literacy and cultural identity. *Harvard Educational Review.* 60 (2), pp. 181-204

Franklin, K (2005). Let it out. EMI Music Publishing.Franklin, K (2011). Smile. Sony/ATV Music Publishing LLC.

Freire, Paolo (2015). *Quotes by Paulo Freire.* Retrieved from http://www.freire.org/paulo-freire/quotes-by-paulo-freire

Gates, H.L., & McKay, N.Y. (1997). *The Norton anthology: African American literature.* New York, NY: W.W. Norton and Company.

Greenberg, D. (1995). *Free at last.* Sudbury, MA: Sudbury Valley School Press

Groff, J. (2016). Plot summary in program for *The Table*

Hansberry, L., & Nemiroff, R. (1969). *To be young gifted and black.* New York, NY: Vintage Books

Harper, D. (2010). www.etymonline.com

Heidegger, M. (1962). My way to phenomenology. In D. Moran & T. Mooney (Eds.), *The phenomenology reader* (pp. 251-256). New York, NY: Routledge.

Heidegger, M. (1962). *Being and time* (J. Macquearrie & E. Robinson Trans.).
New York, NY: Harper and Row.

Heidegger, M. (1968). What calls for thinking. In D. F. Krell (Ed.), *Basic writings.*
New York, NY: Harper Collins.

Hicks, D. (1981). *Norms and nobility: A treatise on education.* New York, NY: Praeger.

Hill, L. (2002). Mr. Intentional. Sony

Hirsch, E.D. (1988). *Cultural literacy: What every American needs to know.* New York, NY: First Vintage Books

Hopkins, J. H. (1857). We three kings. Retrieved from http://www.hymnary.org/text/we_three_kings_of_orient_are

Horton, G.M. (1829). On hearing of the intention of a gentleman to purchase the poet's Freedom. in H.L. Gates & N.Y. McKay (Eds.), *The Norton anthology: African American literature* (pp. 192-193). New York, NY: W.W. Norton and Company.

Huey P. Newton Bio Retrieved from http://www.penguin.com/author/huey-p-newton/234951

Hurston, Z. (1929). How it feels to be colored me. In H. L. Gates & N. Y. McKay (Eds.), *The Norton anthology: African American literature.* New York, NY: W. W. Norton and Company.

Johnson, D. (1991). Three wise gifts. *National Wildlife.* 30 (1), 34.

Johnson, J.W., & Johnson, J.R. (1926). *The books of American Negro spirituals.* New York, NY: The Viking Press.

Johnson, K. A. (2000). *Uplifting the women and the race.* New York, NY: Garland Publishing. Inc.

Kaiser, K. (1969). Pass it on. Bud John Songs.

Kakutani, M. (2009). From books, new president found voice. Retrieved from
http://www.nytimes.com/2009/01/19/books/19read.html?pagewanted=all&mtrref=www.politico.com

Kennedy, J.F. Letter to the Audubon Society. Retrieved from
https://www.va.gov/opa/publications/celebrate/eagle.pdf

King, J. (1991). Dysconscious racism: Ideology, identity and the miseducation of teachers. *Journal of Negro Education,* 60(2), 133-146.

King, M. L. (1963). I have a dream. Retrieved from http://www.huffingtonpost.com/2011/01/17/i-have-a-dream-speech-text_n_809993.html

Krell, D.F. (2008). *Basic writings.* New York, NY: HarperCollins.

Ladson-Billings (1994). *The dreamkeepers.* San Francisco, CA: Jossey-Bass.

Lauria, M., & Miron, L. (1999). *Urban schools: The new social spaces of resistance.* New York, NY: Peter Lang.

Lee, C. (1995). A culturally based cognitive apprenticeship: Teaching African American
high school students skills in literary interpretation. *Reading Research Quarterly.* 30 (4), 608-630.

Lennox, J. G. (2001). *Aristotle: on the parts of animals I-IV.* New York, NY: Oxford University Press.

Lerner, A. B. ( 2015). Obama, America's reader in chief, expands his list of favorite books. Retrieved fromhttp://www.politico.com/story/2015/04/obama-favorite-books-117524

Levin, D.M. (2003). *The body's recollection of being: Phenomenological psychology and the deconstruction of nihilism.* New York, NY: Routledge.

MacArthur, J. (1986). Birth of the king: Who were the wise men? retrieved from www.biblebb.com/files/mac/sg2182.htm

MacKethan, L. H. (1986). From fugitive slave to man of letters. *The Journal of Narrative Technique, 16, 55-71.*

Major, C. (1936). On watching a caterpillar become a butterly. In H. L. Gates & N.Y. McKay (Eds), *The Norton anthology: African American literature* (pp. 2246-2247). New York, NY: W.W. Norton and Company.

May, V. M. (2012). *Anna Julia Cooper, visionary black feminist: A critical introduction.* New York, NY: Routledge.

Mercy Me. (2014). Dear younger me. Fair Trade/Columbia

Merleau-Ponty, M. (1962). *Phenomenology of perception.* London: Routledge & Kegan Paul.

Mills. H., Stephens, D., O'Keefe, T., & Waugh, J.R. (2004). Theory in practice: The Legacy of Louise Rosenblatt. *Language Arts,* 82, 47-55.

Moore, M. J. (2015). Test scores show achievement gaps in large Md. counties.Retrieved from http://wtop.com/education/2015/11/test-scores-show-achievement-gaps-in-large-md-counties/

Moran, D. (2000) *Introduction to phenomenology.* New York, NY: Routledge.

Morrell, E. (2002). Promoting academic literacy with urban youth through engaging hip-hop culture. *Journal of Adolescent and Adult Literacy,* 91, 88-92.

Morrell, E. (2002). Toward a critical pedagogy of popular culture: Literacy development
of urban youth. *Journal of Adolescent and Adult Literacy,* 46, 72-77.

Morrell, E. (2005). Critical English education. *English Education,* 37, 312-321.

Morrell, E. (2010). Critical literacy, educational investment, and the blueprint for reform:An analysis of the reauthorization of the elementary and secondary education act. *Journal for Adolescent & Adult Literacy*, 54, 146-149.

NASA. Why do stars twinkle? Retrieved from https://starchild.gsfc.nasa.gov/docs/StarChild/questions/question26.html

Nelson, C. A. (2001). *Radical visions.* Westport, CT: Bergin & Garvey.

Niequist, S. (2013). *Bread and wine: A love letter to life around the table with recipes.* Grand Rapids, MI: Zondervan

O'Donohue, J. (1990). *Anam Cara: A book of Celtic wisdom.* New York, NY: Cliff Street Books.

Pancoon. (2014). Plant seed retrieved from http://allpoetry.com/poem/11518670-Plant-Seed--Haiku--by-Pancoon

"Pedrolino" Retrieved from http://shane-arts.com/Commedia-Pedrolino.htm

Plato ( 1976) *Meno* (G.M.A. Grube, Trans.). Indianapolis, IN: Hackett Publishing Company.

Plato ( 1987). Laches. *The roots of political philosophy.* In T. L. Pangle (Ed.)., *Roots of political philosophy* (pp. 240-268). Ithaca, NY: Cornell University Press.

Poe, E. A. (1827). Evening star. Retrieved from http://www.eapoe.org/works/poems/estara.htm

Pradle, G. M. (2005). In memoriam: Louise Rosenblatt. *English Journal,* 94, 11-14

Probst. R.E. (2005). In memoriam: Louise Rosenblatt. *English Journal,* 94,11-14.

Rall, G. (1995). The stars of freedom. *Sky and telescope, 89, 36-38.*

*Risser, J. (2012). The life of understanding: A contemporary hermeneutics.* Bloomington, IN: Indian University Press.

Roberts, P.W. (2007). *Journey of the Magi.* New York, NY: Tauris Park Paperbacks.

Rosenblatt, L. (1983). *Literature as exploration*. New York, NY: Modern Language Association.

Rosenblatt, L. (2005). In her own words: Remembering Louise M. Rosenblatt 1904-2005.
*English Journal,* 94, 93.

Rudlin, J. (1994). *Commedia dell'arte: An actor's handbook.* New York, NY: Routledge.

Safranski, R. (1998). *Martin Heidegger: Between good and evil.* Cambridge, MA: Harvard University Press.

"Sankofa" Retrieved from www.adinkra.org

Sayers, D. (1948). *The lost tools of learning.* London: E.T. Heron & Co., Ltd.

Schaaf, F. (2008). Lost lore of the little dipper. *Sky and telescope, 115, 48.*

Shakespeare,
Retrieved
From http://shakespeare.mit.edu/asyoulikeit/full.html

Sisco, L. (1995). Writing in the spaces left: Literacy as a process of becoming in the narrative of Frederick Douglass. *ATQ*, 9, 195-231

Smalls, C. (1975). Home. Warner/Chapell Music Inc.

Smith, J.A. (1941). De anima. In Richard McKeon (Ed.), *The basic works of Aristotle*
(pp. 533-603). New York, NY: Random House.

Stearns, M. W. (1958). *The story of jazz.* New York, NY: Oxford University Press.

Stevenson, R. L. (2006). *Strange case of Dr. Jekyll and Mr. Hyde and other tales.* New York, NY: Oxford University Press Inc.

St. John's College (2014). *Academic Programs.* Retrieved from http://www.sjc.edu/about/why-sjc/

Tetteh,V.A.
Retrieved
From
stlawu.edu/.../education/f/09textiles/a dinkra_symbols.pdf

Tippet,K.
Retrieved
from
http://www.mundanefaithfulness.com/home/2014/03/31/bre
ad-and-wine-shauna-niequist

Tolstoy, L. (1904). Education and culture. In *The complete works of Count Tolstoy.* (pp.
143-144) Boston, MA: Colonial Press.

Townsend, D. (2015). Freedom upon an Achillean shore. *The College,* 16-19.

Voltaire (2010). Character. In H. I. Woolf (Ed.) *Voltaire: Philosophical Dictionary* New York, NY: Dover Publications, Inc.

Winter, J. (1988) *Follow the drinking gourd.* New York, NY: Dragonfly Books.

Wise, J., & Wise-Bauer S. (1999) *The well-trained mind.* New York, NY: W.W. Norton & Company, Inc.

van Manen, M. (2007). *Researching lived experience: Human science for an Action sensitive pedagogy.* Ontario, CA: The University of Western Ontario.

van Manen, M., & Levering, B. (1996). *Childhood's secrets: Intimacy, privacy and the self considered.* New York, NY: Teacher's College, Columbia University.

van Manen, M. (2002). *Writing in the Dark: Phenomenological studies in interpretive inquiry.* Ontario, CA: The University of Western Ontario.

Made in the USA
Columbia, SC
03 February 2023